O. M.
(d)93

SUN, MOON
AND
STANDING
STONES

JOHN EDWIN WOOD

SUN, MOON AND STANDING STONES

1978

OXFORD UNIVERSITY PRESS

OXFORD LONDON NEW YORK

Oxford University Press, Walton Street, Oxford OX2 6DP

OXFORD LONDON GLASGOW
NEW YORK TORONTO MELBOURNE WELLINGTON
IBADAN NAIROBI DAR ES SALAAM CAPE TOWN
KUALA LUMPUR SINGAPORE JAKARTA HONG KONG TOKYO
DELHI BOMBAY CALCUTTA MADRAS KARACHI

British Library Cataloguing in Publication Data

Wood, John Edwin
  Sun, moon and standing stones.
  1. Megalithic monuments—Europe   2. Astronomy,
  Prehistoric
  I. Title
  936   GN792.E/   77–30457

ISBN 0–19–211443–3

*Printed in Great Britain
by Hazell Watson & Viney Ltd
Aylesbury, Bucks*

Dartmoor

Stone and grass on the blasted moor
are dead.
We are alive and living pulled back
by men who lived four thousand years before
Tom Pearce and his grey mare.
Stone rows and pieces of plaited string
traced movements of the lunar disc across
the cloudless sky against the tor
before
the climate changed to what foreigners call
the English summer.

Why must they know the one night of that year
when their moon god was eclipsed?
To lug those stones was quite an undertaking
technology worth some remark
but triangulation with woven ropes finding root
two over two by string and Pythagoras—
that really was something, by eye and rule of thumb.
Was Tom Pearce's father's grandfather not a woad-clad savage
but a Bronze Age chieftain skilled
in astronomical prediction?

PAT WOOD

Toutes les histoires anciennes, comme le disait un de
nos beaux esprits, ne sont que des fables convenues.

VOLTAIRE

Contents

List of Illustrations

Plates

(*between pages* 82 *and* 83)

Text Figures

Acknowledgements

I am grateful to Mr Chris Jennings for allowing me to use eighteen pictures (Plates 5b to 22) from his collection of photographs of standing stones and megalithic sites, and to Mr Alan Penny for photographing Neolithic and Beaker Pottery (Plates 4a and 4b), kindly made available by Mr Roger Peers, Curator of the Dorset County Museum.

I thank Professor A. E. Roy for reading the script and making a number of valuable comments. My thanks are also due to my family and friends for their help and encouragement, and particularly to Pat Wood for editorial assistance during the writing of the book and for the use of her poem 'Dartmoor'.

1 Shedding Light on Stonehenge

In many wild and remote places in the British Isles, we can still come across relics from the distant past. It is not too difficult to recognize some of them, such as hill-top forts and Roman roads, for what they are; in spite of their antiquity their purpose is familiar, for roads and fortifications are with us to the present day. But there are other remains as well, strange and mysterious, without apparent purpose and having no obvious counterpart in our twentieth-century culture. Chief among these are the standing stones. Whether singly or in groups, in rows or in circles, they bear silent witness to vanished communities whose practices have long been forgotten.

In the many hundreds of years before the advent of modern archaeology, men could only look and wonder at the vast numbers of stones which their ancestors had erected in the mountains and moorland. People invented stories to account for their existence, often explaining them away by supernatural events. They were thought to be the Devil's thunderbolts, or meeting places of the 'Little People', and in the eyes of country folk the stones came to be endowed with magical properties, a belief which persists in some parts even today. Sometimes, when people dimly recalled the earlier inhabitants of Great Britain, the stones were attributed to the Danes or the Romans, but back beyond the Romans they knew of nothing except the woad-covered savages briefly mentioned by the classical writers.

The science of archaeology has dispelled many of the myths. As knowledge of the prehistory of the British Isles was gradually built up, it became clear that the builders of the stone monuments, whoever they were, must have lived many centuries before the Romans. Standing stones were put into a chronological framework which has been refined many times, but their purpose remained largely a matter of guesswork. Stone circles were assumed to be ritual sites, where people gathered for religious or other ceremonies, and stone rows were thought to be processional ways, but solitary stones defied any reasonable explanation. Antiquarians quoted the myths and the folk-lore, and archaeologists tended to turn their attention to remains which could be more easily understood.

The situation has changed dramatically in the last twenty years. Archaeology, like many other fields of learning, has been able to make use of and benefit from the explosion in scientific research in the middle decades of this century. The fusion of research in archaeology, astronomy, statistics, climatology, biology, and physics is leading to an unexpected and exciting interpretation of the period when the standing stones were erected. Many of the sites are now thought to be places where men in the Neolithic and Early Bronze Ages devised a kind of geometry, where they made systematic observations of the sun and moon, and where they developed elaborate techniques for predicting lunar eclipses. A few of their main sites, like Stonehenge in southern England, became cultural centres for élite groups of astronomer-priests, and the influence of these men extended from Brittany in the south to the Orkney Islands in the north.

This book is about astronomy and geometry in north-west Europe during the period from 3500 BC to 1500 BC. It is not exclusively, or even mainly, about Stonehenge. But Stonehenge is the best-known of the prehistoric monuments in Britain and has caught the popular imagination since the early Middle Ages. It has also been the monument which has attracted the most speculation and theorizing, though much of this has not been very scientific. But because Stonehenge is spectacular and well known, it has come to the attention of specialists in the physical and mathematical sciences, most of whom might never have heard of Stonehenge's equally puzzling, but comparatively insignificant, contemporaries. Stonehenge has provided the sharpest spur in the study of prehistoric, or archaeo-, astronomy in the British Isles, and therefore that is where we shall begin.

Stonehenge, even more than English cathedrals, is a composite survival from several different periods of construction and reconstruction. Between the first building on the site and the last was a period of more than one thousand years, and during most of that time the large stones which we spontaneously associate with the site had not been erected. The first construction, around 2800 BC, was a circular bank and ditch. The ditch was merely an irregularly shaped quarry for the bank, or rather banks, because there was a low bank outside the ditch as well as the main bank within it. From the size of the ditch it is possible to calculate that the bank was originally about two metres high. Its diameter is 98 m (Fig. 1.1).

There is a gap in the bank towards the north-east, which seems to form an entrance to the enclosure. Lying flat in the entrance, but not in the middle of it, is a large stone, popularly known as the Slaughter Stone, though there is no reason to believe that this was its purpose; more likely it was once vertical and has either fallen or been deliberately pushed over. About 30 metres beyond the bank is the Heel Stone (number 96 on the official plan, reproduced as Fig. 1.1), surrounded by a small ditch. It stands also between two banks of earth, about 16 m apart, which point directly away from the centre of Stonehenge, as though forming a processional route up from the valley towards the monument. The Avenue, as it is called, and the Heel Stone are usually reckoned to belong to the earliest phases of construction on the site. They are not contemporary with the circular bank and ditch, and do not quite line up with the original entrance.

At the inner edge of the bank there are two large stones, called the Station Stones, positioned so that they are on a diameter of the circular bank. There are also two mounds just inside the bank, and the centres of these mounds form a rectangle with the two Station Stones. The southernmost of these mounds was excavated in the nineteen-twenties and a stone hole found beneath it; it doesn't seem unreasonable to suppose that both mounds were originally marked by stones like the two station stones, and in the official guide book numbers have been allotted (91, 92, 93, and 94) to the four stations in a similar way to the numbering of the other stones. If they are all contemporary, the stations date to a later phase of building than the bank because the ditch surrounding mound 92 cuts into it.

The circle of large stone blocks with horizontal lintels belongs to a later period of construction than anything described so far, probably dating to 2100 BC. Like the other large stones, they are a type of sandstone known as sarsen, which

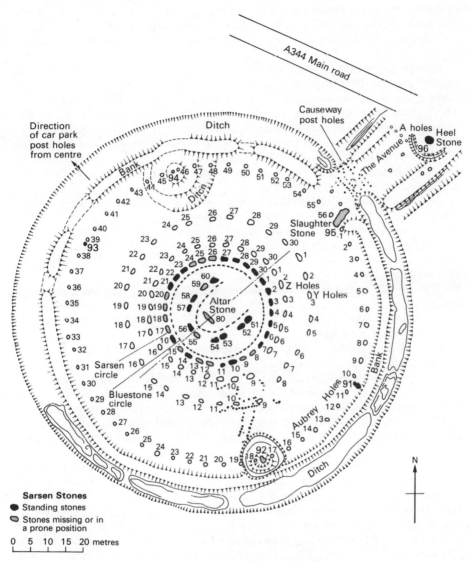

FIG. 1.1   Plan of Stonehenge

occurs naturally as huge irregular boulders on parts of Salisbury Plain. There were originally thirty of these in the 31 m-diameter circle, but now only seventeen are standing and some of these have fallen and been re-erected. Six lintels are in position. The construction is considerably more subtle than appears at first sight. The lintels are shaped so that their vertical faces are curved to the shape of a circle. They are held in position by mortice and tenon joints, each lintel having two holes on its under side so that it locks in to projections on the upper ends of the verticals. The lintels are also keyed in together by a projection on one end and a slot at the other. The whole would have produced a very secure form of construction, although it uses techniques more appropriate to timber than to stone.

The largest stones at Stonehenge are the ten huge sarsens set in pairs inside the sarsen circle. Each pair had originally a lintel across the top, and because they make a group of three blocks the word 'trilithon' was invented to describe them. Three of the five trilithons are standing today, one having been restored in 1958. Like the sarsen lintels, the flat stones are held firmly to the uprights by mortice and tenon joints. The general arrangement of the trilithons is a horseshoe, with the open end pointing towards the Avenue and the Heel Stone. The stones increase in size towards the toe of the shoe, and the largest uprights are 5 m high and are estimated to weigh 50 tonnes.

Within the sarsen circle there is the remains of another circle of much smaller stones. Twenty of these still remain above ground, though there are the stumps of more beneath the soil. These are the 'bluestones', so called because they have a bluish tint in wet weather. They are in fact a mixture of different types of igneous rock, quite foreign to the area of Stonehenge, and their origin was eventually traced to Preseli Mountain in South Wales.

There is another setting of bluestones inside the trilithon horseshoe, and these are of some interest because although they are erected as individual standing stones, several have been prepared as trilithons, and presumably in an earlier phase of Stonehenge were used in this way. It is generally accepted that the erection of the bluestone circle and horseshoe in their present positions took place in the very last phase of the construction of Stonehenge, about 1600 BC. Finally, inside the bluestone horseshoe, but not at the exact centre of the monument, is a recumbent stone, the Altar Stone. It, too, comes from South Wales, from a sandstone outcrop on the shores of Milford Haven, and presumably was transported to Salisbury Plain at the same time as the bluestones. There is some evidence that originally it was vertical; it could have been either a single stone or one of a pair.

This cursory description of Stonehenge deals for the most part with what can be seen by the casual visitor and omits many of the findings of recent archaeological research. Visitors in previous centuries would have seen these features, but unfortunately the value of accurate description was not appreciated until as late as the nineteenth century and the early accounts lean more towards speculation than fact. But one writer, if he really was writing about Stonehenge, made an interesting observation. The classical historian Diodorus Siculus (the Sicilian), writing in Greek about 40 BC, and referring to an earlier writer Hecataeus of Thrace (4th century BC), says:

Amongst the writers who have occupied themselves with the mythology of the ancients, Hecataeus and some others tell us that opposite the land of the Celts there exists in the ocean an island not smaller than Sicily, and which, situated under the constellation of the Bear, is inhabited by the Hyperboreans; so-called because they live beyond the point from which the north wind blows. . . . The inhabitants honour Apollo more than any other deity. A sacred enclosure is dedicated to him in the island, as well as a magnificent circular temple adorned with many rich offerings.

The first certain reference to Stonehenge appears in the writings of Henry of Huntingdon about AD 1130. Some ten years later Geoffrey of Monmouth gave a vivid account of how Stonehenge was transported from Ireland to England by the magic of Merlin, a folk legend that Professor Stuart Piggott has suggested may include some vestige of an oral tradition handed down from the time of the transport and erection of the bluestones two and a half thousand years before. Although there were further references to Stonehenge in the next three centuries, there was no serious study until King James I instructed the architect Inigo Jones to make a plan of the remains. The results were not published until after Jones's death, and then were clearly very imaginative, for the trilithon horseshoe was interpreted as a regular hexagonal figure, bringing the prehistoric monument into line with seventeenth-century notions of good architectural design.

Stonehenge was also visited by the diarist John Aubrey, who made a sketch of the site as he saw it in 1666, and in particular he noticed some shallow depressions arranged in a circle concentric with the bank and just inside its inner edge. Several of them were excavated by Col. Hawley in the nineteen-twenties and they were found to be the positions of roughly circular pits. He called them the Aubrey Holes to commemorate their original discoverer. There are 56 Aubrey Holes, set regularly in an accurate circle 87·8 m in diameter. They are believed to belong to an early phase in the construction of Stonehenge, because they are covered by the mounds of two of the four stations, and the Aubrey circle is not set out from the same centre as the sarsen stones. The locations of 32 are now marked on the ground by white discs.

The Aubrey Holes have proved to be one of the most puzzling features of Stonehenge, and we shall return to them later. They seem never to have contained stones or wooden posts, and they certainly were not left exposed for long, because their sides are not weathered. In general they are filled by the chalk that came out of them, and some have been excavated and filled more than once. Most contained cremated human bones; in others there were flint flakes and small bone objects presumed to be hairpins. On average they are 0·76 m deep and 1·06 m across.

John Aubrey suggested that Stonehenge was built by the Druids, an idea that was grasped with enthusiasm by William Stukeley, who published a book on Stonehenge in 1740. His belief that the Druids were responsible was totally without supporting evidence, but he made a new plan of the site, discovered the Avenue, and excavated several archaeological remains in the area. More importantly, Stukeley recorded the fundamental fact that is crucial to an understanding of Stonehenge and led eventually to a reappraisal of Late Neolithic and Early Bronze Age culture: *the axis of Stonehenge is aligned to the midsummer sunrise*.

Many people visited Stonehenge during the remainder of the eighteenth century, and wrote about it. Famous men saw and speculated; they included John Wood the architect of Bath and Dr Samuel Johnson. The alignment towards the midsummer sunrise was noted particularly by a Dr John Smith who was more specific than Stukeley, for he not only stated in 1771 that the axis of the monument was aligned on the longest day of the year, but he assumed that this was a deliberate orientation and that the purpose of the sarsen stone circle was a calendar.

Stonehenge continued to attract the learned and the curious in the nineteenth century. The eminent antiquary Sir Richard Colt Hoare, who excavated many prehistoric sites in southern England, made the best plan of Stonehenge to date when compiling his book *The Ancient History of Wiltshire*, published in 1812. Although he did not excavate at Stonehenge, he dug several of the round burial mounds, or barrows, in the area, and found in some of them fragments of the Stonehenge stones in heaped-up material covering the interments.

The next astronomical discovery seems to have been made by the Rev Edward Duke in 1846. He noted the midsummer sunrise was also marked by station stone 91, when viewed from the centre of the mound, 92. Similarly the midwinter sunset was marked by stone 93, if the observer stood in the centre of mound 94. These two alignments would divide the year into two six-monthly periods and could presumably have formed the basis of a rudimentary calendar. No more facts of astronomical significance came to light in the nineteenth century in spite of intensive study until Sir Norman Lockyer became interested. He was a professional astronomer who had already made his reputation in spectroscopy and solar physics.

He devoted several years of his life to examining, measuring, and speculating about ancient monuments, not just Stonehenge but also the stone rows on Dartmoor and in Brittany, temples in Babylonia, Egypt, and Greece, stone circles and burial chambers. He was interested in folklore and ancient cults, sun worship and early calendars. Apart from his letters and papers in learned journals, the results of his studies are assembled in a potpourri of astronomy and archaeology called *Stonehenge and other British Stone Monuments, astronomically considered*, published in 1906. Lockyer rediscovered the Station Stone alignments first noted by Edward Duke, and a few more besides. He saw that from the centre of Stonehenge, stone 93 marks the position of the sunset on about 6 May and again on 8 August; stone 91 marks sunrise on 5 February and 8 November. Thus four more dates can be put into the calendar roughly 45 days or one eighth of a year before and after the solstices. We have here the beginning of an eight-'month' calendar. However, Lockyer did not find an alignment for the spring and autumn equinoxes, which would have completed the set.

Lockyer's studies of Stonehenge are chiefly noted for an ingenious attempt to date the monument by astronomical means. The astronomical background to the method will be explained in Chapter 4, but at this stage it is sufficient to know only that at midsummer's day the position on the horizon where the sun first appears is the furthest towards north it can get in the course of a year, and that over a period of several thousand years the midsummer sunrise position has been slowly changing so that it now rises a fraction of a degree east of its position in prehistoric times. In fact the difference in rising position between AD 1900 and 2000 BC is about 0·85°. The rate of change is only about 0·02° per century. It is clear that to give a date of any value at all, this method had to be extremely precise.

Lockyer makes several initial assumptions, the most important being that the first flash of the sun's disc over the distant horizon marks the instant of sunrise. Later work would tend to confirm this, but before comparison between Stonehenge and other sites was possible, he might equally well have taken the instant when the sun was sitting tangentially on the horizon, or even the mid-disc. He assumed also that the sighting line was marked by the axis of the Avenue, and set out pegs at intervals along the Avenue, putting them as nearly as he could in the centre. He then determined the bearing with a theodolite, and got a mean value 49·5975°. Actually he did not use this value in his subsequent calculations, but he took 49·5717°, which was the bearing of a distant Ordnance Survey benchmark, for no better reason than that it was near an Iron Age earthwork, though since it would make a difference of less than 150 years, it is probably unreasonable to quibble.

However, if the centre of the Avenue is to be taken as the sightline it must be marked positively and precisely. One way of doing this is to erect a large pole at some distant point along the Avenue. If it is accurately set up, and distant enough for movement of a few inches in the position of the observer not to matter, it could be used as an accurate indicator of the midsummer sunrise. No such posts were known at Stonehenge until 1966, when the sites of three large posts came to light during the extension of the car park, and so the archaeological community had regarded the astronomical alignment of Stonehenge as a rough and approximate alignment, for some unspecified purpose, presumably ritual.

With his rather arguable assumptions, it was remarkable that Lockyer's date for the Stonehenge Avenue alignment was even in the right millennium. He gives the date of 1680 BC, and allowing for uncertainties in his measurements, suggests a span from 1900 to 1500 BC. More accurate knowledge of the astronomical constants would now revise his dates, making them about 200 years earlier.

Lockyer's method is sound in astronomical principle, but was severely criticized by archaeologists. In their eyes he committed the grave error of mixing up constructions from different periods, for although he measured the alignment of the Avenue, he regarded the result as applying to the sarsen stone circle and the trilithons, which are several hundred years later. It is only by luck that the date he gives for the construction of the stone circle is about right.

So Lockyer's work was rejected by archaeologists for good reasons, but not all the criticisms were equally justified. One objection was quite unsound and it reveals a lack of understanding of his technical approach. It was argued that Lockyer's surveys were carried out with high-precision instruments that were not available to the builders of Stonehenge, who had only their naked eyes to assist them. Since it is obvious that naked-eye measurements are considerably less accurate than those with optical aids, how, it was asked, can conclusions based on these very accurate measurements possibly be valid? And for that matter how could the original builders have erected sightlines with sufficient accuracy if it required the use of elaborate instruments to check them?

The answer is that setting up the original sightlines and checking them afterwards are two very different problems. It is possible to get an extremely accurate line using the unaided eye simply by patience and repetition. Suppose that the Stonehenge builders had decided to use a large post somewhere down the Avenue to mark the midsummer sunrise, they could have erected the post in approximately the correct position, tested its location at midsummer, and moved it if it was not correct. This could, if necessary, be repeated the following year. (There is no evidence that posts were erected in the Avenue beyond the Heel Stone, but some were put up in other parts of the Stonehenge complex.) It would be sensible to site the post so that a fraction of the disc of the rising sun just appeared for an instant in the angle between the post and the ground, and since the human eye can see the bright flash from a tiny fragment of the sun, it would be possible to locate the post with considerable precision. In effect we would be using the sun as an optical instrument. If the post is far enough away from the observer, the angle of the alignment is accurately defined.

How is this checked afterwards? If the post had still been there when Lockyer made his measurements, he could have waited until midsummer's day and observed the sunrise. Had it not been for the change in astronomical constants since the erection of the post, this would have led to a direct verification without the use of optical instruments. Unfortunately direct checks are not possible; the sun no longer rises in the same place. We have to measure the alignment of the stones with optical instruments to the same accuracy as the builders of the monument achieved by sighting on the sun. We can then calculate the position of the sunrise as it used to be. There is no escaping from very careful measurements, and because modern scientists and archaeologists need to use precision instruments, it does not imply that the builders did. Regrettably, this misunderstanding has persisted to the present day, and is sometimes used as an argument against modern investigators.

During the first sixty years of this century Stonehenge was excavated several times, and gradually more and more information came to light. There were new discoveries about earlier constructions on the site, when rings of filled-in stone holes were discovered. The sequence of building, the origins of the stones, and the ways they were shaped and erected became much clearer, and modern dating methods have refined the chronology of the various phases. Yet the astronomical aspects of the structure were almost completely ignored by professional archaeologists, and in several books of the period get no more than a passing mention. It is easy to understand why. From the time when William Stukeley introduced fanciful notions about the Druids, there have been many books of speculation and hypothesis, and the building of Stonehenge has been attributed to almost every tribe, both real and mythological. The orientation towards midsummer sunrise has been seized upon and incorporated into unsubstantiated theories, and archaeologists have come to recognize that their subject, more than most, suffers from the imaginative writings of a 'lunatic fringe'. As the 1959 edition of the official guidebook stated, 'the orientation of ancient monuments is not popular with some archaeologists', and no wonder; they have professional reputations to maintain, and so much rubbish has been written about orientations and alignments that anyone discussing these matters in the nineteen-fifties risked being regarded as yet another crank.

Outside the world of professional archaeology, a few men continued to study the astronomical features of Stonehenge. One of these was Mr C. A. Newham (always known as Peter), who retired from the post of Group General Manager of the North Eastern Gas Board in 1959 and from that time made the study of Stonehenge almost a full-time occupation. He looked again at the four stations and discovered that their positioning was much more subtle than had previously been supposed. Not only do they indicate the positions of the horizon where the sun rises at midsummer and midwinter, but they also show the rising positions of the moon at certain important points in its cycle of movement through the sky.

We will defer the astronomical explanation for these movements until Chapter 4, and just mention for now how the movements of the sun and moon appear to an observer on the ground. In Figure 1.2 the circle represents the horizon, and the observer is assumed to be standing at its centre. In midsummer the sun rises quite a long way towards the north, in fact in the direction marked by the line 'midsummer sunrise'. In midwinter the sun rises well to the south, and its line is indicated by 'midwinter sunrise'. The sun sets in the western half of the horizon and the sunset directions can also be shown by two lines. The midsummer sunrise is almost (but not quite) in the reverse direction to the midwinter sunset. These are the four limiting positions for the rising and setting of the sun. The sun never rises or sets along the part of the horizon to the north or south of these lines. The diagram is drawn to be approximately correct for a place on the earth's surface with a latitude the same as Stonehenge. If the observer went further south the two sunrise lines would be closer to east, and if he went further north, they would open out and be closer to north and south.

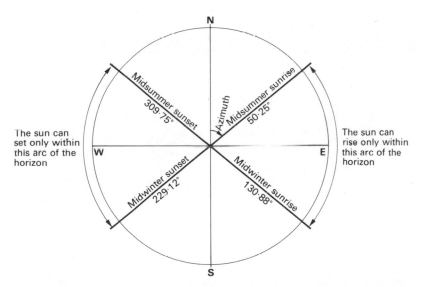

FIG. 1.2 The limiting directions of sunrise and sunset for a site with the latitude of Stonehenge

The moon's movements are quite complicated and it has eight limiting rising and setting directions instead of four. Its movements during a month echo those of the sun during a year, so that in the course of only twenty-eight days the moonrise direction goes from a maximum northerly one to a maximum southerly one; the moon's rising and setting positions swing across two arcs of the horizon, just as the sun's do in a period of twelve months. Sometimes the moon rises and sets over wide arcs on the horizon. It is then said by astronomers to be at its 'major standstill'. Sometimes the rising and setting arcs are much narrowed, and

the moon is then said to be at a 'minor standstill'. It takes the moon 9·3 years
to go from a major to a minor standstill; after 18·6 years it completes the full
cycle.

The most northerly and southerly moonrise and moonset directions at the
major and minor standstills are shown on Figure 1.3. They are approximately
correct for Stonehenge, and again, the lines that look opposite to each other are
very nearly so (but not quite). Anyone can find these twelve important directions
from his own home by patiently watching the sun and moon rise and then marking the directions permanently in some way, but he would have to observe for at
least ten years to see the moon rise in all possible directions.

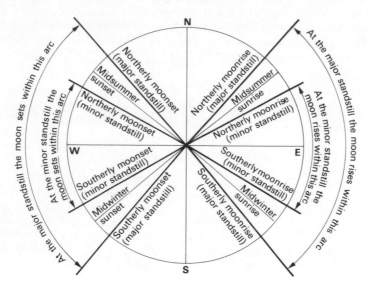

FIG. 1.3   The limiting directions of moonrise and moonset for
a site with the latitude of Stonehenge

This seems to have been what happened at Stonehenge when the Station
Stones were erected. Edward Duke had already discovered in 1846 that the
midsummer sunrise and midwinter sunset directions were shown by the alignments of stones along the shorter sides of the quadrilateral formed by the four
stations. Peter Newham found that the longer sides of the quadrilateral gave the
directions of the most northerly setting of the moon and, looking the other way,
the most southerly rising of the moon at the major standstill (Fig. 1.4). He also
discovered another very surprising fact. The four stations make a rectangle, with
the short sides at right angles to the long ones. It is possible only at the latitude
of Stonehenge to lay out a rectangle which will mark these sun and moon alignments. At other latitudes it would be a parallelogram.

We have already mentioned Lockyer's discovery about the diagonals of the
rectangle dividing the year, and that an alignment on the Spring and Autumn

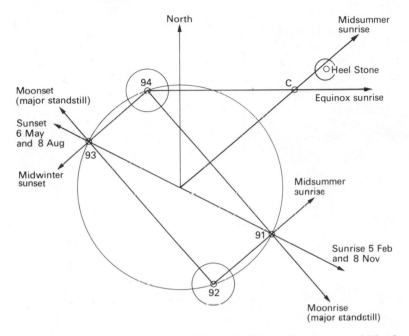

North

Midsummer
sunrise

Heel Stone

94   C

Moonset
(major standstill)

Equinox sunrise

Sunset
6 May
and 8 Aug

93

Midwinter
sunset

Midsummer
sunrise

91

Sunrise 5 Feb
and 8 Nov

92

Moonrise
(major standstill)

FIG. 1.4   Alignments at Stonehenge claimed by Duke, Lockyer, and Newham

equinoxes would give all the sightlines needed for an eight-month calendar. This missing alignment was also discovered by Newham, when he noted the position of a hole between the ditch and the Heel Stone that is believed by archaeologists to have once held a stone. Standing on mound 94 and looking to this stone gives the sunrise position for the two equinoxes in March and September.

The new discoveries about Stonehenge made almost no impact. Peter Newham published them in the *Yorkshire Post* in March 1963, and the next year he had a little book called *The Enigma of Stonehenge* privately printed. He was unable to get it sold at the Ministry of Works bookshop beside the monument, although you can now buy his later book there, *The Astronomical Significance of Stonehenge*.

Meanwhile Professor Gerald Hawkins, a professional astronomer from the University of Boston, Mass., was also thinking about Stonehenge and adopted what can only be described as the 'brute force' method of solving its problems. He selected a large number of pairs of stones and then, using a digital computer, compared their alignments with the rising and setting positions in 1500 BC of the sun, moon, the planets, and some bright stars. He could find no lines which marked the rising and setting points for the planets or stars, but for the sun he claimed to have found ten alignments closer than 1° and for the moon, fourteen closer than 1·5° (Fig. 1.5). In these calculations Hawkins included the Station Stones, the Heel Stone, and several holes (D, F, G, and H) which have been discovered during excavations of Stonehenge, but are not identified on the official plan. (There is some doubt as to whether D, F, G, and H are natural or artificial.)

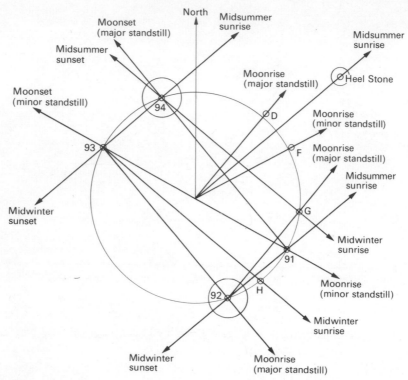

FIG. 1.5   Alignments included by Hawkins in *Stonehenge Decoded*

Hawkins also found alignments connected with the sarsen circle and the giant trilithons. He claimed that looking out through the trilithons and the corresponding gaps in the sarsen circle significant alignments were defined in every case. Going round the trilithon horseshoe in a clockwise direction: from the first trilithon a midwinter sunrise is marked; from the second, the southerly moonrises for both the major and minor standstills; from the third, the midwinter sunset which is on the axis of the monument and opposite the midsummer sunrise alignment; from the fourth, the two northerly moonset alignments for the major and minor standstills; and finally from the fifth trilithon the midsummer sunset.

These results were published in the scientific magazine *Nature*, a periodical of great prestige which frequently announces substantial discoveries in science, and is very widely read. It was impossible not to be aware of this piece of work, and it provoked considerable discussion. Almost every archaeologist treated it with extreme scepticism.

To anyone dubious about his first paper on Stonehenge, Hawkins's second paper, in June 1964, was a real shock. Having looked at the alignments and come to the conclusion that Stonehenge was intended as a solar and lunar observatory, Hawkins advanced the idea that it was designed in part as a computer for predicting eclipses of the moon. The feature of Stonehenge he called upon for eclipse prediction was the ring of Aubrey Holes, for which no reasonable explanation had ever been proposed.

Eclipses of the moon take place when the moon is cut off from the light of the sun by passing through the shadow of the earth. Thus they can only occur when the moon and the sun are in the opposite directions in the sky, and this is the time of the month when the moon is full. So eclipses of the moon happen only when the moon is full, but not every month because usually the moon passes either above or below the earth's shadow. On the average there is about one lunar eclipse each year, not all of them visible, because sometimes the moon is below the horizon during the hours of the eclipse. Eclipses can take place at any time of the year, and usually happen about three weeks earlier each year, so that after eighteen or nineteen years they have worked right round the calendar.

It is no accidental coincidence that this period is the same as the time it takes for the moon's rising and setting positions to go through their cycle; it is the same motion of the moon's orbit that is at the root of both effects. Given precisely, the time from major standstill to minor standstill and back again is 18·61 years, and three times 18·61 = 55·83. To the nearest whole number this is the number of the Aubrey Holes.

Professor Hawkins computed the position of the moon from 2001 BC to 1000 BC, working out when the moon would appear to rise over the Heel Stone. Because 18·61 is not a whole number, there is some irregularity in the intervals between risings in a particular direction. But after 56 years the cycles repeat more accurately, and the directions of moonrise in a particular year are a copy of those on the corresponding day 56 years before. He also worked out where the nearest full moon to the winter solstice would appear to rise, and concluded that when it rose over the Heel Stone an eclipse of the sun or moon would occur (though they would not all be seen from Stonehenge). He deduced that eclipses would occur after 56 years on the very same day of the year. Professor Hawkins suggested that perhaps the Aubrey Holes were used as a counting device, for keeping a tally of the years in the 56-year lunar cycle. A marker stone would be placed on the Aubrey Hole No. 56 (this is the hole in the same direction from the centre as the Heel Stone) when a winter eclipse had occurred, and it would be moved round clockwise by one hole every year. After 56 years it would again predict a winter eclipse.

By putting six marker stones round the ring of Aubrey Holes, at intervals of 9, 9, 10, 9, 9, 10 holes, intermediate winter eclipses could be predicted and Hawkins also proposed a method by which eclipses could be predicted for other times of the year.

In retrospect we can say that there are flaws in Hawkins's interpretation of the use of the Aubrey Holes. The 56-year period is not an eclipse cycle, and though eclipses can repeat on the same day after 18 years, they very rarely do so twice, and never three times. However, this was not generally appreciated in 1964, and certainly not by archaeologists who were already having problems trying to understand the somewhat simpler matter of lunar alignments.

There was a third strand in the thread of discoveries concerning the astronomical interests of prehistoric men in the British Isles. From the nineteen-thirties onwards, a professor of engineering at the University of Oxford, Alexander Thom, had been studying megalithic sites in England, Scotland, and Wales. (The term 'megalithic' simply means 'large stone' and is correctly applied to edifices like Stonehenge. By common practice the word has now become used to describe sites where the stones are not particularly large, if they date approximately to the same period as truly megalithic constructions, say the Late Neolithic and Early Bronze Ages. We shall use the wider definition in this book.)

Professor Thom first became interested in megalithic sites early in the century and visited and surveyed hundreds of them. As a practical engineer, who at one time worked on the construction of the Canadian railways, and a keen small-boat sailor, he fully appreciated the need for accurate observation and recording. Indeed his surveys were always meticulous and usually far exceeded in accuracy any that had been done before.

He had slowly come to three conclusions about stone rings. His first was that they were not all circular, and those that were not true circles were intentionally laid out in the form of other geometric figures, with the perimeter either extended to make an egg-shape, or squashed to make a flattened circle.

His second conclusion was that a common unit of length was used in laying out these shapes. He called it the megalithic yard, and its length he claimed as 0·83 m.

His third conclusion was that many of the stone circles and rings were associated with other stones or prominent natural features, such as an outcrop on a hillside, to indicate directions on the ground, and these directions were astronomically significant. They point to the directions of sunset at midsummer's and midwinter's day or at the solstices, and some indicate the limiting rising and setting positions of the moon.

Professor Thom's conclusions are amenable to statistical tests, though exactly what tests were valid became a subject of discussion among statisticians. When eventually Thom was able to find journals to print his papers, they were astronomical and mathematical journals, not archaeological ones. For a non-mathematician his scientific writings are very difficult to follow, and some archaeologists felt that somehow they were being bamboozled with scientific and mathematical jargon, and they were cautious if not actually hostile to these new ideas.

The first reason why archaeologists regarded the hypotheses of Hawkins and Thom with alarm was therefore that, with a few exceptions, they did not understand either the astronomy or the mathematics. They could not really be expected to. Original scientific papers make no concession to the uninitiated, mainly because if they are not as brief as possible they will not get printed. It was natural on reading these papers to think, 'If I, a twentieth-century man, can't understand it, how could it have been done four thousand years ago?' This is the same fallacy as we have noted over the use of optical instruments. The techniques that were developed for laying out and measuring geometrical shapes could have been very simple. The complexity of the modern scientific papers is introduced in order to test the hypotheses; megalithic man needed no statistics.

Nevertheless, if these astronomical observations were made as Thom and Hawkins claimed, the observers would have been intelligent men. Were people intelligent enough in 2000 BC? The answer is almost certainly yes. Four thousand years is a very short span in the one or two million years of human evolution. There is no reason to suppose that intelligence had got greatly out of step from one part of the world to another, and the great pyramids of Egypt, which were highly complex and sophisticated feats of engineering, had already been built for seven hundred years before the peak of megalithic astronomy. High standards of technical ability are clear enough in the mechanical construction of Stonehenge, the shaping and joining of the stones and the ability to transport and erect them. In any community there is a spread of intelligence, and the innovators are a small proportion of the population. It must have been the same in the megalithic period: a few geniuses were certain to have lived and invented things and directed their fellow men.

A more serious problem for archaeologists was to see how this knowledge could be assimilated, if at all, into what was already known about the period. It implies an organized society, with a group who had specialist knowledge of geometry and astronomy well in advance of their successors, a thousand years later. There would have been a need for recording observations and handing them down over several decades, yet no writing is known or even suspected. If the same units of length were used from one end of the country to the other, there would be difficulties in transporting the standards, and all for no apparent reason. It just did not square with the accepted idea of an illiterate farming community, whose technology had not developed beyond stone and bronze metal-working, and who lived apparently in unhealthy squalor, had a short expectation of life, and scraped a living from rudimentary farming.

The controversy reached its zenith in 1966. Professor Hawkins wrote a popular book, *Stonehenge Decoded*. It was far from popular among archaeologists. Hawkins's ideas were made the subject of a CBS television programme, 'The Mystery of Stonehenge', and thereby received much publicity throughout Britain and America. The archaeological establishment counterattacked with an article by Richard Atkinson in *Antiquity*. Professor Atkinson is one of the great authorities on Stonehenge. He has dug extensively on prehistoric sites in England and Scotland, and from 1956, in collaboration with Professor Stuart Piggott and Dr J. F. S. Stone, he conducted excavations at Stonehenge. His book *Stonehenge* is the standard work on the monument, and no one could have been better equipped to put forward the archaeological point of view.

His review of *Stonehenge Decoded* had the title 'Moonshine on Stonehenge'. He criticized Hawkins on several grounds, such as incomplete acknowledgement of his sources of information, inaccuracies in the archaeological sections of the book, and also because the confident style of *Stonehenge Decoded* was likely to give the general reader no inkling of the tentative nature of the author's hypotheses. More to the point was the criticism of the alignments that Hawkins had claimed. Atkinson rejected the disputed F, G, and H holes and argued that some of the remaining alignments were not nearly as accurate as Hawkins had claimed. He recalculated the probability of getting Hawkins's alignments by chance and concluded that instead of the probability being less than one in ten thousand, it was more like evens. Finally he admitted that Hawkins's work included some useful suggestions, especially concerning eclipses, and by implication he accepted the validity of the major alignments involving the four stations.

The archaeological quarterly *Antiquity* for 1966 and 1967 includes several articles on megalithic astronomy and geometry. Professor Thom wrote a paper in which he described the geometric construction of the shapes of stone rings, and put forward the suggestion that the reason why these curious shapes were chosen was to make the perimeters as well as their other dimensions equal to integral multiples of the megalithic yard. It is not possible with a perfect circle to have both the circumference and diameter equal to a whole number of units (though certain diameters approximate to this), but by distorting the shape it can be achieved to a high degree of accuracy. Thom also claimed to have discovered evidence for the use of right-angled triangles in these constructions; not just any right-angled triangle but the special ones which have their three sides in simple mathematical proportions. The best-known of these triangles, and one favoured in the megalithic period, has sides 3, 4, and 5 units in length.

Later in 1966 *Antiquity* published an article by the noted British astronomer, Professor Sir Fred Hoyle. After a rather mathematical résumé of the astronomical background, which was unlikely to have eased the problems most archaeologists had in following the controversy, he recalculated Hawkins's alignments. Hoyle's conclusion was that the builders could have made the alignments much more accurate than they actually did. Perhaps they had been made deliberately in-accurate, he suggested, to make the observations easier. There is very little movement in the sun's rising position from day to day as it approaches the maximum at the solstices. Instead of trying to find the exact day by sighting on the absolute maximum position, Hoyle thought they could have set the sightlines so that the sun rose over a stone a few days before and after the solstice. This would be much easier to observe and the solstice would be half way between the two dates. It is a good way of observing the sun's maximum, and could have been done at Stonehenge. With moon observations there are other problems, as we shall see later.

And what about the Aubrey Holes? Hoyle thought they represented a large protractor, or instrument for measuring angles. The Stonehenge Eclipse Prediction Unit would use the 'protractor' as a celestial model, and put on the appropriate Aubrey Holes markers to indicate the positions of the sun and moon in the sky. They would move the sun marker round anticlockwise two holes every thirteen days so that it did a full revolution in the year. They would move the moon marker anticlockwise two holes each day, so that it completed its circle in twenty-eight days. This is difficult, but would not have been impossible for the megalithic astronomers. The real problem is to place correctly two more stones which represent the positions where the moon, in its orbit round the earth, crosses the path that the sun traces out in the sky during the course of the year. These two markers, which we shall call the nodal markers, have to be moved clockwise three holes each year. When the sun and moon markers are exactly opposite each other, and the two nodal markers are on the same Aubrey Holes as the sun and the moon, there will be a lunar eclipse. There is no doubt that the Aubrey Holes could be used in this way, and setting out the markers with the aid of an astro-nomical almanac would be no great problem. There are, however, several objections to this idea. It is a very sophisticated method, requiring the formaliza-tion of astronomical concepts which it would be difficult for any primitive society to have attained. They would have had to represent points in the sky that were not directly observable, and whose existence could only be inferred from a long series of observations. Moreover, it would have been most difficult to set the stones in the correct positions to start the cycles. Finally, although a circle of fifty-six holes is a good number for this method, other numbers can also be used. Perhaps the *coup de grâce* for this proposal is that there are other and simpler methods of eclipse prediction not requiring this high degree of intellectual sophistication.

In 1972 the Royal Society and the British Academy jointly held a conference in London with the title 'The Place of Astronomy in the Ancient World'. Speakers talked about astronomy in Babylonia, Egypt, Polynesia, and China, but the real excitement came on the second day when the subject turned to megalithic astronomy in north-west Europe. At last, in one large assembly, were those who fervently believed in the ability of Bronze Age men to make accurate and ingenious astronomical observations and those who just as strongly pooh-poohed it. Would this conference resolve the conflict? It did not.

Nevertheless, the evidence for megalithic astronomy seemed to be building up steadily. For the first time there was an account of an archaeological dig deliberately planned to test the supposed observing site. Professor Thom had already published details of a site at Kintraw in Argyllshire, where he claimed that the midsummer sunset was observed from a small area of level ground on the side of a steep hill. Dr Euan MacKie excavated to see if this was a natural feature or a deliberately cut platform. If natural, there would be no evidence either way, but if artificial it would be strong support for the observatory hypothesis. Although MacKie found no pieces of pottery or other man-made objects, the platform turned out to have a cobbled surface, and the stones appeared to be set in a way that could not have happened by natural processes. This provided the first direct archaeological support for the astronomical theory.

Professor Thom, in the next four years, published a torrent of papers in the *Journal for the History of Astronomy*. With his son, Archibald, and as many other members of his family as he could persuade to join in, he studied the Carnac alignments in Brittany, the Ring of Brodgar on the Mainland of Orkney (Pl. 7), and finally Stonehenge. Up to then he had deliberately kept away from Stonehenge so that he could concentrate his attention on monuments he thought were quite as important but very neglected. He resurveyed the site with the thoroughness and accuracy characteristic of all his work and once again Stonehenge had a surprise in store. The arrangement of the trilithons, thought up to that time to be a rough sort of horseshoe, turns out to be a precise ellipse. Another discovery was that in the countryside surrounding Stonehenge there are distant markers on the horizon, correctly positioned for very accurate observations of the sun and moon. Maybe the inaccuracies in Hawkins's alignments are not important at all. Professor Thom's work showed that in spite of all the studies and investigations, we still have a lot to learn about Stonehenge.

What of the effect of this on professional archaeologists and traditional archaeology? In the face of accumulating evidence, archaeologists began to change their views. Professor Atkinson, who nine years earlier had written the critical paper on Hawkins's book, published, in the *Journal for the History of Astronomy*, a review of the work of Professor Thom and his collaborators. His comments are favourable and complimentary; he accepts most of Thom's conclusions and courageously admits he has changed his mind.

This paper marks a turning point in the study of megalithic astronomy. Not all the ideas will be substantiated with further investigation, but at least the subject is respectable and can be discussed in archaeological circles without creating embarrassment.

The problems now lie elsewhere. If the ideas about megalithic astronomy are accepted in principle, what are the implications for our picture of the Late Neolithic and Early Bronze Ages? What sort of a society was it that produced the conditions where, for a few centuries, such intellectual pursuits could flourish? These and similar questions are the ones waiting to be answered in future research.

2 The First Farmers of North-West Europe

Archaeology is the study of the activities and the development of the human race by examination of the remains that people have left behind. Archaeological techniques can be applied just as validly to modern communities as to ancient ones, and then are used to supplement the information that comes from the written records. In the case of prehistoric communities, which by definition are those that have no written or historical records, archaeology is usually the only source of information. The maximum amount has to be deduced from the stones, small finds, and remains of earthworks that are now left to us and therefore it becomes necessary for archaeologists to pore over unexciting material like bits of old, broken, and often badly manufactured pottery, to try to reconstruct from these fragments something about the people who made them. On the assumption that they were rather conservative in their habits, and made pots or spearheads or huts in much the same way as their fathers and mothers, archaeologists look for both continuity and change in style and manufacturing methods, and then try to interpret these to throw light on the communities who made the objects. With luck it is sometimes possible to deduce important facts about how different societies related to each other and how they moved or changed their character, grew or decayed away.

We must be careful not to equate archaeology with its techniques. The study of prehistoric pots or burial places is not the totality of archaeology. These are techniques, and archaeology should be the study of people. In the same way that the techniques of pottery analysis may lead to broader conclusions, so the study of prehistoric astronomy should be regarded, not as something special and mysterious, but as another technique available to the practising archaeologist to help him find out a little more about the people who lived and worked on his site.

The real value of trying to piece together what is known about the astronomical and mathematical activities of men in early Europe is to give additional information about their way of life. It is something that has to be added to our general knowledge of prehistory. It should neither be neglected, nor given too much emphasis. Conventional archaeological books have generally ignored the astronomical discoveries until now, and books about the astronomical significance of prehistoric monuments tend to give the impression that the earth was populated by super geniuses whose sole occupation was computing with great refinement the movements of the heavenly bodies. This can't be true; we have to try, through a long fog of time, to see these astronomically-minded people in the context of the other facts that archaeologists have found out about them during a hundred years of excavation and research.

We must confine ourselves rather strictly in both space and time. Astronomical measurements and observations have been made by many different communities in all parts of the world, from Europe to the Pacific Ocean, and over a very long period indeed, from 3500 BC to the present day. But the observational methods that are described in this book are centred on a small part of north-west Europe, mainly the British Isles from the Shetland Islands to Cornwall, including Ireland, and an area of northern France roughly equivalent to present-day Brittany. During the period we are interested in, say from 3500 BC to 1500 BC at the outside, there were cultural links with a rather wider area of Europe, including Spain, most of France, northern Germany and Denmark, and parts of southern Sweden. Although it would not be in any way surprising for astronomically important sites to be discovered in these last areas (especially the more northern ones), so far they do not seem to have been identified, and for the most part we shall concentrate on the British Isles, where the majority of studies have taken place, with occasional attention to the monuments in Brittany. (Locations of places mentioned in this and subsequent chapters are shown on Figures 2.1, 2.2, and 2.3; a chronological chart is given on Figure 2.4.)

It is not necessary to begin with the earliest occupation of the area. The first human habitations in the British Isles were many thousands of years ago, and faint traces of their occupancy have been found, showing that during the warmer spells of the last Ice Age small groups of people lived by hunting and gathering food. The most recent advance of the ice sheets did not finally begin to withdraw northward until perhaps 12000 BC, and it is only since the climate improved at the end of the last Ice Age that there has been continuous occupancy of these islands.

Before about 4000 BC there was no settled agriculture in Great Britain or Ireland. The inhabitants gained their living from what they could kill or gather. They hunted the wild animals, fished, snared birds, dug out insects, and ate whatever wild plants were found to be palatable, following a way of life similar to the Australian aboriginals of a century ago. In some places there was an abundant supply of food throughout the year, such as by rocky coastlines where they could always be sure of finding shellfish. Inland, they moved from camp to camp, living in one place during the winter, in another in the summer, following the wanderings of the animals they hunted, and stripped the trees of nuts and fruit. They developed the technique of chipping flints until they had a wide variety of tools: axes, scrapers, knives, flint-tipped arrows, awls for boring holes in wood and bone, and even saws, and their finely shaped and barbed harpoons have been found at several sites. We presume they made wooden objects too, for at Star Carr in Yorkshire an oar was discovered, and perhaps their boats were skin-covered coracles kept watertight with animal fat.

But these people had no pottery, no knowledge of cultivating the ground, and as far as we know did not domesticate animals. About 4000 BC another culture arrived in these islands that could do all these things and more besides. They brought with them a totally different way of life. Although they still had not discovered metals, and therefore the new culture was stone-age like its predecessor, archaeologists distinguish them by calling the earlier culture the Mesolithic (Middle Stone Age) and the later one the Neolithic (New Stone Age).

The most important change was the introduction of farming, which brought with it the need to remain more or less in one place. The countryside was mainly covered with woodland, oak, elm, lime, and alder, which had to be cleared by felling and burning. A primitive wheat, called emmer, was planted out for the main cereal crop, and a little barley was also grown. The people of the Mesolithic

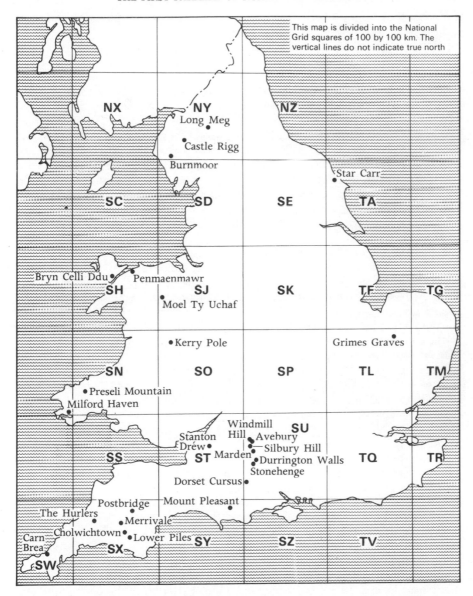

This map is divided into the National Grid squares of 100 by 100 km. The vertical lines do not indicate true north

NX

NY
Long Meg
• Castle Rigg
Burnmoor

NZ

• Star Carr

SC

SD

SE

TA

• Bryn Celli Ddu
SH
• Penmaenmawr

SJ
• Moel Ty Uchaf

SK

TF

TG

• Kerry Pole

Grimes Graves•

SN

SO

SP

TL

TM

• Preseli Mountain
Milford Haven

Windmill
Hill
Stanton
Drew•
SS

SU
• Avebury
•—Silbury Hill
ST • Marden
•Durrington Walls
Stonehenge

TQ

TR

Dorset Cursus•

Postbridge •Mount Pleasant
The Hurlers •Merrivale
Carn •Cholwichtown•
Brea •Lower Piles SY
SX

SZ

TV

SW

FIG. 2.1 Locations of some of the places in England and Wales which are referred to in the text

Period almost certainly lived, like the Red Indians, in transportable tents made of animal skins over a wooden framework, but the neolithic tribes did not need to migrate in search of food; they had to be static to tend the crops. Thus settlements began, and sites of early houses are known, dating from about 3500 BC.

Probably they were timber-framed, with walls made of split planking and roofs either thatched or covered with turves.

The new way of life did not of course arise spontaneously in the British Isles. Farming began in the lands around the eastern end of the Mediterranean Sea, in what is now Israel, Iran, and Asia Minor, perhaps around 7000 to 6000 BC, when the mesolithic tribes were just beginning to repopulate northern Europe. Slowly the new methods spread towards the west, not by a massive migration of warlike armies, as occurred in central Europe at the end of the Roman Empire, nor by streams of settlers trekking their way across the continent like the American pioneers, but more probably by the children of each generation clearing and cultivating land just a little bit further west than their family home. As the population expanded there was a need for more farming land, and so where the forest was not too thick to clear, and the land not too heavy to work, there was a slow drift towards the coast of the Atlantic.

Looking back from this distance in time it is difficult to appreciate the enormity of the change that had taken place. The Neolithic Revolution, as it has been called, was a major turning-point in the history of the human race, even though it took hundreds of years, as far-reaching in its consequences as the Industrial Revolution was in the eighteenth century. For the first time men became settled in particular localities; in the Near East villages and towns were established thousands of years before the end of the Mesolithic Period in Britain. The increasing population led also to social organization of some sort, and men co-operated in the construction of large earthworks, whose remains can be seen to this day. The interested tourist in the twentieth century will find nothing to see from the Mesolithic Period, but there are many impressive remains from the Neolithic that he can locate without difficulty.

With the end of the migratory life-style, manpower became available and the neolithic people began to construct enclosures on the chalk hilltops of southern Britain. The first to be excavated and recognized as a neolithic earthwork is on Windmill Hill, near Avebury in Wiltshire, and since we have no idea what its builders would have called themselves, archaeologists sometimes talk about the Windmill Hill culture, though it would be assuming too much to regard this term as an indication of a family, tribal, or political unit. The Windmill Hill enclosure, and others like it, are also known as causewayed camps. In general they have one or more irregularly shaped banks, with an external ditch. The ditches seem to have little function other than as quarries for the material of the banks, because they are not continuous round the outside, and they give the impression of having many entrances, or causeways. In fact the banks are continuous where the ditches are not, except for one or two deliberate entrances, and the enclosures seem to be fortified for the protection of the community and its livestock. They may of course have been just as much for protection against wild animals as against human enemies. Causewayed camps do not usually provide a lot of archaeological material in the way of small finds, bone and pottery, nor do they have foundations of houses, and this has led some researchers to the view that they were not permanently occupied but were used seasonally for cattle-herding, sheep-shearing, and social activities. We must remember, however, that in chalk uplands the land surface has been eroded by half a metre or more since 3000 BC and many of the fragments of bone and pots would have disappeared along with the soil. Unless the houses had been constructed with posts set deep into the ground, their traces would also have vanished, and there is now little hope of recovering evidence for buildings from these sites.

Whatever the primary purpose of causewayed camps, they certainly confirm that in southern England, by 3500 BC, societies had become organized to the extent that medium-sized projects could be undertaken. The outermost banks of a multibanked enclosure are typically about 600 m long and surround five or six hectares of land. With antler picks, bone or wooden shovels, and baskets for carrying the excavated chalk, they probably took several tens of man-years to complete. The communities who built the camps are thought to have been very small, not more than fifty people, and we must bear in mind that they had to put the business of farming before building.

Because very few of the houses of this period have been found, not much is known about them. They seem to have been generally rectangular, both in the British Isles and on the mainland of Europe. One, at Ballynagilly in Ireland, was $6\frac{1}{2}$ m by 6 m in dimension, made of wood with walls of vertical split planking. At Carn Brea in Cornwall there is a neolithic enclosure with ample evidence of living sites, and the remains of hearths and a mass of stake holes. Carn Brea was a neolithic hilltop village occupied around 3700 to 3300 BC.

These and other sites produce evidence of the technology of the Early Neolithic. Pottery was very crude. It was moulded into shape by hand and the earliest forms were round-bottomed, shaped like bags, and look as though they were attempts to reproduce in clay the leather containers that must have been a traditional pattern from the Mesolithic Period (Pl. 4a). They were often decorated with lines made by bone scrapers, or by punctured patterns made by pricking, which are common ways of decorating leather goods, even to this day. Sometimes they are ornamented with turned-over rims, formed with finger and thumb. Pots of this period could not be fired to a very high temperature and are consequently rather fragile and crumbly.

In this long span of the Neolithic Period, the pottery developed into many different styles. Decorations include the impressions made by twisted or whipped cord; sometimes lugs were added, which must have made for easier lifting, and pots with lugs or collars could have been suspended over the cooking fire. Towards the end of the period, flat-bottomed pottery, known as grooved ware, came into use (Pl. 5a). It is found in many places in Britain and is dated to a few hundred years on either side of 2500 BC.

Stone was the important source of material for tools. In the Great Langdale district of Cumbria there was a flourishing axe factory which exported polished axes as far as the south coast of England, 450 km away. It was only one of more than twenty axe factories scattered from Brittany to the Lake District, which have been located by petrological methods. As well as igneous rock, flint was used. The neolithic people of southern England opened up a considerable flint industry, which reached its peak in the Late Neolithic Period at Grimes Graves in Norfolk. They dug shafts down to the best layers of flints and mined horizontal galleries, taking care to leave pillars of unexcavated rock at intervals to support the roof. The flint nodules were extracted from the chalk by levering with antler picks and often the preliminary working was done at the bottom of the mine-shaft, the mines exporting roughly shaped axes. In their finished form the axes

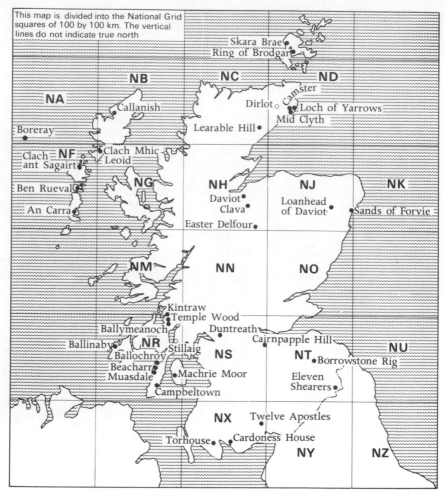

This map is divided into the National Grid squares of 100 by 100 km. The vertical lines do not indicate true north

FIG. 2.2   Locations of some of the places in Scotland which are referred to in the text

were ground and polished to make tools which are handsome as well as effective.

Though the dating evidence is still sparse, the earliest flint mines began before 4000 BC and the axe factories in the igneous rock areas were in use by 3500 BC. Grimes Graves was mass-producing axes around 2600 BC. We can draw two conclusions from the existence of the axe industry. Mining is a difficult job, demanding much specialized knowledge and experience, not only for the selection of the best raw materials, but also in providing for the safety of the miners. It would seem that even in the Neolithic Period some groups of men had specialized in a branch of technology and were probably working at it full-time. The second conclusion concerns trade. The stone axes are found hundreds of miles from their points of origin. It is possible that in the early days they were traded between adjacent settlements, never moving more than a few miles at each transaction. However, the mines at Grimes Graves were producing large quantities of axes, and the industry could not have continued without a regular means of distribution of its products. Either traders were setting out from the mining areas to sell the axes, or possibly the communities who needed them were buying in bulk directly from the mines. In either case, the implication of this in archaeo-astronomy is that the existence of trading patterns from early in the Neolithic Period would account for the spread of knowledge as well as goods over a wide area of Britain.

There were links even with the neolithic people of the far north. In 1866 a storm on the Orkney Islands exposed a group of neolithic houses at Skara Brae, on the west coast of the Mainland of Orkney. The site was excavated in 1928–30 by Professor Gordon Childe, who uncovered a tightly packed complex of seven stone huts. They had been buried by drifting sand in prehistoric times, and although the roofs had disappeared, the walls were still $2\frac{1}{2}$ m high in places. The sand had protected the contents, as the volcanic ash preserved the Roman town of Pompeii. Inside the huts were suites of neolithic 'furniture': beds, dressers, shelves, and water tanks, all made of slabs of stone (Pl. 5b). In the Orkneys timber was hard to come by, and the resourceful occupants had made for themselves useful everyday equipment that would have been made out of wood in more hospitable parts of the British Isles. The link with other neolithic sites is found in the pottery. At Skara Brae the earliest levels contain grooved ware, thus showing either that there was direct trade or that fashion spread from one end of Britain to the other before 2000 BC. The site is also important because of the vivid picture it reveals of the domestic scene in neolithic times.

The most numerous remains of the Neolithic Period are, however, not evidence of their way of life, but of the rites of death. From the Shetland Islands to Spain, neolithic communities built large and impressive tombs for the remains of their dead. Although the style of construction varies considerably from place to place, there is a consistency of theme: there is a chamber, or small room, above ground rather than dug into the earth, covered with a mound far larger than the actual chamber, and usually off-centre. Differences are found in the building materials, which may be small stones, enormous slabs, or heaps of earth; in the size and shape of the internal chambers, which can be long thin passages or vaulted; in the shape of the mound, which can take any proportions between a long bank and a circular heap; and in the treatment of the entrances to the tombs, which can be deliberately impressive, or quite hidden.

In southern England, on the chalk downs where there was little stone, the typical burial mounds are earthen long barrows. Not uncommonly, the beginnings of the structure would be a wooden mortuary house, maybe a copy of their ordinary houses, where the dead bodies would be left for years, gradually accumulating in numbers until perhaps twenty or more were present. The memorial mound would then be heaped up over the mortuary house and possibly the tomb would be sealed. The mounds in this region were always longer than they were wide. They vary in length from 15 to 30 m.

Where stone was more plentiful there are stone structures inside the earthen mounds. The most famous is the West Kennet long barrow, with its 12 m-long passage leading to five separate burial chambers. The passage is nearly $2\frac{1}{2}$ m high and is basically two rows of vertical slabs of stone with horizontal capstones making the roof. Its entrance was in the centre of an imposing forecourt, with more large upright slabs forming a retaining wall for the end of the barrow. The entrance was deliberately sealed in antiquity with a blocking stone, though judging by the quantity of human remains inside the chambers, this was not done until the tomb had been in use for a long period of time.

West Kennet is usually described as a chambered long barrow. The two main types of stone-built neolithic tombs are passage graves and gallery graves. Passage graves are those with a large burial chamber approached by a passage which is narrower and with a lower roof than the chamber itself (Pl. 11). There are examples in Ireland, the most famous being at New Grange in County Meath; in Scotland, particularly in the far north; and in Brittany. Gallery graves have the passage, but no widened chamber at the end, and these too can be found from Scotland to France.

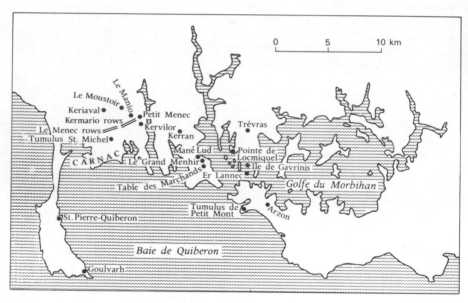

FIG. 2.3   Locations of some of the places in Brittany near the town of Carnac which are referred to in the text

One of the most spectacular groups of neolithic tombs is found in southern Brittany around the Golfe du Morbihan. The tombs here can truly be described as megalithic. The vertical sides of the passages are often huge slabs of roughly shaped rock and they are capped with enormous stones, some of them weighing many tens of tonnes. Several graves have lost their covering mounds in the centuries since they were constructed, and the capstones are clearly seen, perched on their uprights, as though defiantly mocking the force of gravity. It is impossible to gaze at these monuments without the feeling that their builders were intentionally showing off their technical expertise in handling huge masses of stone. They were meant to impress, and impress they do.

Although most of the megalithic tombs are not decorated in any way, a small number are spectacularly ornamented with carved stones. In Brittany, on the tiny island of Gavrinis, is a passage grave with a circular mound 6 m high. No fewer than twenty-three of the twenty-nine upright slabs that form the walls of the passage and chamber are covered with patterns of inscribed lines, with spirals, zig-zags, ellipses, concentric semicircles and other, more complicated, geometrical figures. A few carvings are pictures of stone axes, and these are the only ones that can be interpreted with any certainty; if the rest are intended to represent faces, animals, or other everyday objects, the abstract styling effectively disguises their meaning. Very similar patterns are found on stones in passage graves in Ireland. The entrance to New Grange has a large horizontal stone decorated with chiselled geometrical designs, including spirals and concentric semicircles strongly resembling the patterns at Gavrinis. Naturalistic carvings are quite absent, and the overall effect is more of geometric doodling than of artistic talent.

In north-west Europe building of neolithic tombs probably began in Brittany, about 4000 BC. The earliest earthen long barrows also date to 4000 BC and they were constructed for perhaps a thousand years. The Irish graves are a little later, beginning about 3500 BC, and the few datings that have been obtained from the Scottish tombs are roughly contemporary with the Irish. Archaeologists have made several attempts to classify them into different types and put them in sequences with cultural affinities, using the same methods that have proved useful with pottery and flints, but so far with little success. For many years it was believed that megalithic tombs originated in the eastern Mediterranean, and that an earth goddess religion spread, carrying with it the knowledge of megalithic engineering into Spain and then along the Atlantic coast to Brittany, Great Britain, and the adjacent islands. We now know that this simple scheme cannot be true. Improvements in dating techniques have revealed that the megalithic tombs of western Europe were built before the large stone structures in the east, and furthermore they appear to be almost contemporary over the whole of the area in which they are found. Some of the constructional methods may well have been passed from one region to another, but not the detailed designs. The decorations on the tombs show so much similarity of style that it would be a remarkable coincidence if they were quite independent; yet we must not jump to quick conclusions, because we cannot always be sure that the stones were carved at the time the graves were built.

Local variations in tomb construction are in part due to the availability of different building materials, but they also show independent interpretations of the basic idea of a large, impressive, communal grave. The mystery of the megalithic tombs is why, at this particular period, social forces should have made it necessary to divert substantial resources from the essential tasks of feeding, clothing, and housing people to building large and extravagant monuments for the receipt of the dead.

If it has been difficult to understand the reasons for the large tombs, other remains from the Neolithic Period have proved even more puzzling. In England there are about twenty recognized examples of a type of monument known as a cursus. These are superficially just parallel banks of earth, thrown up from material out of external ditches, which run for considerable distances across the country-side. They are not boundaries (but were sometimes used as such later), nor a sensible shape for agricultural enclosures, and antiquarians of the last century speculated that they were prehistoric racecourses, hence the name cursus. They are found in association with long barrows, and have come to be regarded as some sort of processional way for funerary rites. The largest is the Dorset Cursus, whose banks are 80 m apart and extend for 10 km, up and down hillsides, on Cranborne Chase. Whatever its original purpose, it must have been important to its builders, for it must have taken at least 200 man-years of effort to construct. The Dorset Cursus may be one of the early examples of a feature for making astro-nomical observations, and we shall return to it in later chapters.

In Europe the largest prehistoric mound, and the greatest neolithic engineering work of all, is Silbury Hill. It looks like a conical round barrow with a flat top, and it is of quite surprising dimensions, nearly 40 m high and covering an area of 2·2 hectares. The weight of material used in its construction is not far short of half a million tonnes, and it is estimated to have required 5,000 man-years of work. Excavations have shown that it is not just a heap of chalk piled up in a crude mound, but that it has been skilfully constructed with internal walls of chalk blocks to make a stable structure. It seems not to be a burial mound, for no primary interment has been found in spite of several excavations, and its purpose remains a complete mystery. It was built between 3000 BC and 2500 BC, which is quite consistent with the grand architectural schemes of the megalithic period. Even by comparison with the Great Pyramid of Giza it is a commendable achievement, for it is about 10 per cent of the volume of the pyramid, and may be a few hundred years older.

There is yet one more type of remains from the Neolithic Period, the henge. The name comes in a circuitous way from the word Stonehenge, meaning 'hanging stone'. Because Stonehenge started as an earth-banked enclosure, other similar enclosures have been called henges, whether they had internal stones or not. There are different varieties of henges, and the earliest, the Class I henges, were first built at the time of the neolithic causewayed enclosures. They are smaller than causewayed camps and have the ditch inside the bank which is a weaker arrangement defensively. (Stonehenge, in spite of being the origin of the word 'henge', is untypical because it has the ditch outside.) Class I henges have one entrance and appear to be ceremonial meeting places. They are almost all located in southern England and are not known outside Great Britain and Ireland.

Towards the end of the Neolithic Period, around 2600 BC, men began to build another type of henge. These, the Class II henges, are larger and have two or more entrances. Four henges are very big compared with the others, having diameters greater than 350 m. They are all in southern England, and three, Avebury (Pl. 3), Marden, and Durrington Walls, are within 30 km of Stonehenge. The fourth is at Mount Pleasant, near Dorchester, in Dorset. A most interesting feature of the super-henges is that they have internal structures, stone circles in the case of Avebury, wooden buildings in the other three. The buildings were substantial; their ground plans show concentric circular, or nearly circular, rings or postholes with the posts larger near the centre than at the outside. It is difficult to reconstruct the whole of a structure from its ground plan alone, yet the arrangement of posts is quite consistent with what would be needed for roof supports. Many archaeologists think that they had conical roofs, low on the outside and rising to a point in the centre, like the native huts in parts of Africa. A lot of pottery, especially grooved ware, has been found in the ditches, and the picture begins to emerge of a small number of permanently occupied centres, where possibly a chieftain and his family, or a group of priests, had their base.

Not quite all the neolithic round houses were in Class II henge enclosures. The first site to be interpreted as a large roofed building is at Woodhenge, a curious and fascinating site which we shall study later, where the builders made use of a small Class I henge, not more than 100 m outside the bank of Durrington Walls. Another famous example is the Sanctuary, 2½ km from Avebury, where there has been a long sequence of wooden buildings, each one bigger than its predecessor. By the end of the Neolithic Period we see many signs of a highly organized and vigorous society, capable of large civil engineering works which could not have been accomplished without technical knowledge and logistic planning. These people had advanced a long way beyond the popular notion of ignorant savages.

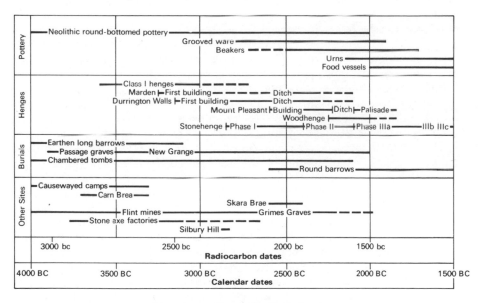

FIG. 2.4 Chronological chart

This chart is only an approximate guide to the chronology of the Late Neolithic and Early Bronze Ages. For the relationship between radiocarbon and calendar dates, see Appendix B.

The Neolithic Period was followed by the Early Bronze Age. Not long after 2500 BC another group of people began to populate the British Isles. They can be distinguished anatomically as well as culturally. They were tall and had characteristic round heads, contrasting with the shorter stature and long-headedness of the neolithic population. They brought with them the knowledge of bronze metal-working and also a distinctive style of pottery, a decorated drinking cup or beaker, which has led to their being called the Beaker Folk (Pl. 4b). They also cultivated barley; these two facts have led archaeologists to suggest that the art of brewing beer was one of the Beaker Folk's contributions to civilization.

Their movements can be traced through continental Europe. From Spain they migrated northwards and eastwards, eventually reaching England via the Rhine basin. Researchers are still discussing whether there were two main waves of immigrants or a more complex pattern of arrivals. Attempts to reconstruct the order of events have relied on interpreting sequences of the varieties of Beaker pottery, and they are not yet sufficiently supported by dating evidence.

Remains of domestic settlements are very scarce from the Early Bronze Age and this is a problem for archaeologists. Whereas a few neolithic houses have been excavated and studied, houses from the Early Bronze Age are almost unknown. There are only a few places, such as Downton in Wiltshire, where the postholes of Beaker huts have been found, and Dartmoor, where small round stone huts possibly date to the right period, that give a clue to the home life of the Beaker Folk. Perhaps this was because Beaker agriculture reverted to more nomadic methods of cultivation, but another explanation could be that they no longer had need of permanent and strongly built houses because the climate had improved. During the period from 2500 BC to 1500 BC there was a warm spell and this would have allowed them a more outdoor existence than the neolithic people had. The Beaker Folk possibly survived comfortably with temporary shelters made of hides like those of the Mesolithic Period, using them for shelter only during the worst of the weather, and sleeping in the open when it was fine.

Most of our knowledge of Beaker Folk has come from excavating their burials. Although occasionally Beaker remains are found associated with long barrows, the usual Beaker custom in England was to inter the dead either singly or in very small numbers in a crouched position in round barrows. Sometimes a pit was dug first, sometimes the bodies were placed directly on the ground and covered by a mound or small cairn. They did not leave many possessions in the grave: a pot perhaps, and now and again a bronze article such as a dagger or a clothes pin. The Beaker burials span hundreds of years and a wide area, so it is not surprising that evidence of different customs is found. In the north and west of the British Isles stone boxes, called cists, were used, and cremation, rare with the early Beaker graves, gradually became a more common practice.

The Beaker Folk were once thought to have been dominant and warlike invaders who suppressed the indigenous tribes and forcibly established their own culture in place of the neolithic. The current view is that this is altogether too simple an interpretation. Fragments of Beaker pottery turn up at some neolithic sites, such as Durrington Walls, with apparently no break in continuity. At other sites, such as Mount Pleasant, there seems to be a gap between neolithic and Beaker occupation. The entrance to the West Kennet long barrow was not blocked until after the Beaker arrivals, and they used and modified many of the henges. The relationship between the old and new cultures must receive more study before it can be properly understood.

Nevertheless one result of the impact of the Beaker Folk on the indigenous tribes is clearly seen by the changing styles of native pottery. There are two main groups of pots, the food vessels and the urns, and as with the Beaker Folk, in default of anything better, the pottery has given its name to the cultural groups who made it. The Food Vessel people were the more strongly influenced by the new arrivals. Their pottery has a hybrid style, often bearing decorative motifs 'borrowed' from beakers as well as a strong resemblance to the designs used in the Late Neolithic Period. They followed closely the Beaker burial customs, especially where the Beaker population was densest. They put their dead in round barrows in the south-east, and in stone cists in the north-west of the British Isles. Quite commonly they used existing Beaker round barrows, putting their corpses in pits dug into the sides of the mound.

The Urnfolk were much less influenced and preferred to cremate their dead, following a custom that had begun to appear towards the end of the Neolithic Period. They seem to have clung as best they could to the old customs; to individual graves they preferred cemeteries, for which they often used the old henge enclosures.

Early Bronze Age graves are very poor in material possessions, apart from one small group of barrows in southern England, the Wessex group, dated to about 1500 BC. Although the majority of graves of this date were not particularly rich, and contain the everyday pottery of food vessel and urn, from the richest barrows have come finely worked gold plates for personal adornment, bronze daggers, curiously decorated cups looking like pomegranates, dress pins, beads, tweezers, and a ceremonial mace. These are not the graves of another wave of invaders, wealthy as their owners certainly were; they are the signs of a short era of local prosperity that came about after the merging of the Beaker and the earlier traditions. For many years archaeologists regarded the Wessex graves as the burial places of the chieftains who were rich and powerful enough to organize and afford the sarsen circle of Stonehenge. This view can be held no longer; the Wessex culture came too late for the building of the sarsen circle and if the Wessex chieftains were involved at all in the construction of Stonehenge, it was with some relatively minor rearrangement of the bluestones at the very end of the Early Bronze Age.

Stonehenge is only one of more than 900 stone circles in the British Isles. The building of stone circles started in the Neolithic Period, and one of the earliest is a ring of stones surrounding the passage grave at New Grange. Whether the circle is contemporary with the tomb and therefore dated to about 3300 BC is not known—it is notoriously difficult to date standing stones. Except for the lucky chance of finding a datable object in the original packing material at its base, chronology has to rely on comparison and association. It is not always possible to state with certainty whether a stone circle belongs to the Late Neolithic or Early Bronze Ages. However, the general trends are becoming clearer. Perhaps one third of the known stone circles were constructed before the end of the Neolithic Period. These tend to be the larger and more spectacular ones, such as the Stones of Stenness on Orkney and the circles at Avebury. In both these cases the stones were set up inside neolithic henges.

Avebury, with a diameter of 370 m, is the largest stone circle in the British Isles. In addition to the ring of stones going the whole way round the Class II henge just inside the ditch, there were two smaller, but still large, circles inside the main one, and yet more stones inside one of these. The largest stones were over 40 tonnes, and before they were deliberately broken up for building material between the fourteenth and eighteenth centuries, there were about 170 stones in all. Now unfortunately only 43 remain.

The Beaker Folk and their successors took over the techniques for handling large blocks of stone, and although they no longer built communal graves, they set up stones in circles, rows, and as solitary megaliths from Shetland to Brittany. Stone settings have great architectural diversity, for the rings are not all true circles, the stones may be big or small, and they are different in their archaeological associations. Few circles have stones as large as Stonehenge or Avebury and many have stones barely half a metre tall. In moorland areas the small stones may appear even smaller than they are, owing to the accumulation of peat that has occurred since the Early Bronze Age. On the whole, the later stone circles are smaller and less imposing than the earlier ones.

To the men who built them these circles must have had great ceremonial and religious significance. Many of them are associated with burials. It has been suggested that the very idea of stone circles came originally from the kerbstones incorporated into megalithic tombs and round barrows to stabilize the construction, though this is not now a widely held opinion. In many cases there are cairns within stone circles, not closely adjacent like the kerbs but occupying only a small fraction of the area defined by the ring of stones. It is not easy to decide with these whether the cairns were built inside an existing circle because it was a sacred enclosure, or whether the stones were erected round the cairn to emphasize its importance. Stone circles quite commonly have casual burials and cremations within them, unmarked by cairns, and remains of incomplete human skeletons imply that rather unpleasant religious ceremonies took place.

In Scotland there is a distinctive variety, the recumbent stone circle, in which one of the stones lies flat and is flanked by two tall uprights. The other stones, all standing, diminish in size towards the opposite side from the horizontal stone. The recumbent stone circle at Loanhead of Daviot in Aberdeenshire surrounds a ring cairn which has been found to contain burnt human bone. It has been dated to 2200 BC, and though this may be later than the stone circle, it is one of the few datings available so far.

Outside Great Britain and Ireland stone circles are rare. In Brittany there are very few and they differ from those we have just been considering in the spacings between the stones. In the British stone circles the stones are well spaced out, and while they may adequately delineate an area, they could not be said to form an enclosure. At Er Lannec in the Golfe du Morbihan there are two rings set so that they form a figure-of-eight. The stones are close together, if not touching, and appear to make a crude wall. They are not very visible now because the sea level has risen since megalithic times and one circle is covered by water at high tide. The other is exposed on its northern half, where the ground level is a little higher. The rings have been dated only by the pottery found in the cists on the site and are believed to be from 2500 BC or a little earlier, contemporary in fact with the oldest of the British stone circles. The ashes of fires were found inside the cists during the excavations of 1923–6, and perhaps this is evidence of nocturnal or midwinter ceremonies, since no cremated human remains were discovered.

Although they are not as common as stone circles, there are many sites where stones are arranged in rows or avenues. The henge at Avebury once had a very impressive pair of stone rows, called the Kennet Avenue, which ran from its southern entrance to the Sanctuary, already referred to as one of the multi-posted Late Neolithic buildings. At the period of the Kennet Avenue, however, the building was demolished and two concentric stone circles were erected in its place. Though the two rows are parallel they are not straight, and they have the appearance of simply marking out a convenient route from one important place to another. The width of the Avenue is about 25 m, and one can easily imagine a ceremonial procession making its way with dignity between the lines of standing stones.

There are rows of standing stones leading to circles in several other places in the British Isles. At Stanton Drew in Somerset, for instance, the large stone circle, 112 m in diameter, has an avenue and nearby another avenue connects to a smaller stone circle. In the Hebrides, at Callanish on the Isle of Lewis, one of a particularly important set of circles has a stone avenue leading northwards (Pl. 6). Here there are some obvious differences, for the avenue does not lead to a ceremonial entrance to the ring of stones, and other stone rows project from the circle in several different directions. Whatever their purpose, they are not in the least like processional ways.

Stone rows are numerous on Dartmoor in Devon. Large stones, like those at Avebury and Callanish, occur in only a few rows; for the most part the rows are composed of stones up to half a metre high with larger ones marking the ends. Rows can be single, double, or even triple. Where they are double the space between the lines of stones is usually too narrow for two or more persons to walk comfortably side by side, and they would hardly be suitable for a dignified procession. Although some rows have small cairns at the ends, others have 'blocking stones', and the rows do not apparently go anywhere in particular or have any clear purpose. For more than two centuries they have been regarded as one of the mysteries of Dartmoor.

In the far north of Scotland, in Caithness, at a few enigmatic sites we find large numbers of small stones arranged in a fan-shaped pattern. The best-known site of this type is Hill o' Many Stanes at Mid Clyth. The positions of the two hundred or so low slabs still remaining have been surveyed by Professor Thom, who interprets the layout as a grid with the stones arranged at the intersections of the rows and columns. The twenty-two rows, each about 42 m long, converge towards one end. The closest modern analogy would be to compare them to a sector of polar co-ordinate graph paper (Fig. 7.8).

Nothing like this is known in the rest of the British Isles, but the great alignments at Carnac in Brittany closely resemble the Scottish fans of stones in their disposition, if not in their scale. There are several sets of alignments in the Carnac area. The Menec alignments consist of twelve converging rows, 1,167 m long, extending from a ring of stones at one end to the remains of a ring at the other (Pl. 23). The largest stones are at the western end, where the rows are also widest apart, and they gradually diminish in size from 4 m tall down to 0·6 m as one goes along the rows. At the very eastern end the stones are once more taller than a man. The pattern is repeated almost exactly in the Kermario alignments a short distance further east. There are yet more alignments on a smaller scale within a few kilometres. In all, there are more than 2,000 stones in these rows and several tens of thousands of tonnes of rock have been quarried, transported, and erected to realize the ambitions of the builders.

Not all standing stones are in rows and circles, they also occur singly and in small groups. They can be associated or not with prehistoric remains such as burial cairns. When not near other remains there may be difficulty in identifying them positively as prehistoric, though if they are more than 2 m high they are not too likely to be modern boundary stones or gateposts. The distinction of having the largest 'standing' stone, now unfortunately fallen, goes to Brittany. It is Le Grand Menhir Brisé, a few kilometres from Carnac (Pl. 24). (Menhir is simply standing stone in Breton.) The Grand Menhir lies in four pieces, where according to folklore it was brought down by an earthquake hundreds of years ago. Its length is 20·5 m and it weighs 330 tonnes. Of all the stones moved in the megalithic period, this is the biggest. It is almost certainly the heaviest object ever moved without powered machinery anywhere in the whole world.

The stones of the megalithic monuments were very rarely dressed. They were either erected in their natural state or split by wedges or heat along cleavage planes to make crudely shaped blocks. This does not mean that the shape was unimportant. One can find many sites where tall, thin stones alternate with fat ones, for example the Kennet Avenue, and it is thought that these are symbolic representations of male and female. The few fully-dressed stones were shaped by light hammering and grinding with hand-held boulders of hard stone, and this tedious method was employed at Stonehenge to make the mortice-and-tenon joints on the sarsen lintels. More often only part of a stone was shaped, with one side flat and the other left rough. Several of the menhirs in the Carnac area appear to have been partially smoothed.

Sometimes the stones were decorated with shallow carvings similar in style to the ornamentation of the megalithic tombs. The same motifs occur and they are just as unfathomable on standing stones as they are inside passage graves. Sometimes the carvings are nothing more sophisticated than circular pits about 10 cm across, and from their size and appearance they are now called cup marks. Often they are surrounded by sets of three or more concentric circles, the 'cup and ring' marks (Pl. 18, 19). This was a very popular symbol, especially in Ireland, Scotland, and the north of England. It occurs on small stones as well as megaliths and can convincingly be dated to the Early Bronze Age because cup and ring marks have been found on stones in the mounds containing food-vessel burials.

A few carvings are more representational, such as the daggers and axes, which surprisingly were not noticed on the stones at Stonehenge until 1953. The dagger strongly resembles a type known to have been in use at Mycenae in Greece about 1600 BC and for a while these carvings were cited as evidence for the date of the last phase of building at Stonehenge. Since then radiocarbon dates have been revised (see Appendix B) and Stonehenge is believed to have been completed before the great days of Mycenae. The daggers, if they are Mycenaean, could in any case be a later addition and it is certainly fair to point out that their style is different from the carvings we normally associate with the Early Bronze Age.

This is as far as we need to go with the brief sketch of the prehistoric communities in north-west Europe. At the start of the Middle Bronze Age fundamental and profound changes occurred affecting religious and economic matters alike. Stone and bronze artifacts, the types of pottery and the burial customs all changed, and, with their passing, communities lost interest in the great monuments of the earlier periods. No longer did men know how and why the henges, cursuses, circles, and stone rows were built and what use was made of them by their constructors. Men came to regard them as visible evidence of the work of super-natural powers, from where it was a small step to deliberate destruction to lessen the forces of evil. With the technical background of the twentieth century we more readily appreciate the civil engineering and logistic planning of these massive projects. We recognize the intelligence and determination of people who were able to work together in such an organized and methodical way. None of this is disputed by archaeologists. The controversy arises when we look more closely at the surviving monuments and try to deduce the astronomical and mathematical knowledge that was a hidden facet of the megalithic culture.

3 Megalithic Mathematics

We must be very cautious how we approach the subject of mathematics in the Neolithic and Early Bronze Ages. We are hampered by the breaks in cultural tradition as well as by the lack of documentary evidence. There is nothing to help us except the remains of the monuments, and they themselves are often damaged, incomplete, or have even been partially 'restored' by well-meaning antiquarians before modern scientific methods of analysis could be applied. We look at these remains through the eyes of twentieth-century men, and are susceptible to seeing in them a reflection of our own ideas of space, time, religion, and cosmology. Our society often prefers complicated methods of organization or construction to simple ones, for economic or social reasons, and we forget that the basic crafts of the pre-industrial era ever existed. When we do remember them, we do not always appreciate how effective they could be.

An example of a simple solution to an apparently difficult problem will make the point, even if it is not from the period or the region we are considering in this book. Before the first courses of stones in the pyramids were laid, the Egyptians had to prepare a level area sufficiently extensive to take the whole base. The sides of the Great Pyramid at Giza are 230 m long, and the site was prepared with such accuracy that the perimeter was level to better than 2 cm. Stop for a moment and ask yourself how this could have been done without any modern surveying instruments, or indeed without any measuring equipment at all. The Egyptians did it this way. They built a mud bank around the site, filled the enclosed area with water and allowed it to evaporate in the sun. As islands appeared in the artificial lake they were removed by chipping until all the area had been brought to the desired level.

As far as we know, this technique was not used in north-west Europe; it is cited merely to illustrate that a simple method can sometimes be effective for solving what at first thought may seem a difficult task. The way to look at megalithic monuments is to ask the question 'What is the minimum amount of technical knowledge needed to do this job?' and then maintain a clear separation between fact and speculation. On this basis we can deduce what are the likely, or possible, bounds of knowledge of megalithic mathematicians.

It is not easy to divorce ourselves from the patterns of modern thought. We use mathematical models based on the discoveries of many great mathematicians from Euclid to Einstein. We are familiar with the technique of inductive logic, which is to deduce one fact from another, reasoning step by step. This is taught at school and used when we prove, for example, geometrical theorems involving congruent or similar triangles, and many others. We are also taught symbolic logic, and use this in algebraic equations, manipulating expressions which have both letters and numbers. These are very powerful methods of problem-solving, and after practice they become so familiar that it is sometimes difficult to recall that many problems can be solved, or at least approximate solutions obtained, without using them.

There is no reason to suppose that people of the Neolithic and Early Bronze Ages had any of our modern ideas about mathematics, but there is no escaping the fact of their fascination for geometry. Although the spirals, semicircles, and other shapes on the standing stones and in the tombs indicate their interest, the strongest evidence comes from studying the stone circles and rings. Many of the stone settings are true circles, precisely laid out and constructed, whilst some, though appearing to be circular at a casual glance, are clearly not so when they are accurately surveyed. Neither are they examples of sloppy megalithic workmanship. The non-circular stone rings are sometimes well-constructed ellipses, and quite often are deliberately modified circles, with arcs that are either flattened to give the shape of a slightly squashed orange, or pulled out to make an egg. Looking closely at these shapes yields rather surprising results, because they have some interesting mathematical properties that could hardly have come about by chance.

The first scientist to point out the complexity of megalithic geometry was Professor Thom. In his publications he explains his discoveries in scientific language of the present day and he uses conventional mathematical methods to show the geometrical relationships inherent in the stone circles. Unfortunately many of his readers have assumed that a similar knowledge of mathematics was necessary to produce the complicated shapes at the time of their erection. Unable to accept this idea, they have become sceptical about the actual shapes of the stone circles, and have tended to the view that the people who surveyed the sites have imposed on them over-elaborate and fastidious interpretations that are not genuine. They have overlooked the possibility of simple methods being adequate to create the sophisticated shapes.

The spiral can be taken as an example of a shape which is much simpler to draw than to describe in mathematical terms. Stone rings were not laid out in spirals, but the figure occurs frequently in the decoration of carved stones. Although the mathematical equation for a spiral of constant pitch is not very difficult, it requires an understanding of co-ordinate geometry that would not be reached now until the final years of secondary school education. It is, however, very easy to draw this type of spiral. Take a post and hammer it into the ground, then fasten one end of a rope round the post so that it will not slip. Tie a sharpened stake to the other end and walk round and round the fixed post, letting the rope wind up as you go. The sharp stake will scratch a spiral on the ground, and it will gradually get smaller until all the rope is wound tight. The person who draws a spiral this way may not recognize its geometrical properties, that it decreases its diameter by the same amount each revolution, or that the distance between the lines is equal to the circumference of the central post, or that tangents to the spiral make a constant angle with the radius, but these relationships are inevitably present. The lesson is to beware of assuming that because a mathematical relationship is found at a site, it was known to the builders and deliberately incorporated by them.

In spite of the other varieties of stone rings, the commonest shape by far is the true circle. Throughout its long development, Stonehenge retained the circular shape which began with the earthen bank of the original henge. The

Aubrey Holes were laid out on the circumference of a circle 43·2 m radius, and 1,800 years later the pattern was repeated when the sarsen circle was built round a circle 14·79 m radius, although the new centre was displaced 0·55 m to the north.

It is important to establish how accurately the builders of stone rings were able to work. We have already mentioned the critical view that the builders of the stone rings did not have enough mathematical knowledge to make more complicated shapes than the circle; other critics have said that they were technically unable to lay out stones with the accuracy that modern surveyors claim was achieved. Everyone seems to agree that the circles were intentional; therefore if we know the precision of their construction, it helps in interpreting the more complicated shapes.

The circle of Aubrey Holes has recently been resurveyed with great care. The edges of the holes were found by careful probing, and each centre marked with a metal stake. The circle was found to be remarkably accurate. The error in positioning the centres of the holes is about 0·17 m (strictly speaking the standard deviation of the error is 0·17 m). This error is approximately 0·4 per cent of the radius. It is more difficult to give a precise figure for the accuracy of the sarsen circle, because only three of its stones have never been disturbed, but the dishing of their inner surfaces to fit the curve of the circle is an indication of precise intentions on the part of the builders.

The important megalithic site in the far north of the British Isles, the Ring of Brodgar on the Mainland of Orkney, is a true circle of radius 51·83 m. There are 58 stones, some of them now reduced to stumps. All but nine of the 58 lie within 0·5 m of the circumference of the circle, and only two are more than 1 m off the line. Unfortunately, some of the stones were re-erected in the nineteenth century, and others have tilted away from the vertical, so the Ring of Brodgar was probably erected with greater precision than appears from the existing remains. Without excavation to find the original sockets of the doubtful stones, it is not possible to state the degree of accuracy obtained by the builders. We can say only that most of the stones were placed within half a metre of the perimeter of the circle. (If all the stones are included, the standard deviation is 0·55 m, and if the two badly displaced ones are excluded the standard deviation becomes 0·4 m.) This accuracy is not as good as was obtained at Stonehenge when the Aubrey Holes were set out, but nevertheless the radius of the circle at Brodgar was maintained to 1 per cent. The circles at Stonehenge and Brodgar suggest that the megalithic engineers were quite able to erect accurate stone circles, and it therefore seems likely that, when they did not do so, the departures were intentional.

The simplest way to lay out a stone circle on the ground is to begin by making a loop of rope or hide, twice as long as the radius of the circle to be drawn. The loop is put over a post firmly hammered into the ground, and in the other end of the loop is a sharpened stake for inscribing the shape. The circle is drawn by walking round the central post keeping the rope tight all the time. It is much easier to use a loop rather than a single rope tied between the central post and the stake, especially if the post has a rough surface, because the loop does not need to slip round as the circle is drawn.

It is not all that easy to draw large circles accurately using a rope. One snag is that the rope stretches if the tension varies, and the thinner the rope, the more stretch is likely. Therefore a strong, thick, and heavy rope would be preferable to a light one, but more difficult to use. A further difficulty is that both vegetable fibres and hide change their dimensions when they get wet. Measured lengths would change during the course of a day, if operations started on a wet dewy morning and continued while the sun dried out the grass. The workers could overcome this by frequently checking their rope's length against the first centre-to-circumference distance pegged that day. Finally, the uneven ground would degrade the accuracy, and the rope may have had to be held horizontal by several people, to avoid the errors associated with sagging.

Before we describe the non-circular stone rings, let us see how the men of the Early Bronze Age constructed right-angled triangles. Schoolchildren today learn about one of the most famous discoveries in classical geometry, the Theorem of Pythagoras: 'the square on the hypotenuse of a right-angled triangle is equal to the sum of the squares on the other two sides'. In Figure 3.1, the triangle ABC illustrates this theorem. If the right angle is the corner at A, then $AC^2 + AB^2 = BC^2$. The best-known Pythagorean triangle has sides of 3 units, 4 units, and 5 units, and is right-angled because $3^2 = 9$, $4^2 = 16$, and $9 + 16 = 25 = 5^2$.

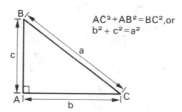

FIG. 3.1 Geometry of the right-angled triangle

The 3,4,5 triangle is the simplest right-angled triangle, with its three sides having lengths in ratios of small whole numbers. Early Bronze Age men were certainly familiar with it. The triangle occurs over and over again in stone constructions from this period. Sometimes it is incorporated into stone rings, and quite often in the relationships between several stone rings or standing stones at a particular site. Megalithic geometers evidently knew that this triangle has special properties.

There are other Pythagorean triangles with sides in ratios of larger whole numbers, for example 5,12,13; 8,15,17; 7,24,25; 20, 21,29; and 12,35,37. Not all of these have been discovered at megalithic sites, although the largest, 12,35,37, was known and used, and perhaps sites incorporating all of them will one day be discovered.

At some sites they used triangles that are not quite true Pythagorean ones, for example 8,9,12. In this case $8^2 + 9^2 = 145$, while $12^2 = 144$. The angle between the two shorter sides is 89·6° instead of 90°, and it is doubtful whether the small discrepancy would have been noticed. In more modern times carpenters have used 10,10,14 triangles for constructing roof joints, giving an angle of 88·8° for a similar though less accurate approximation. We cannot say from the evidence of the use of these triangles that the Theorem of Pythagoras had been pre-empted in the Bronze Age. Indeed, because approximations to Pythagorean triangles were used, it implies that the mathematical relationship between the sides had not been discovered, and that they had arrived quite empirically at a set of triangles which gave them easy ways of drawing a right angle on the ground. Having discovered accidentally that certain triangles gave them right angles, they memorized the lengths of their sides and used them again and again.

The method of laying out the right angle is exceedingly simple. It is to make a rope triangle with sides of the chosen lengths and place it flat on the ground, making sure it is held quite taut. Better accuracy can be obtained with a set of poles all cut to the same length, using, for example, three end-to-end for one side, four for another, and five for the third. Naturally the longer the poles, the more accurate the final result will be. Examples of the use of right-angled triangles will occur when we come to the non-circular stone rings.

The next most simple curved shape after the circle is the ellipse. An ellipse can be thought of as a circle with two centres. If two posts are hammered into the ground and the loop of rope goes round both simultaneously, a stake in the loop will mark out an ellipse. The further apart the posts are, the more elongated it will be. In mathematical terminology the positions of the posts are called the foci of the ellipse, and in Figure 3.2 the foci are at F_1 and F_2. The distance AC is called the major axis, and BD is the minor axis. The ratio F_1F_2/AC is the eccentricity of the ellipse; its maximum possible value is 1 (the ellipse being exceedingly thin) and its minimum value is 0 (the ellipse is now a circle). The eccentricities of megalithic ellipses are generally between 0·3 and 0·7. More than twenty stone ellipses have been discovered; they include the stone settings at Postbridge, Devon (the least elliptical, with an eccentricity only 0·29), Penmaenmawr, Gwynedd (eccentricity 0·31; Pl. 9), and Machrie Moor on the Isle of Arran (eccentricity 0·5), so they have a very wide geographical distribution. About another twenty settings are less definite ellipses, unproved as yet either because the stones have been moved or because they have not been accurately surveyed.

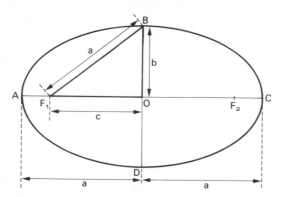

FIG. 3.2   Geometry of the ellipse

It is tempting to speculate on how ellipses might have come to be drawn in the first place. The ellipses could have been discovered quite accidentally if circles were drawn using a loop of rope as suggested above. Almost certainly at some time or other the loop would have caught on an obstruction, a stone, a tree stump, or even the leg of an onlooker. The resulting shape may well have been interesting enough to arouse the curiosity of the stone circle builders and to start them experimenting in drawing ellipses.

One of the properties of an ellipse is that the distance BF_1 is equal to half the length of the major axis. On Figure 3.2 OB is given the length b, OA is a, and the distance from the centre to the foci is c. In these symbols, $BF_1 = a$. (The proof comes directly from the way the ellipse is drawn. When the stake is at A, the loop goes from F_2 to A and back again; its length is therefore $2a+2c$. When the stake is at B, the loop of rope goes round F_1, F_2, and B; its length is $2BF_1+2c$. By subtraction, $BF_1 = a$.)

The triangle BOF_1 is right-angled, and if the builders of stone settings were interested in triangles, it would not be particularly surprising to find Pythagorean triangles incorporated into megalithic ellipses. There are in fact several of these. The 3,4,5 triangle is the basis of one of the ellipses at Callanish, two ellipses at Stanton Drew in Somerset are both based on the 5,12,13 triangle, and the 12,35,37 triangle occurs in an ellipse at Daviot near Inverness. A few ellipses are based on triangles that are nearly Pythagorean, such as another of the ellipses at Callanish, incorporating a triangle with sides in the ratio 7,11,13 ($7^2+11^2 = 170$, $13^2 = 169$). Nevertheless, the majority of megalithic ellipses are not based on simple triangles with their sides in whole-number ratios. Professor Thom has put forward suggestions why the dimensions of ellipses were chosen as they are, and we shall come back to this a little later.

As well as circles and ellipses, the megalithic builders invented two types of flattened circle and two egg-shapes. The flattened circles are relatively common. They have been called Type A and Type B by Professor Thom and are illustrated

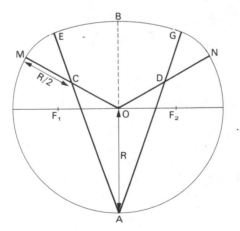

FIG. 3.3   Type A flattened circle

F_1 and F_2 are not involved in the construction of the flattened circle, but are the foci of the ellipse which most closely fits the non-circular portion of the ring (see Fig. 3.9)

in Figures 3.3 and 3.4. Basically they are very similar, in that they are composed of arcs of circles with three different radii. Type B (Fig. 3.4) is the simpler of the two; it is made up of a semicircle with radius OA, two segments of circles with radius CM centred on C and D, and finally a joining arc with radius AE and centre at A. The secondary centres, C and D, both lie on the diameter MN and they are one third of the basic radius from the centre O. How can this be constructed without knowledge of formal geometry?

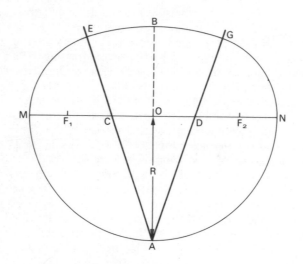

FIG. 3.4   Type B flattened circle

F_1 and F_2 are not involved in the construction of the flattened circle, but are the foci of the ellipse which most closely fits the non-circular portion of the ring (see Fig. 3.9)

(a) Draw a complete circle with a loop of rope turning about a post at O.

(b) Hammer a post into the ground at a point on the circumference of the circle, say the point A.

(c) Measure a right angle from OA and lay out the line MN. By folding the rope into thirds, find the points C and D and hammer in two more posts.

(d) Now take another loop of rope, so that it goes over the post at A, both strands go round the post at C, and its length is just right to bring the other end of the loop to M.

(e) Put a marking stake in the loop and swing it round so that it first draws a circle centred at C, then as it clears the post at C it will begin to draw a circle of radius AE.

(f) Continue the movement as far as G (taking care not to snag the loop on the post at O on the way), then let the loop pivot about D to complete the arc GN.

There is a variation of this method that does not even require the use of two loops of rope. The posts at O, A, C, and D can all be put in the ground by measuring with rods, so the construction can follow the steps (*d*), (*e*), and (*f*) without actually drawing the initial circle. Having completed the flattened part of the figure, a post can be put in at B by sighting along the line AO. Then to draw the rest of the circle, put the loop over B and allow it to pivot around O giving the arc MAN.

More than a dozen stone circles of this type are known, including the Twelve Apostles stone circle near Holywood in Dumfriesshire, the famous 'Long Meg and her daughters' circle in Cumbria, and the stone ring at Merrivale in Devon.

The Type A flattened circle differs from the Type B in that the secondary centres are not on a diameter of the basic circle, but are half way along two radii with an angle of 120° between them (Fig. 3.3). These secondary centres are easily located once the circle is drawn and a post is hammered into the ground at A. With the same loop of rope that was used for the basic circle, its perimeter can be divided into sixths (as when making flower patterns with a pair of compasses), and this gives the positions of the points M and N. By halving OM and ON, we find the positions of C and D; two more posts are set in the ground and the flattened circle is completed in exactly the same way as the Type B, with a second loop of rope going from A via C to M.

This circle, too, has an alternative method of construction requiring only one loop of rope. The first step is to construct an equilateral triangle (all three sides equal in length) out of ropes or poles. Two equilateral triangles side by side will give the direction of OM from OA, and by direct measurement pegs can be located at A, O, M, N, C, and D. The arc MEGN can be drawn with the loop of rope, and finally the basic circle, using the same loop hooked over B and allowed to pivot about a peg at O.

Although Type A is a little more complicated to construct, there are more Type A stone circles than Type B. They include the Castle Rigg circle near Keswick in Cumbria (Pl. 8), and the Standing Stones of Torhouse near Wigtown in Scotland. The largest stone circle in the Burnmoor group, in Cumbria, is also of this type, and it is particularly interesting because inside the circle are five small cairns. The centres of four of the cairns lie on the perimeter of an ellipse with eccentricity 0·72, and the centre of the fifth is on the axis of the ellipse. Combinations of different geometric shapes at the same site is not at all uncommon, though it is unusual to find one shape actually inside another.

The egg-shapes are based on Pythagorean triangles. The Type I egg (Fig. 3.5) has two triangles placed back to back. Its perimeter is a combination of the arcs of three circles, one centred at A with radius AE, two sections centred at C and D with radius DE, and the sharp end of the egg is an arc of a circle centred at B with radius BG. The figure is surprisingly easy to set out.

(*a*) Lay out the Pythagorean triangle on the ground using measuring poles or ropes and then put pegs at the corners, A, B, C, and D.

(*b*) Having decided what size the egg is to be, take a loop of rope, place it over the post at C, take it round the post at A and back to E, where the marking stake is at the start of drawing the shape.

(*c*) Draw the large end of the egg, taking the stake right round to F, but on reaching F, lift the rope over the post D and carry on anticlockwise. The radius of the circle now automatically changes as the loop of rope clears the post at A.

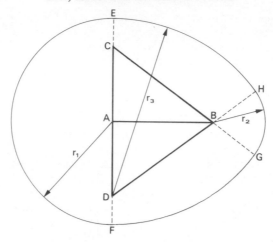

FIG. 3.5   Geometry of the Type I egg-shape

(*d*) Carry on to the point G, and this time allow the rope to pivot about B, so that the stake marks out the sharp end of the egg as far as H.

(*e*) Now unhitch the loop from C and put it over the post at D to trace the remaining arc HE.

There are many variations of the proportions of the egg. To begin with, any right-angled triangle can be used for the initial setting of the four posts, and then the length of the loop can be either small, giving a very pointed egg, or long, giving a rounded egg. The 3,4,5 triangle was the most popular one used in the construction of stone eggs, examples being found at Cairnpapple Hill, West Lothian, and at Clava in Inverness, where the stone egg-shape actually surrounds a circular passage grave. As with ellipses, there are sites where Pythagorean 'near misses' were employed, such as at Burgh Hill in Roxburghshire. The basic triangle has sides in the ratio 11,13,17 ($11^2+13^2 = 290$, $17^2 = 289$) and the difference between it and a true Pythagorean triangle would be quite unmeasurable.

The most remarkable layout based on this type of egg-shape seems to be Woodhenge (Fig. 3.6). If Professor Thom's interpretation is correct, the triangle selected for the contruction was 12,35,37, which we have already noted was used in the ellipse at Daviot. Woodhenge is not a stone circle, but is believed to be the site of a large wooden building with a roof. It was discovered by aerial photography in 1925 and later excavations revealed six concentric rings of post-holes: each hole is now marked by a concrete pillar. The positions of these holes can be quite well represented by six egg-shapes based on the same triangle, the different eggs being obtained by increasing the length of the loop of rope each time a new ring was marked out. The innermost egg, as would be expected if they were drawn this way, is quite thin, and the outermost nearly circular, with the others intermediate in shape. It is quite easy to work out the lengths of loops required when laying out the lines of holes. They were (starting at the inside) 18·61 m, 21·24 m, 23·90 m, 26·54 m, 31·82 m, and 34·46 m. The loop was increased

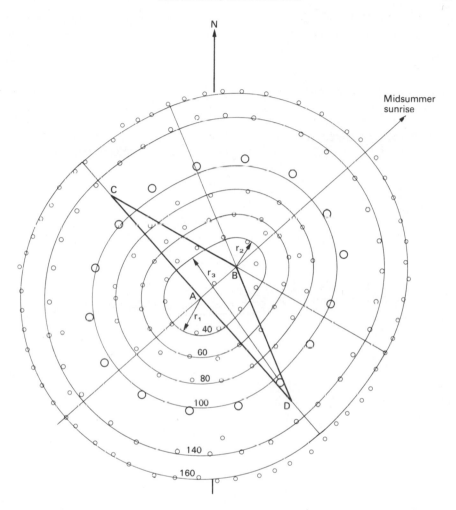

FIG. 3.6   Plan of Woodhenge

The numbers beside the rings are the perimeters in megalithic yards. The superimposed construction is a Type I egg with a basic triangle AB $= 6$ MY, AC $= 17\frac{1}{2}$ MY, and CB $= 18\frac{1}{2}$ MY. Based on a diagram in Thom, *Megalithic Sites in Britain*.

by the same length, 2·64 m, each time the builders progressed from one ring to the next, except between the fourth and fifth rings, when there was twice the usual increment. Woodhenge is particularly interesting because it gives a hint about possible reasons for the choice of these strange geometrical constructions, and we shall return to this point later.

The Type II eggs are similar to the Type I eggs, in that they are based on a pair of right-angled triangles, though the triangles are now placed with their hypotenuses together (Fig. 3.7). They are set out in the same way as for the Type I eggs, beginning with two Pythagorean triangles with posts at their corners. The loop of rope is put over the post at B, goes outside C, and has the inscribing stake at its other end, initially at the point E. The arc of the large circle is drawn from E to F, allowing the loop to rotate about C. The same rope is used for the smaller arc, being taken this time over A, round C, and rotating first on one side, then on the other side of B to inscribe the arc GH. The two straight parts of the figure, FG and EH, have to be completed separately with rods or taut ropes.

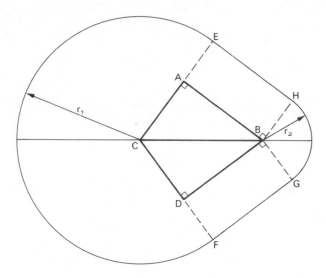

FIG. 3.7   Geometry of the Type II egg-shape

Only a few eggs of this type have been identified so far, but like all the other non-circular shapes they are found from one end of Great Britain to the other. There is for example a Type II egg among the three rings known as The Hurlers, on Bodmin Moor in Cornwall, about 6½ km north of Liskeard. This egg is based on the 3,4,5 triangle, as is the one at a nearby site, Buckland Ford on Dartmoor, about 9 km east of Buckfastleigh.

In Scotland near the town of Lauder in Berwickshire is the inconspicuous stone ring of Borrowstone Rig. Its right-angled triangle is not quite Pythagorean, for it has sides of 7·88 m, 10·17 m, and 12·87 m, which are in the ratio 3·06: 3·95: 5. The departure from the simple 3,4,5 triangle is small, and the decrease in length of one of the adjacent sides is compensated by the increase in length of the other, so that the triangle is right-angled to a high degree of accuracy. Whether this change was intentional or not is a matter for speculation, but the choice of these particular dimensions together with a loop length of 33·6 m, gives the additional sophistication of the circumference of the smaller circle passing through the centre of the larger one. It begins to look as though the team who designed and erected the stone ring at Borrowstone Rig were displaying their technical virtuosity and showing to their contemporaries their mastery of the techniques that had been discovered (Fig. 3.8).

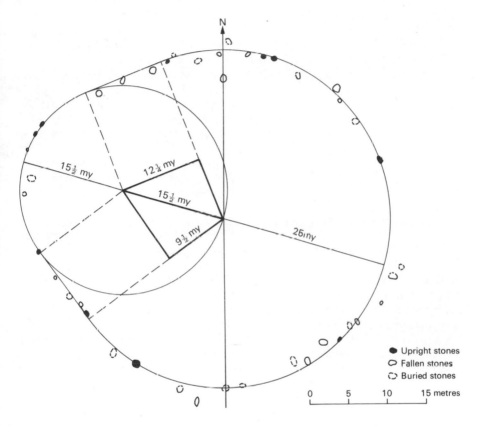

FIG. 3.8   Plan of Borrowstone Rig

The plan is based on one by Professor Thom and the dimensions on the figure are his interpretations of distances in megalithic yards.

Finally there are a few, possibly only four, much more complicated stone rings. Professor Thom has called these compound rings because, although they are based on true circles, they include arcs laid out with several different radii. Two examples of this type are found in the county of Powys in Wales, Moel Ty Uchaf near Welshpool (Pl. 10) and Kerry Pole near Newtown. In Scotland there is a compound ring at Easter Delfour near Aviemore in the county of Highland. Like the flattened circles and the egg-shapes, they can be drawn on the ground with loops of rope passing over and round correctly positioned posts. Their geometrical constructions will be found in Thom's books.

The single example of a compound ring in England is the great stone circle at

Avebury. It is unusual in several ways: its large size (370 m diameter), its extensive internal constructions (two stone circles each 103·6 m diameter and other arrangements of standing stones), and the fact that it has angles in its perimeter. Professor Thom has done a precise survey of Avebury and he interprets the geometry of the stone ring as consisting of the arcs of seven circles, all with different radii and different centres. Three of the centres lie at the corners of a 3,4,5 triangle and all seven are geometrically interrelated. His analysis of the ring has been criticized by Freeman, who claims that other circular arcs with different radii fit the positions of the stones more precisely, but this ruins the geometry connecting the centres. On archaeological grounds, there are also problems. Avebury is not yet firmly dated, but it is an early stone ring, possibly 26th century BC. It is difficult to accept that there was such a subtle geometrical shape at a time when non-circular rings had hardly begun to evolve. Some archaeologists suspect that Avebury has no systematic layout and the complex interpretation is the result of trying to impose order where none exists.

We remarked at the beginning of the chapter that not all archaeologists were happy about accepting that megalithic men set out stone rings in deliberately designed flattened circles, eggs, and ellipses, and this is a suitable point to review the evidence. To begin with, hundreds of sites have now been examined, mainly though not entirely by Professor Thom, and multiple examples have been found of all the non-circular rings. We know that truly circular stone settings could be laid out accurately and easily, therefore it is reasonable to assume that the non-circular settings were also intentional. We do not know for sure how it was done, but the method just described using posts, loops of rope, and marking-stakes is simple even for the more complicated figures. You can check this yourself by experimenting on a beach or football field. All that is required is a capability for accurate measurement of lengths and a knowledge that if triangles are set out with the lengths of their sides in certain proportions, the triangle will be right-angled. We can be sure techniques for accurate measurement had been developed, otherwise it would never have been possible to fit together the stones at Stonehenge, to name the most spectacular example. It would not have been necessary to know the theorem of Pythagoras, but merely to find out by trial and error that some triangles were more useful than others. In summary, the skill and knowledge needed to draw the various shapes is not very great. It pales beside the engineering ability demanded of the builders of the megalithic tombs or of Silbury Hill. The evidence is strongly in favour of non-circular geometric shapes being deliberately used by those who constructed the megalithic stone circles and rings.

Nevertheless it is legitimate to ask if any other geometric arrangements, possibly simpler ones, could give the same shapes. Could the flattened circles and egg-shapes be made up from a combination of semicircles and ellipses? For the two flattened circles it is straightforward to draw the ellipse which has the closest resemblance to the flattened part of the ring. On Figures 3.3 and 3.4, mark off two points (F_1 and F_2) on the horizontal diameters of the rings, at a distance from B equal to the radius of the main circle, i.e. so that $BF_1 = BF_2 = OA$. F_1 and F_2 are now the foci of the ellipses, which can be drawn using a loop, as already described. The eccentricities of the ellipses can be calculated from the right-angled triangle BF_1O (they are OF_1/OA in both cases) and they are found to be 0·567 for the Type A and 0·693 for the Type B flattened circles. In Figure

3.9 these ellipses are superimposed on the original constructions for the flattened circles so that the reader can see how they compare. The ellipse makes quite a reasonable approximation for the Type B ring, though it does not match the curvature of the Type A. Ellipses with these eccentricities are not found elsewhere, and on the whole it seems unlikely that these alternative constructions for the flattened circles were the ones used in the Early Bronze Age.

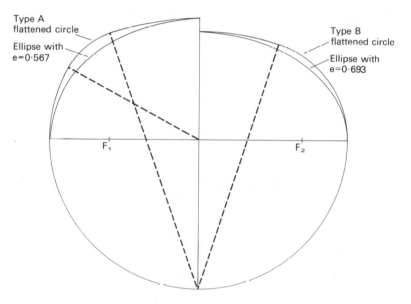

FIG. 3.9   Flattened circles approximated by ellipses

It is not so easy to make a similar approximation for the eggs, because there are too many variable lengths involved. In addition to the different shapes of the basic triangles, the length of the loop of rope could also be changed, and in effect each egg is a unique shape. One comparison only is given: the semi-ellipse approximating to the egg-like end of the ring at Clava (eccentricity 0·574) is superimposed on its plan. The two curves are almost indistinguishable (Fig. 3.10).

Further information on how the stone rings were set out may come eventually from careful excavation of sites. With good fortune an excavator may find the marks made in the ground by the temporary posts which were used in the initial stages of the work. Their position would go a long way towards making clear whether these or quite different constructions were used by the builders.

If we are willing to believe that the stone rings were intentionally set out in special geometric shapes, the inevitable question arises, 'Why did they do it?' What was wrong with the simple circle that made it necessary to go to the trouble of more complicated stone settings? It certainly was not for the appearance of the rings, because no one standing in the centre of a flattened circle, or in the ellipses of lower eccentricity, will notice the distortion. Professor Thom suggests the

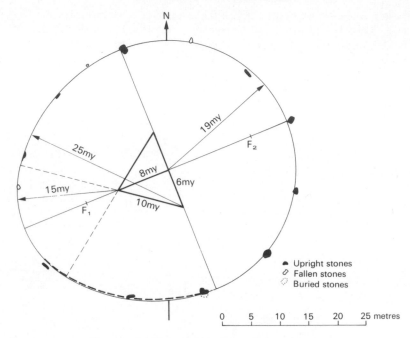

FIG. 3.10   Geometry of the ring at Clava

The plan is based on one by Professor Thom and the dimensions on the figure are his interpretations of the distances in megalithic yards. The dotted line in the south-west quadrant is a
section of an ellipse with foci F_1 and F_2

explanation for the ellipses and egg-shapes is that the builders of the stone rings
had devised their own unit of length, and they wanted as far as possible to make
circles and rings with perimeters equal to $2\frac{1}{2}$ times a whole number of these units.
As if this were not difficult enough, they tried simultaneously to make the
diameters equal to a whole number of units. Thom calls the unit the Megalithic
Yard, abbreviated MY, and claims 1 MY = 0·829 m: hence $2\frac{1}{2}$ MY, the Megalithic
Rod, = 2·073 m.

It cannot be done in the case of a circle. The circumference of a circle is given
by $2\pi \times$ radius, the Greek letter π (pi) representing the number 3·1415926 . . .,
which is approximately $3\frac{1}{7}$ but can never be expressed exactly as either a fraction
or a decimal. A number of this sort is called irrational.

By selecting diameters carefully it is possible to find combinations of diameter
and circumference which almost fit the requirements. For example, a circle with
diameter 4 units in any system of measurements has a circumference of 12·566
units, equal to $2\frac{1}{2} \times 5$·0265 units, and 5·0265 is less than 3 per cent of a unit
from a whole number. Or another circle, with diameter 27 units, has a circumference $2\frac{1}{2} \times 33$·93 units, and 33·93 differs from 34 by only 0·02 per cent. Professor
Thom has analysed the sizes of very many stone circles and concludes that
particular diameters (in megalithic yards) giving these and other combinations
were strongly favoured by the stone circle builders. This analysis is one of the

main sources of data from which he deduced the size of the megalithic yard. Statisticians' opinions on the validity of the megalithic yard will come up later; in the meantime let us accept Professor Thom's idea and see if it helps to explain the other shapes.

It may be thought that the flattened circles were deliberate attempts to make rings with a circumference nearer to three times the diameter and so avoid the irrationality of π. The Type A flattened circle has a perimeter $2 \times 3 \cdot 0591 \times$ radius of the circular portion, and for Type B it is $2 \times 2 \cdot 8746 \times$ radius. But $2 \cdot 8746$ is no nearer to $3 \cdot 0$ than is π, and the multiplying factor in the Type A flattened circle, though within 2 per cent of $3 \cdot 0$, could have been nearer still with a minor change to the construction. This does not seem to be the explanation of the flattened circles.

Did the builders look for combinations of diameter and circumference giving whole numbers as they did for the true circles? Apparently not. If they had, we would expect to find a concentration of Type A diameters at say 18 MY, giving a perimeter $22 \cdot 03$ MR, and at 27 MY, giving a perimeter $33 \cdot 04$ MR. Similarly with the Type B flattened circles we would look for diameters at 20 MY and its multiples, whose perimeters are multiples of $22 \cdot 997$ MR. These diameters are not found. Although Thom claims that there is a preference for diameters to be in whole numbers of megalithic yards, there is no evidence of perimeters being multiples of $2\frac{1}{2}$ MY. From studying their geometry, we have not yet found any reason why these shapes were chosen.

The ellipses and egg-shapes are a different matter. An ellipse can be any shape from a circle at one extreme to a straight line at the other, and its circumference can take any value from $\pi \times$ its diameter (when it is a circle) to twice its length (when it has narrowed to a line). So by adjusting the eccentricity it is quite possible to get the major axis of the ellipse and its circumference to be simultaneously whole numbers in any unit one likes. According to Thom, the megalithic architects were not even satisfied with this. We have seen how every ellipse incorporates a right-angled triangle (F_1OB in Figure 3.2) and that in the stone ellipses these triangles were sometimes Pythagorean; the difficult task they set themselves was to make all three sides of the triangle whole numbers of megalithic yards all at once. Of course it is impossible to do this exactly, and very difficult even to do it approximately. A good attempt was made at Loanhead of Daviot, near Meldrum in Scotland, where the recumbent stone 'circle' is an ellipse with an eccentricity of $0 \cdot 36$. (This is not the same site as the ellipse at Daviot near Inverness.) The Loanhead ellipse is based on a near-Pythagorean triangle with sides 14,5,13·08 MY (very nearly 14,5,13) which has a perimeter $42 \cdot 54$ MY, i.e. $17 \cdot 016$ MR (very nearly 17 megalithic rods).

It was not always possible to be as close as this to whole numbers. In general, either the ellipse was based on a Pythagorean triangle and the perimeter was allowed to depart from a multiple of $2\frac{1}{2}$ MY, or they kept the length of the perimeter $2\frac{1}{2}$ times a whole number of megalithic yards and modified the triangle. In the latter case they let the minor axis be an awkward length, and had both the major axis and the distance between the foci equal to a whole number of yards. This ensures that the length of rope used for laying out the ellipse is also integral in MY. Thus the Callanish ellipse based on the 3,4,5 triangle has a perimeter $14 \cdot 18$ MY, i.e. $5 \cdot 67$ MR, and this is not near enough to 6 to be considered a well-adjusted perimeter. On the other hand, at Sands of Forvie on the coast about 20 km north of Aberdeen, an ellipse is based on the triangle 16½,6,15·37 MY and its perimeter is very accurately set to a multiple of 2½ MY, being 20·03 megalithic rods.

The egg-shapes have similar circumferential properties to the ellipses. The Clava egg was based on a triangle with sides 6, 8, and 10 MY. The radius of the semicircular portion is 19 MY and therefore the egg was drawn with a loop of rope 25 MY long. The perimeter of the egg is calculated to be 125·36 MY, i.e. 50·14 MR. If this is the correct interpretation of its construction, it is a remarkable achievement to get the perimeter, the sides of the triangle, and consequentially the length and breadth, all nearly whole numbers at the same time.

Yet it is when we turn to the complicated multiple rings of postholes at Woodhenge that we see the most subtle features incorporated into egg-shapes. The length of loop required for setting out the pattern increases by the same amount from one ring to the next. The effect of this on the perimeter of the rings is to increase their length by an equal distance from ring to ring. Using the data originating from Thom's survey, the perimeters of the rings are 32·9 m, 51·2 m, 66·7 m, 87·0 m, 115·4 m, and 134·4 m. The significance of these numbers is more apparent if we put the lengths of the perimeters of the six rings as a fraction of the length of the third one from the inside. Then we find the values 0·49, 0·77, 1·00, 1·30, 1·73, and 2·01. Within a few per cent error, they form the series ½, ¾, 1, 1¼, 1¾, and 2. Once the basic triangle is chosen, the perimeter, length, and maximum width of the rings depends only on the length of loop, and it might be argued that the loop lengths were picked to make the lengths and widths of the rings increase, as they do, by a fixed amount each time. But neither of these dimensions has the tidy series of ratios we find in the perimeters and it is very reasonable to conclude that the main aim in laying out Woodhenge was to make the perimeters increase in length by simple increments from the centre outwards. Woodhenge gives a lot of support to Thom's hypothesis that the perimeter lengths were most important to the builders of megalithic circles.

This conclusion can be reached without introducing megalithic yards, but if we accept Thom's length for the megalithic yard as 0·829 m, the perimeters become 39·7, 61·8, 80·5, 104·9, 139·2, and 162·1 MY, which he believes was the outcome of attempts to make them 40, 60, 80, 100, 140, and 160 MY.

There has been a lot of scepticism about these results. Although the general shape of the rings of postholes is very well represented by the egg-shapes, some of the holes on Thom's survey are two metres or more off the lines. If the geometrical construction of Woodhenge had been important to its builders we would expect the setting out to be precise. But Thom surveyed the positions of the concrete posts, which may not coincide with the original postholes. There are some differences between the survey made at the time of the excavation by Mr and Mrs Cunnington and Thom's survey; we do not know how precisely the original survey was made. Furthermore the third ring in is rather too large to fit the sequence, an anomaly which Thom explains by the fact that this is the ring with the largest holes, and therefore the fattest posts, and if the dimensions are taken to the inside edges of the holes rather than their centres, they match the pattern quite well.

There are a few other interesting features about the design. Its axis is aligned, like Stonehenge, to the midsummer sunrise, with the narrow ends of the eggs towards the north-east. The numbers of posts in the rings, 12, 18, 18, 16, 32, and 60, were chosen to allow equal numbers on either side of the axis. And finally the Cunningtons found a child's grave on the axis, in a position which appears to be near one of the corners of the basic triangle.

None of the geometrical features of Woodhenge precludes it from being the foundation of a large, roofed building. Indeed, the huge postholes of the third ring have ramps indicating that substantial timbers were in them originally. But the other sites where there are the remains of timber buildings, Marden, Mount Pleasant, Durrington Walls, and the Sanctuary, have none of these complexities in their plan. They were laid out as simple circles, though with some precision and care, as is shown by the symmetrical design at Mount Pleasant, where there were equal numbers of posts in each quadrant of the building.

One reason for the complexity of Woodhenge compared with the other timber buildings may be that it had special ritual significance. It is believed to be of relatively late construction, about 2250 BC whereas the others date to the 26th century BC. The date of Woodhenge shows by what stage the geometry of the egg-shapes had been perfected, and this is particularly valuable in view of the paucity of dates from stone circles themselves. It is not yet possible to put forward a firm chronology for the different types of stone rings, nor to relate them to other cultural characteristics. The evidence, such as it is, has been collected by Aubrey Burl, who draws a few tentative conclusions.

Whatever the period of construction, the majority of stone rings were truly circular. The rough proportions for the different shapes are $\frac{2}{3}$ true circles, $\frac{1}{6}$ flattened circles, $\frac{1}{9}$ ellipses, and $\frac{1}{18}$ eggs. The earliest rings are true circles, as one would expect since these are the easiest to set out. A few flattened circles may have been built in the Late Neolithic Period, but the other developments, ellipses and eggs, belong to the Early Bronze Age, with most of them later than 2000 BC. With the development of the more elaborate shapes there was a general reduction in size of stone circles, and the Early Bronze Age circles include a much smaller proportion of large ones than do those from the Late Neolithic Period.

Megalithic geometry was not always on such a large scale. Thom has studied the cup and ring marks with the same dedication as he shows towards the stone circles and rings. The majority by far are simple circles and depressions, but some are interesting non-circular shapes, including spirals, ellipses, and eggs. The same rules of construction apply to the carvings as to the stone monuments: eggs and ellipses are both based on Pythagorean triangles. One set of four carved rings, at Cardoness House, near Kirkcudbright in Scotland, is egg-shaped (Type I) and is based on the ubiquitous 3,4,5 triangle with sides of 1·55, 2·07, and 2·59 cm. The radii of the semicircular ends of the eggs are 3·11, 4·66, 7·24, and 9·57 cm, giving 20·7, 31·05, 46·6, and 62·1 cm for the perimeters. The similarities between this and Woodhenge are obvious. Thom deduces that a small unit, the megalithic inch (MI), equal to one fortieth of the megalithic yard, i.e. 2·07 cm, was the basis of the design. In this unit the perimeters become 10, 15, 22½, and 30 MI.

There are other examples, which need not be described because they follow so closely the geometry of the stone rings. Rocks are very hard, and it would not be feasible to make these designs using strings as is suggested for the larger work. Thom proposes compasses, or trammels, with fixed scribing points of flint or quartz set into a wooden stick. A different trammel would be needed for each circle, but since it appears that the inscribed circles were always in units of the megalithic inch, only a small number of tools would be required. Perhaps the ring marks were made not just for intellectual pleasure but for testing out new designs and instructing novices in the art and practice of megalithic geometry.

The megalithic yard is the most contentious of the proposals put forward by Professor Thom. According to his view it is a very accurate unit of measurement of 0·829 m, and it was used over the whole area of north-west Europe in the construction of stone circles, rings, and rows. He finds the same size of megalithic yard, to within half a centimetre, at Carnac in Brittany, Avebury in England, and at Brodgar on the Mainland of Orkney. At Stonehenge he finds the same length for the megalithic yard in the circle of Aubrey Holes as in the sarsen circle, even though they span nearly 2,000 years in time. If Thom is correct, this exceedingly precise measure was used by different tribes over a wide area and for a long period. The implications of this on our interpretation of the Late Neolithic and Early Bronze Ages are enormous.

We know from similarities in pottery and in the distribution of axes that there was some contact between different peoples of northern Europe during these periods, and the wide distributions of the different types of stone rings confirm that this contact was rather closer than would be needed simply for trade. The adoption of the same exact standard of measurement, however, would imply strong cultural links that are not confirmed by archaeological investigations. For example, units as precise as those claimed by Thom could only have spread throughout the area if physical replicas of the standard, say in the form of a wooden pole, were made centrally and then taken to the various groups who were building the rings. Somehow these people had to be forced to use them or persuaded that it was to their advantage to do so. The standards would have to be renewed at intervals, because they would become worn or broken in a long period of use, and this indicates a continuity of purpose and tradition surviving the arrival of the Beaker Folk and the cultural changes which ensued. Clearly archaeologists are opposed to accepting the megalithic yard without the strongest of evidence.

We shall never be in the fortunate position of finding marks on a block of stone with an inscription saying that the distance between them is a megalithic yard, and therefore we must look to the circles and rings to see if we can deduce from their existing dimensions whether a particular unit of measurement was used. The methods employed are statistical. They have to be able to deal with imperfect information, because many of the stones have been shifted since their original erection, and the surveys of the circles are not always of high accuracy.

The first papers on the search for a common unit, or quantum, as it is generally called in this context, were by Mr S. R. Broadbent, whose main field of research was connected with the biological sciences. He pointed out that there are two different situations which have to be dealt with by different mathematical methods. The first case is where we already believe, or know from other sources, that there is a quantum and we have an idea of its magnitude. Broadbent thought up a statistical test, which can be applied to Thom's list of stone circle diameters, to try to see whether the assumed value for the quantum is present or not. In the second, and more difficult, case there is no preconceived idea about the existence or value of the quantum and the list of diameters has to be searched statistically to see if a quantum of any value is present. The two approaches, when applied to the stone circle data, give rather different results: the existence of the megalithic yard is supported more strongly by the first method of analysis than by the second. Some statisticians think the first method is misleading and therefore the results given in the following table are for the second method only.

A somewhat different method of tackling the problem was developed by Professor Kendall and explained at the 1974 conference on 'The Place of Astronomy in the Ancient World'. His lecture, for non-specialists, gave an explanation of the statistical problems encountered when looking for quanta, and is a good source for readers who wish to go into more detail.

The figures in Table 3.1 are from the results (stone circles only) obtained by Broadbent and Kendall. Beside each value found for the quantum is an indication of the statistical significance of the result. In plain words, if the significance is 0·01, there is only one chance in a hundred of the results arising by accident. Broadbent and Kendall reached similar conclusions. They both found a quantum of about 1·66 m in the dimensions of the Scottish stone circles, which we would interpret as 2 megalithic yards. The English and Welsh stone circles did not give clear-cut results; more than one quantum was produced by the analysis at fairly low significance levels. When the results from the whole country are combined, the Scottish data swamp the rest, and the 2 MY quantum is again revealed. Kendall's conclusion was that whilst the results did not completely verify Thom's hypothesis, at least they were sufficiently encouraging to make it worthwhile to survey the sites more accurately and to gather information from other stone circles. There are not really enough measurements yet to give conclusive results, especially when the data are split into samples from different parts of the country.

| | Broadbent | | Kendall | |
	quantum (metres)	significance	quantum (metres)	significance
Scottish stone circles (109)	1·658	0·05	1·657	0·02
English and	3·238	not given	1·381	not given
Welsh stone circles (60)	1·382	not given	1·665	not given
All the stone circles (169)	1·653	0·05	1·659	0·01

Table 3.1

The most recent study of Thom's stone circle dimensions was by P. R. Freeman, using yet another method. His results for the Scottish stone circles agree well with Kendall's; he thinks there is evidence for a megalithic yard being used in Scotland, but the stone circles of England and Wales give him no indication that there was a universal unit there. He applied his tests also to the spacings between the stones in the rows at Carnac, using the distances from one of Thom's own surveys. He concluded that there was no sign of any unit having been used consistently in the setting out of these stone rows, and that there was nothing to support Thom's claim that their geometry was based on the megalithic rod.

Although the arguments and discussion will certainly go on, the recent conclusions are in line with common sense. There is no doubt that measurements had to be made to set out the geometrical shapes, and the more complicated sites, like Woodhenge, could not have been created unless the measurements had been accurate. But why the unit of length at one site needs to be the same as that at another is far from obvious, and the further the separation of the sites in space and time, the less credible the idea becomes. Yet at the Scottish sites a common unit does seem to have been adopted, perhaps by a single cultural group for a limited period of time.

The statistical analysis does not tell us about the use of units that were only approximately the same. We can readily imagine a group of Early Bronze Age men deciding to set up a stone ring like the one they had heard of in another village. If they wished to depart from a simple circular design, they most likely would have needed the services of a specialist from a place where they had traditional rules for setting out stones. He would know that accurate work was needed, but instead of bringing a standard length with him, he would make it when he arrived, using some dimension of the human body as his starting point. He could have taken for his 2 MY ruler the height of a man, or the average height of several men, or the spread of a man's arms when outstretched. Alternatively he could have used an average pace for his version of the megalithic yard. Any of these ways would give him a practical measuring rod without the need of sophisticated scientific methods.

Though we may find it difficult to accept the idea of the widespread use of the standardized megalithic yard, we must not go to the other extreme and deny or belittle the achievements in geometry and measurement during the Late Neolithic and Early Bronze Ages. The interrelationship between the three units of length, 1 megalithic rod = $2\frac{1}{2}$ megalithic yards = 100 megalithic inches, gives a practical and sensible set of units. If they were as accurate and well-defined as Professor Thom claims, even locally, the Beaker Folk had a better scale of linear measurement than at any time until the invention of the metric system after the French Revolution.

4 The Sun and the Moon

On a clear dark night, if you look up at the sky, you will see a few thousand stars. Because they are very far away they look like faint points of light, but if we were to come closer to them we would find each star was really a very large and hot ball of incandescent gases, giving off light and heat. Our sun is a star, the only one near enough for us to be able to see that it is a spherical object. It is about 150 million km away and its diameter is 1,392,000 km.

Surrounding the sun is a family of smaller bodies, which are dragged along by the sun in its journey through space. There are many hundreds of these, mainly lumps of rock and metals, quite cold except for the sun's heat radiated on them, and invisible unless shining by reflecting the light of the sun. The largest and best-known are the nine planets, Mercury, Venus, Earth, Mars, Jupiter, Saturn, Uranus, Neptune, and Pluto. The planets all revolve round the sun in the same direction, in elliptical orbits of small eccentricity.

From the Earth the motions of the other planets appear complicated and wayward. For most of the year they move from west to east against the background of stars, the nearer ones quite quickly, and their positions change noticeably from night to night. At times, when they are at their brightest, they appear to stop in their tracks and reverse direction, their paths tracing out loops in the sky. This is due to the fact that the Earth is also moving and their apparent movements are the result of the combination of the motions of two planets.

The brightest planets, Mercury, Venus, Mars, Jupiter, and Saturn, were known to the ancient astronomers of Egypt, Babylonia, and Greece, who were quite unable to understand their movements and raised them to the status of gods. The Neolithic and Bronze Age peoples of north-west Europe must also have been familiar with these planets, because at times they can be the most conspicuous objects in the night sky, apart from Mercury, which is always close to the sun and difficult to observe in northern latitudes. Whether they worshipped the planets or not we do not know, nor have we any means of telling if they attempted to follow the planetary movements systematically, but we can safely assume that they made little progress in understanding their complicated behaviour. In megalithic astronomy we have to disregard the planets.

The earth's orbit, with an eccentricity of 0·017, is one of the most circular. The sun is not at the centre of the ellipse, but at one of the foci. The consequence of this is that the distance of the earth from the sun varies from about 146 million km in January to 151 million km in July, so we are rather nearer the sun in the northern winter than we are in summer. This variation in distance is not the cause of the seasons.

As well as going round the sun once each year, the earth also spins like a top, revolving once each day. In the course of twenty-four hours every place on the earth's surface gets carried round to the sunny side of the earth, where it is day, and then back to the dark side, where it is night. The axis of the earth is an imaginary line passing through the north and south poles, and if we looked at the earth from a space vehicle somewhere above the north pole, the earth would appear to be rotating anticlockwise. North America is west of Europe, and anticlockwise rotation brings it into the sunlight after Europe. Thus the same time of day is later the further west you go (until the dateline in the mid-Pacific is reached). An astronaut on the way to the moon sees the sun as stationary in the sky and the earth as rotating, but we on the earth's surface are carried round as it rotates, and to us the earth seems stationary and the sun rotating. It appears to rise in the morning in the eastern part of the sky and set in the evening in the west.

Now if the earth's axis were exactly perpendicular to the earth's orbit, we would have a very simple situation. The sun would rise due east and set due west no matter where we were on earth. The days would be exactly the same length throughout the year, and we would have no seasons, except for the slight temperature changes caused by the earth varying its distance from the sun. Fortunately it is not like that. The earth's axis of rotation is tilted and makes an angle of about $66\frac{1}{2}°$ to the plane of the orbit. It is customary not to measure the angle of tilt from the plane of the orbit, but to measure it from the perpendicular to the orbital plane, and then it has the value $23\frac{1}{2}°$. Since the earth's equatorial plane is perpendicular to the polar axis, this is also the angle between the plane of the earth's orbit and the equator. The astronomical term invariably used is the angle of the ecliptic, and it has its own symbol, the Greek letter epsilon, ε (Fig. 4.1).

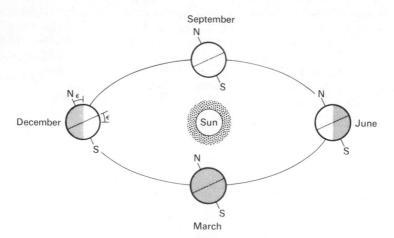

FIG. 4.1   The formation of the seasons (not to scale)

It is the tilt of the earth's axis that gives us the seasons. In June the earth's north pole is tilted towards the sun, so that it and the regions immediately around the pole never get carried by rotation into the darker side; they have perpetual day. The south pole meanwhile is tilted away from the sun and has perpetual night. Throughout all the northern hemisphere the sun is at its highest in the sky in June, whereas in the southern hemisphere the sun is much lower. The higher the sun in the sky, the warmer it feels, and so we have the northern summer coinciding with the southern winter.

Now as the earth goes round the sun, the direction of its polar axis remains fixed in space, so that by the time six months have passed, and it is December, the situation has reversed. The south pole is now pointing towards the sun and the north pole is tilted away from it. We have come to summer in the southern hemisphere and winter in the northern hemisphere.

Mid way between June and December, in September and March, the tilt of the earth's axis is neither towards nor away from the sun. The axis is still at $66\frac{1}{2}°$ to the plane of the orbit, but in a direction at right angles to the line joining the earth and the sun. We are back temporarily to the simple situation of the sun rising due east and setting due west everywhere on earth, and all places having twelve hours day and twelve hours night. The two days of the year when this occurs are called the equinoxes, and they are within a day or so of 21 March and 22 September.

If you live in temperate latitudes in the northern hemisphere and you were to watch the sun every day throughout the year, you would see it complete a full cycle of movements (Fig. 4.2). From 20 March onwards, it rises each day just a little further north of east and sets a little further north of west. The sun always climbs at about the same angle to the horizon (90° minus the latitude) so that if it rises further north it reaches a higher point in the sky at midday, and the day lasts longer. As the seasons advance into summer, the sun's rising point moves less each day towards the north, and on 21 June it reaches its limit. For a few days hardly any change is seen, either in the positions on the horizon of sunrise and sunset, or in the maximum height of the sun at noon. For a week around the longest day, the days are all about the same length. The sun appears to stand still before reversing its movements and beginning its daily decline in altitude.

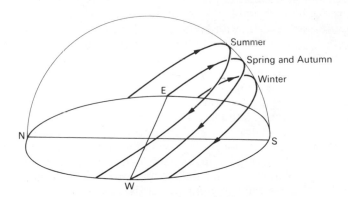

FIG. 4.2 The sun's daily movement through the sky

From midsummer, the positions of sunrise and sunset also move southwards, passing east and west at the Autumn equinox and eventually reaching their southernmost points on 21 December. The sun's midday altitude declines as winter comes, and the days gradually get shorter. Once again, as the sun reaches the limit of its movements, the daily change in rising and setting positions becomes so small as to be barely perceptible, and the short days around mid-winter are all about the same length; the sun appears to stand still in the sky. The times when the sun's movements temporarily almost cease are called the summer and winter solstices.

So far the description has been completely qualitative. If we want to devise a calendar based on the movements of the sun, we must find some way of indicating precisely where it is in the yearly cycle. One way is to follow the method that was invented in the Neolithic Period, by noting the position on the horizon of the sunrise and sunset at different times of the year. Providing the distant horizon is marked with a distinctive feature, it should be possible to do this quite accurately, without the need for elaborate mathematics. We could find sunset positions by repeated observations, if necessary putting up indicators to show other people where to look. If, however, we want to test for alignments made in the past, it is just not practicable to go to all the sites and repeat the observations at different seasons of the year. We are forced to use mathematical methods to test for alignments, and this means we must use precise ways of defining and measuring directions.

A very simple method is to define a direction by its azimuth and altitude. The azimuth is the horizontal angle measured clockwise from true north. Thus east has an azimuth of 90°, south 180°, and northwest 315°. The altitude is the vertical angle above the horizontal: looking up is positive and down is negative. For a mountain top azimuth and altitude are very convenient angles because they are constant values. For heavenly bodies they are not so convenient, because they are always changing.

Another pair of angles is used to indicate the positions of the sun, moon, and stars in the sky. Let us imagine that the sky is a large dome, like the ceiling of a planetarium. If we pretend the sky is a sphere we can draw on it grid lines, like the lines of latitude and longitude on the surface of the earth. Indeed, the lines can correspond exactly with latitude and longitude, because we can extend the plane of the earth's equator until it cuts the sphere and make that our celestial equator. We can project the line through the north and south poles of the earth until in imagination they meet our celestial sphere, and mark the north and south celestial poles (Fig. 4.3). Finally, the celestial sphere can be graduated in degrees to give angular position.

The equivalent of latitude is the angle measured from the celestial equator, which on the celestial sphere is called declination. The corresponding angle to longitude is called right ascension. There has to be an agreed zero line for right ascension, just as the line through Greenwich is internationally accepted for zero longitude. By convention, zero right ascension is the line which goes through the two celestial poles and the point where the sun is at the instant of the spring equinox.

It is easier to visualize the celestial sphere if we think of ourselves on the outside looking in rather than on the inside looking out. Figure 4.3 is drawn this way. It also shows the path of the sun on the celestial sphere during the course of a year. At the spring equinox the sun is at the position marked by the letter W, crossing the celestial equator as it moves from south to north. At the same time its declination changes from a negative to a positive value. From March to June

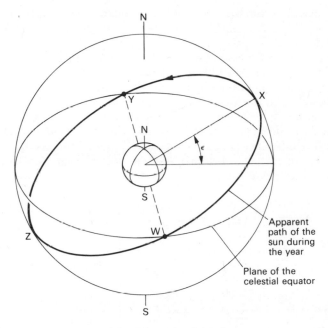

Apparent
path of the
sun during
the year

Plane of the
celestial equator

FIG. 4.3   The celestial sphere

the sun's declination increases to a maximum value of $23\frac{1}{2}°$, and its position at the summer solstice is represented by the point X. The path traced out on the celestial sphere by the sun during the remainder of the year is the curve YZW. On this representation WXYZ is the plane of the earth's orbit, and it is tilted to the plane of the equator by the angle of the ecliptic, ε.

The first stage in the process of checking an alignment is to calculate the apparent rising and setting positions of the sun, for different assumed values of declination. We need to know the latitude of the archaeological site, and the elevation of the sun when it appears on the horizon. All these quantities are related by a trigonometrical equation, in which the Roman letters A and h stand for the azimuth and the angular elevation of the sun at sunrise and sunset. The Greek letter ϕ (phi) represents the latitude, and δ (delta) is the declination of the sun. Then

$$\cos A = \frac{\sin \delta - \sin \phi \sin h}{\cos \phi \cos h}. \tag{1}$$

The meanings of the trigonometrical quantities are explained in Appendix C.

The easiest to find of the three unknowns, ϕ, δ, and h, is the latitude ϕ, because it is given along the vertical margins of all large-scale Ordnance Survey maps. We have to work to quite high accuracy to get useful results, and should aim at estimating the latitude of the site to within one hundredth of a degree. The National Grid lines on maps of the British Isles do not run due north and south, and therefore the two scales of latitude on each side of the maps are slightly displaced vertically. The latitude should always be estimated from the positions of the nearest small crosses which are printed at intervals of five minutes of arc.

The declination of the sun (or moon) on any day of the year can be found from nautical almanacs. Most likely the archaeologist will be interested primarily in the sun's declination at the solstices. At the present time it is about 23·5°, but it has not always had this value. Complicated gravitational interactions between the earth and the other planets have caused the angle of the ecliptic to change slowly over the centuries and it has decreased to its present value from about 24·1° in 4000 BC. The difference is small but it has to be taken into account. The correct value to take for any date between 4000 BC and 1000 BC can be found from Table 4.1, by interpolating for dates not given.

Date BC	Angle of the ecliptic ε	sin ε
4000	24·11°	0·4085
3500	24·07°	0·4079
3000	24·03°	0·4072
2500	23·98°	0·4064
2000	23·93°	0·4056
1500	23·87°	0·4047
1000	23·81°	0·4037

Table 4.1   The angle of the ecliptic from 4000 BC to 1000 BC

It is this small variation in the angle of the ecliptic that Sir Norman Lockyer tried to make use of in his method of dating Stonehenge. We can work out the azimuth of the midsummer sunrise in a simplified way, to explain Lockyer's method, and incidentally show how the equation can lead to the azimuth of the midsummer sunrise. The simplification which we introduce is to assume the horizon is horizontal, thus making the angle $h = 0$ in equation (1), and since $\sin 0° = 0$, and $\cos 0° = 1·0$, equation (1) simplifies to

$$\cos A = \frac{\sin \delta}{\cos \phi} \qquad (2)$$

The latitude of Stonehenge is 51·178°, and therefore $\cos \phi = 0·6269$. We can find the azimuth of midsummer sunrise in 2000 BC by taking from Table 4.1 the value 23·93° for the sun's declination, and hence $\sin \delta = 0·4056$, and $\cos A = 0·4056/0·6269 = 0·6470$. This gives $A = 49·68°$. Repeating the calculation for 1500 BC, we find $A = 49·79°$. These values differ by only just over one tenth of a degree for 500 years of change, or 0·02° per century. When Lockyer tried to date Stonehenge by measuring the azimuth of the axis of the Avenue and then comparing it with calculated azimuths, he was correct in principle but, as explained in Chapter 1, not precise enough in practice. Professor Thom has used the same method in recent years to date archaeological sites other than Stonehenge. He chooses alignments with very precise indication, usually by a notch in a distant horizon.

The calculation of the two values of azimuth was intended to show the rate of change of the alignment, not to give precise values of the azimuths at the two dates. By putting $h = 0$ we will have reached incorrect answers, though the difference between the two azimuths will not have a significant error. When testing a particular sightline, the approximation $h = 0$ is not good enough and should not be used (except perhaps as a quick initial check to see whether a conjectured alignment is in the right general direction).

The elevation of the horizon can be measured directly with a theodolite (the best way), or it can be deduced by drawing profiles of hill tops from a large-scale map. This has to be done with care, because it is remarkably easy to draw a profile for one range of hills and fail to notice that the horizon is wholly or partially the outline of a more distant range. Having drawn the profile, it has to be converted to an angle of elevation and for this it is useful to know that a rise of 1 m in 1 km is an upward angle of 0·057°. When the horizon is very distant the earth's curvature has to be included, and the angles should be reduced by 0·0045° per km distance from the observing site.

The elevation of the horizon is not, however, the value for h to put in equation (1). There are two further factors which must be taken into account, refraction and parallax.

Refraction is the bending of light rays by the atmosphere. The effects of atmospheric refraction are quite often seen in summer when driving along a main road on a warm day. In the distance black 'pools' seem to appear on the road ahead, and if a car happens to be on the far side of one of them its reflection can sometimes be seen as though the pool were actually water. They are in fact mirages, and they disappear as you approach. They can be explained by the bending of a ray of light, which is refracted upwards as it travels through the warm and less dense air in the few centimetres above the hot road surface.

In a similar way, the atmosphere bends the rays coming from the sun. When the sun is on the horizon, although it may appear to have the same elevation as the distant hills, this is not the case. The rays have been bent downwards as they enter the denser atmosphere near the ground and the result is to 'lift' the sun a small amount in the sky (Fig. 4.4). Refraction makes the sunrise earlier and the sunset later than it would otherwise be. It can be taken account of in equation (1) by a small correction subtracted from h. The amount to subtract depends on the altitude of the horizon; if the horizon has zero altitude, the correction is 0·55°, but with higher horizons the correction is less. The actual value can be taken

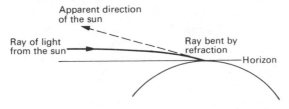

FIG 4.4 Refraction of light by the atmosphere

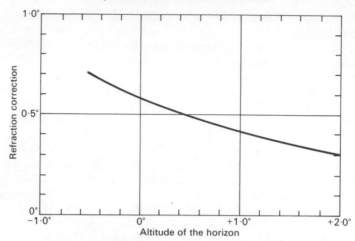

FIG. 4.5   Variation of refraction with altitude

from Figure 4.5, in which the refraction correction is plotted for different horizon altitudes.

The second factor, parallax, is the astronomical term for a very simple thing. If you hold a pencil up in front of your face at about arm's length and alternatively shut first one eye and then the other, the pencil will appear to jump from side to side compared with the background. This is parallax: the apparent position of an object depends on where you are when you are looking at it. Now the figures for declination of the sun and moon, which we get originally from astronomical almanacs, are worked out for observers at the centre of the earth. This may seem strange, but the figures can then be used by anyone, no matter where they are in the world. As can be seen from Figure 4.6, when the sun or moon is low in the sky its apparent position is slightly different for an observer on the earth's surface. As with refraction, parallax can be dealt with by a small correction to h, 0·002° for the sun (so small it can be neglected) and 0·95° for the moon (never negligible). Parallax makes the moon rise later and set earlier than predicted, and therefore works in the opposite direction to refraction. The parallax correction is added to h.

Combining all these factors gives the rule

$$h = \text{(horizon altitude)} - \text{(earth's curvature correction)} + \text{(parallax)} - \text{(refraction)}.$$

When we put this value for h in equation (1), the azimuth we calculate gives the position when the middle of the sun's disc is on the horizon. Unfortunately we do not know what the Neolithic and Bronze Age astronomers took as the moment of sunset: the first touch of the sun on the horizon, the sun half obscured, or the last flash before disappearance. They may even have had different practices at different times. If they thought it was important to fix the direction of the sunset precisely, the last flash would have been the easiest to observe. It can be located very accurately on a level horizon. In contrast, it is difficult to judge when the sun is exactly half set, and not too easy to tell when the bottom of the disc just touches the horizon, mainly because of dazzle and the shimmering effect of variable refraction. It is more difficult to mark the position of first appearance at sunrise than last flash at sunset, unless you know almost exactly where it is going to be.

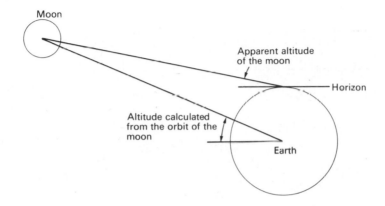

FIG. 4.6   The effect of parallax

There is no problem in amending the value of h to give the azimuth of either the last (or first) flash or where the horizon is just tangential to the disc. For the last flash, subtract from h the angle $0 \cdot 25°$, which is half the diameter of the sun's disc. For the tangential case, add $0 \cdot 25°$ to h. Since the sun and moon, by chance, have almost the same apparent diameter, these figures apply equally to both.

When the horizon is mountainous or rocky, it is more informative to the modern researcher to plot the path of the rising or setting sun or moon. The best way to do this is to begin by plotting on graph paper the profile of the horizon, and then to work out the azimuth of the centre of the disc for a series of different elevations, both higher and lower than the horizon. Refraction and parallax (for the moon) must be included. Pictures like Figure 6.4 can be produced simply by drawing circles to scale and joining their circumferences with tangents. If the horizon is low, the setting path will be slightly curved, due to a different value of refraction being taken each time. Though a little tedious, it is usually well worth making a sketch like this, for it shows the sunset or moonset as it would actually have appeared in megalithic times, and gives the setting paths in correct relation to irregularities on the horizon.

Here is a worked example. Imagine we want to know the midsummer and midwinter sunrises and sunsets, four directions in all, for a site with the same latitude as Stonehenge, and with a level horizon, not very distant, having an elevation all round of $1 \cdot 0°$. Take the instant of sunrise and sunset to be when the sun is just visible as a flash of light. Then the latitude, ϕ, $= 51 \cdot 178°$, hence sin $\phi = 0 \cdot 7791$ and cos $\phi = 0 \cdot 6269$ (from sine and cosine tables). In this example we can neglect earth's curvature because we have a near horizon, and parallax because the sun's parallax is small, and we find

$h = 1 \cdot 0°$ (horizon altitude)$-0 \cdot 4°$ (refraction from Fig. 4.5)
        $-0 \cdot 25°$ (half disc) $= +0 \cdot 35°$.
Hence $\sin h = 0 \cdot 0061$ and $\cos h = 0 \cdot 9998$.

The remainder of the calculation is best tabulated.

	Midsummer sunrise	Midwinter sunrise	Midwinter sunset	Midsummer sunset	Notes
Declination, δ, of the sun in 2000 BC	$+23 \cdot 93°$	$-23 \cdot 93°$	$-23 \cdot 93°$	$+23 \cdot 93°$	from Table 4.1
$\sin \delta$	$+0 \cdot 4056$	$-0 \cdot 4056$	$-0 \cdot 4056$	$+0 \cdot 4056$	
$\sin \phi \sin h$	$0 \cdot 0047$	$0 \cdot 0047$	$0 \cdot 0047$	$0 \cdot 0047$	multiplying the figures given above
$\cos \phi \cos h$	$0 \cdot 6269$	$0 \cdot 6269$	$0 \cdot 6269$	$0 \cdot 6269$	
$\cos A$	$+0 \cdot 6395$	$-0 \cdot 6545$	$-0 \cdot 6545$	$+0 \cdot 6395$	from equation (1)
azimuth, A	$50 \cdot 25°$	$130 \cdot 88°$	$229 \cdot 12°$	$309 \cdot 75°$	from sine and cosine tables.

Table 4.2 Calculation of azimuths of sunrise and sunset

The above table shows that $\cos A$ is the same for midwinter sunrises and sunsets, yet it gives two different azimuths. This is because, for any angle, the cosine of the angle is the same as the cosine of 360° minus that angle. The calculation therefore gives two results from one cosine value, and the midwinter sunset is found by taking the azimuth of sunrise from 360°. The same applies to midsummer sunrises and sunsets.

The four directions plotted on a map would look like Figure 1.2. Midsummer sunrise and midwinter sunset are not exactly opposite each other, and because of refraction, they would not have been opposite even if the elevation of the horizon had been zero all round.

While the movements of the sun as seen from the earth are fairly simple, the movements of the moon are very complicated. The moon goes round the earth in the same direction as the earth goes round the sun. Its orbit can be represented pictorially as in Figure 4.7, where the scales of the orbits and diameters of the astronomical bodies are grossly distorted. The moon's orbit is 1/360th of the earth's and if drawn to scale would be quite invisible. The moon's period of revolution is about $27\frac{1}{3}$ days and its mean distance from the earth is 384,000 km. The plane of its orbit is neither the plane of the celestial equator nor the plane of the earth's orbit, but at an angle of $5 \cdot 14°$ to the latter. The moon crosses the plane of the ecliptic twice a month, and the two points where the orbits intersect are called the nodes of the moon's orbit, represented by N_1 and N_2 on Figure 4.7.

Now we are not really interested in the actual distances of the sun and moon, but in their apparent positions in the sky. It is far more convenient to abandon

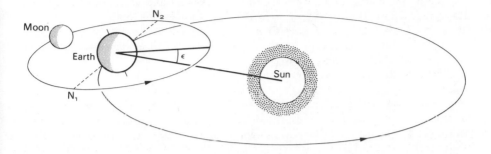

FIG. 4.7 The moon's orbit in space (not to scale)

attempts to draw the moon's movements realistically and to return to the representation of the celestial sphere, as in Figure 4.8. Here the moon's apparent path in the sky is indicated by the circle N_1PN_2Q, and the points N_1 and N_2 represent the nodes of the moon's orbit. N_1 is called the ascending node, because when the moon crosses the ecliptic at this point it is going northwards. N_2 is the descending node. The angle between the plane of the moon's orbit and the plane of the ecliptic, 5·14°, is given the symbol i. This angle is the same now as it was in prehistoric times and, unlike ε, does not have to be corrected for the date.

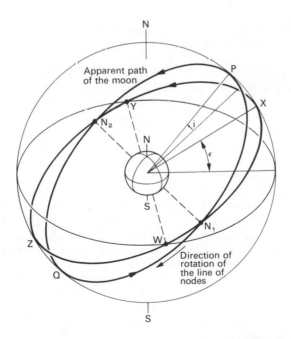

FIG. 4.8 The moon's orbit on the celestial sphere

During the course of a month the moon makes a full revolution of N_1PN_2Q. Its highest declination is when it is at P, and its lowest declination is when it is at Q. In $27\frac{1}{3}$ days the moon goes through a complete oscillation in declination, from high in the sky to low in the sky. Its movements follow the same pattern as the sun's, but thirteen times as fast.

There is, however, a vital complication: the plane of the moon's orbit also rotates. The line of nodes makes one revolution every 18·6 years. Look at Figure 4·9 and compare it with Figure 4·7. They are identical, except that the moon's orbit is tilted in the opposite direction, just as it would be after 9·3 years. In Figure 4.7 the plane of the moon's orbit is much nearer the plane of the earth's equator than it is in Figure 4·9.

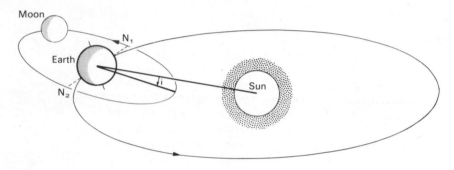

FIG. 4.9   The moon's orbit in space (not to scale) — nine years after Fig. 4.7

The rotation of the nodes of the moon's orbit is more scientifically illustrated in Figure 4.8; the orbit is shown a short while before its maximum inclination to the celestial equator. At the maximum inclination, the angles ε and i are in the same direction, and the inclination of the moon's orbit is therefore $\varepsilon+i$, or about 29°. Half a nodal revolution later, the point P will have gone round to somewhere just above Z, and Q will be between X and the ecliptic. The angles ε and i will be in opposite directions, and the tilt of the moon's orbit will be $\varepsilon-i$, or about 19°.

We have already said that the moon swings each month from a maximum value of declination to a minimum value and back again. We now see that the amplitude of this oscillation will at some time be at its greatest, from about 29° north of the celestial equator to 29° south of the celestial equator. We can say that it swings from $+(\varepsilon+i)$ to $-(\varepsilon+i)$. The time when the moon is swinging its farthest is called the major standstill, because the moon reaches about the same maximum height in the sky every month for something like three years. At the major standstill the moon's movements are at their most dramatic. Not only does it reach its highest possible elevation each month, but two weeks later it is very low in the sky, and barely rises in the high latitudes of the Shetland Islands. These movements would have been very conspicuous to early man.

Just over nine years after the major standstill, the moon's orbit has completed a full half turn and the monthly oscillation in declination will be much smaller:

from about 19° north of the celestial equator to 19° south, i.e. from $+(\varepsilon-i)$ to $-(\varepsilon-i)$. At this time the moon is said to be at the minor standstill, because once more it reaches approximately the same height in the sky for months on end. From the observer's point of view its movements are now far less dramatic than at the major standstill. Its maximum height in the sky is about 10° lower at this time, and its minimum height is 10° higher, so it does not show such a wide swing in its monthly movement.

These motions can be represented on a single diagram such as Figure 4.10 which shows the monthly oscillation of the moon's declination, modified by the effect of the 18·6-year rotation of the moon's orbit. In fact the diagram cheats a little, because there should really be 242 monthly cycles in the period of 18·6 years. If they had been drawn strictly accurately, they would have been too close to picture clearly.

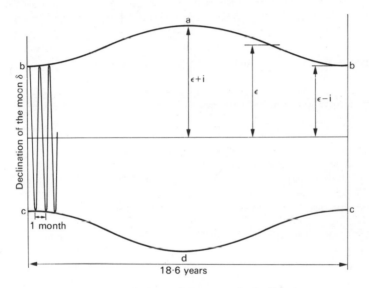

FIG. 4.10   The variation of the moon's declination over a
period of 18·6 years

On Figure 4.10 the moon is at its minor standstill when the declination oscillates between b and c, and at its major standstill when it oscillates between a and d. The moon was last at the major standstill in April 1969 and will be again at the end of 1987. The intervening minor standstill was in August 1977.

Just as we are able to calculate the rising and setting points of the sun by the use of equation (1), we can find the rising and setting points of the moon. The method is exactly the same as before, though we must always remember to include the correction for parallax. There are four limiting directions when the moon is at the major standstill, and four for the minor standstill. Figure 1.3 shows how the eight directions are distributed round the horizon for a site with the same latitude as Stonehenge.

People who write about megalithic astronomy often use a sort of shorthand when describing the direction of the risings or settings of the sun and moon. They speak of a $(\varepsilon+i)$ moonrise, for example, describing it by the declination of the moon at the time of rising. This is more convenient (and shorter) than the descriptions used by Hawkins, such as 'most northerly midwinter full moon rise'. Thom extends this terminology to include the diameter of the moon. In his notation, half the diameter of the moon is given the letter s, so that when he marks a direction on one of his diagrams with $(\varepsilon+i+s)$, he means the direction where the upper limb of the moon appears over the horizon.

I mentioned in Chapter 1 that Professor Hawkins had suggested that Stonehenge might have been used as a computer for predicting eclipses of the moon. To understand this and other similar suggestions, it is necessary to know something of the astronomy of eclipses. An eclipse of the moon is caused by the shadow of the earth cutting off the sun's light from the moon, so that we can no longer see it. In order for this to happen, the sun, moon, and earth must be in the same straight line, and therefore the moon must be on the opposite side of the sky from the sun; it must be a full moon. An eclipse of the sun occurs when the moon passes between the earth and the sun, thus casting its shadow on the earth's surface. Once again the sun, moon, and earth must be in a straight line, and this time the sun and the moon must be in the same direction in the sky. Eclipses of the sun can only take place at new moon.

Now if the moon's orbit did not have its $5·14°$ tilt, we should have eclipses of the sun and moon every month. Because of the tilt, they happen only if the moon is near one of its nodes at new or full moon. It does not have to be exactly at the node, because the earth and the moon are several thousand miles in diameter. The dark part of the shadow of the earth at the distance of the moon's orbit is still about twice the diameter of the moon and the eclipse can occur when the moon is in any part of the shadow. Similarly, an eclipse of the sun happens at some place on earth if the moon's shadow falls anywhere between the north and south poles. As long as the moon is within 17 days of the node at full or new, there will be an eclipse of some sort. The period of 34 days is called an eclipse season.

There is a very important difference between eclipses of the sun and the moon. The shadow of the moon on the earth is quite narrow, and as the earth rotates it sweeps across the surface. The only people to see a total eclipse of the sun are those who happen to be in the narrow band, at its widest not more than 180 km across, traced out by the moon's shadow. Other people will see a partial eclipse of the sun, with the moon obscuring only a fraction of the sun's disc. Partial eclipses of the sun, unless they are almost total or coincide with sunrise or sunset, are not very noticeable, and since no one goes round gazing directly at the sun, it is possible that the inhabitants of north-west Europe in the Neolithic and Early Bronze Ages were unaware of them. In this long period only a few persons could ever have seen a total eclipse of the sun. If they had seen one, it would no doubt have been a very disturbing experience, but one that is repeated so very rarely they would have been quite unable to deduce the periodicities in the recurrence of solar eclipses. We shall not concern ourselves further with eclipses of the sun, because they are not really relevant to megalithic astronomy.

Eclipses of the moon are much more often seen. When a lunar eclipse takes place it is visible simultaneously from half the earth's surface, and since it lasts for several hours, part of the eclipse can be seen (if the skies are clear) from more than half the earth. On the average about one lunar eclipse each year is visible from any part of the earth. A lunar eclipse, though not as spectacular as a total solar eclipse, is quite a remarkable sight, and could scarcely have failed to make a great impression on prehistoric peoples of any period. Taking into account their fairly frequent occurrence, we cannot rule out the possibility of the discovery, in the Neolithic or Early Bronze Ages, of some of the regularities in the sequences of lunar eclipses.

We have already seen that lunar eclipses occur only at full moon, and the moon has to be close to one of the nodes of the orbit. Since there are two nodes, we have a chance of two lunar eclipses each year, separated by an interval of six months. The 18·6 year rotational period of the nodes is equivalent to an annual drift of about 20°. The sun moves along the ecliptic at a rate of 1° per day (360° in 365¼ days), so a change of 20° in the position of the nodes means that the sun will be in the direction of the nodes 20 days earlier each year. (The nodes rotate in the *opposite* direction to the sun's annual motion.) The effect of the rotation of the lunar nodes is therefore to make the lunar eclipses occur on average 20 days earlier each year.

This over-simplifies the situation. The length of the month, that is the time from one new moon to the next, is 29·53059 days, and 12 lunar months = 354·37 days. Twelve lunar months are 10·63 days shorter than one year of 365 days. The eclipses therefore actually recur ten or eleven days earlier each year for a few years, the eclipse missing the node by a few days more year by year, until at last the day of the full moon is too far from the day when the moon crosses the node for the eclipse to occur. There is then a slip of thirteen lunar months and the sequence begins again.

There are other interesting patterns in the cycles of eclipses. In Table 4.3 are listed all the lunar eclipses between 1913 and 1988. For each year the date of the midwinter full moon is given, together with the declination of the midwinter full moon. (Actually the declination given is the maximum for the month, but it is always within one or two days of the midwinter full moon.) The letters t, p, v, and i, in brackets after the dates of the eclipses, mean 'total, partial, visible, and invisible' and describe the lunar eclipses and whether they could be seen from north-west Europe. There are 112 eclipses listed for these years and 62 (55 per cent) are total, 55 (49 per cent) being visible from Europe. On the average one sees rather fewer than one eclipse per year, and one total eclipse every two years.

It is worth noting the links between the dates of the eclipses and the declinations of the moon. The moon was at the major standstill in 1913, 1932, 1950, and 1969. It was at the minor standstill in 1922, 1940, and 1959. (The declination maxima reveal the year in most cases, though one must remember that the table gives the value of the declination maximum in December, not the highest maximum for the whole year.) In the years of major and minor standstills, eclipses, if they occurred at all, were at the full moons nearest to the spring and autumn equinoxes (21 March and 22 September). Half-way between the standstills eclipses took place near the winter and summer solstices (21 December and 21 June).

Even with the few facts mentioned so far, one can go a long way towards making successful predictions of lunar eclipses. It is simply necessary to make sufficient observations of the moon's rising and setting positions to find out what

Year	Date and declination of midwinter full moon	Dates of lunar eclipses	Year	Date and declination of midwinter full moon	Dates of lunar eclipses
1913	13 Dec 28·4	22 Mar (t, i), 15 Sept (t, i)	1932	13 Dec 28·2	22 Mar (p, i), 14 Sept (p, v)
1914	1 Jan 27·9	12 Mar (p, v), 4 Sept (p, i)	1933	31 Dec 27·7	NONE
1915	21 Dec 26·7	NONE	1934	20 Dec 26·6	30 Jan (p, v), 26 July (p, i)
1916	9 Dec 25·7	20 Jan (p, v), 15 July (p, v)	1935	10 Dec 25·1	19 Jan (t, v), 16 July (t, v)
1917	28 Dec 24·1	8 Jan (t, v), 4 July (t, v), 28 Dec (t, i)	1936	28 Dec 23·6	8 Jan (t, v), 4 July (p, i)
1918	17 Dec 22·5	24 June (p, i)	1937	17 Dec 21·8	18 Nov (p, i)
1919	5 Jan 20·8	7 Nov (p, v)	1938	5 Jan 20·3	14 May (t, i), 7 Nov (t, v)
1920	25 Dec 19·5	2 May (t, v), 27 Oct (t, v)	1939	26 Dec 19·1	3 May (t, i), 28 Oct (p, v)
1921	15 Dec 18·7	22 Apr (t, i), 16 Oct (p, v)	1940	14 Dec 18·6	NONE
1922	3 Jan 18·5	NONE	1941	2 Jan 18·6	13 Mar (p, i), 5 Sept (p, i)
1923	23 Dec 19·0	3 Mar (p, v), 26 Aug (p, i)	1942	22 Dec 19·5	3 Mar (t, v), 26 Aug (t, v)
1924	11 Dec 20·1	20 Feb (t, v), 14 Aug (t, v)	1943	11 Dec 20·7	20 Feb (p, v), 15 Aug (p, v)
1925	30 Dec 21·7	8 Feb (p, v), 4 Aug (p, i)	1944	29 Dec 22·3	NONE
1926	19 Dec 23·3	NONE	1945	19 Dec 24·1	25 June (p, i), 19 Dec (t, v)
1927	8 Dec 24·8	15 June (t, i), 8 Dec (t, v)	1946	8 Dec 25·6	14 June (t, i), 8 Dec (t, v)
1928	26 Dec 26·6	3 June (t, i), 27 Nov (t, v)	1947	27 Dec 26·9	3 June (p, i)
1929	16 Dec 27·6	NONE	1948	16 Dec 27·9	23 Apr (p, i)
1930	4 Jan 28·2	13 Apr (p, i), 7 Oct (p, v)	1949	4 Jan 28·3	13 Apr (t, v), 7 Oct (t, v)
1931	24 Dec 28·5	2 Apr (t, v), 26 Sept (t, v)	1950	24 Dec 28·4	2 Apr (t, v), 26 Sept (t, v)

Table 4.3   Eclipses of the moon from 1913 to 1988

Where January dates are given for the midwinter full moon, this refers to the January of the following year.

Year	Date and declination of midwinter full moon	Dates of lunar eclipses	Year	Date and declination of midwinter full moon	Dates of lunar eclipses
1951	13 Dec 28·1	NONE	1970	12 Dec 27·7	21 Feb (p, i), 17 Aug (p, v)
1952	31 Dec 26·4	11 Feb (p, v), 5 Aug (p, i)	1971	31 Dec 26·6	10 Feb (t, v), 6 Aug (t, v)
1953	20 Dec 26·0	29 Jan (t, v), 26 July (t, i)	1972	20 Dec 25·4	30 Jan (t, i), 26 July (p, i,)
1954	10 Dec 24·4	19 Jan (t, v), 16 July (p, v)	1973	10 Dec 23·9	10 Dec (p, v)
1955	29 Dec 22·8	29 Nov (p, v)	1974	29 Dec 22·2	4 June (p, v), 29 Nov (t, v)
1956	17 Dec 21·2	24 May (p, i), 18 Nov (t, v)	1975	18 Dec 20·6	25 May (t, i), 18 Nov (t, v)
1957	5 Jan 19·8	13 May (t, v), 7 Nov (t, i)	1976	6 Dec 19·2	13 May (p, i)
1958	26 Dec 18·8	3 May (p, i)	1977	25 Dec 18·6	4 Apr (p, v)
1959	15 Dec 18·4	24 Mar (p, v)	1978	14 Dec 18·4	24 Mar (t, i), 17 Sept (t, v)
1960	1 Jan 18·8	13 Mar (t, i), 5 Sept (t, i)	1979	2 Jan 19·2	13 Mar (p, v), 6 Sept (t, i)
1961	22 Dec 19·8	2 Mar (p, i), 26 Aug (p, v)	1980	21 Dec 20·4	NONE
1962	11 Dec 21·4	NONE	1981	11 Dec 21·9	17 July (p, v)
1963	30 Dec 23·0	6 July (p, v), 30 Dec (t, i)	1982	30 Dec 23·6	9 Jan (t, v), 6 July (t, i), 30 Dec (t, i)
1964	19 Dec 24·6	25 June (t, v), 19 Dec (t, v)	1983	20 Dec 25·2	25 June (p, i)
1965	8 Dec 26·2	14 June (p, v)	1984	8 Dec 26·6	NONE
1966	27 Dec 27·3	NONE	1985	27 Dec 27·6	4 May (t, v), 28 Oct (t, v)
1967	16 Dec 28·1	24 Apr (t, i), 18 Oct (t, i)	1986	16 Dec 28·8	24 Apr (t, i), 17 Oct (t, v)
1968	3 Jan 28·5	13 Apr (t, v), 6 Oct (t, i)	1987	4 Jan 28·4	NONE
1969	23 Dec 28·3	NONE	1988	23 Dec 28·2	3 Mar (p, i), 17 Aug (p, i)

Table 4.3   Eclipses of the moon from 1913 to 1988 *cont.*

stage the moon has reached in its 18·6-year cycle. Then, providing there is a reasonably accurate calendar and some means of recording the dates of the full moons, most eclipses, or rather most eclipse seasons, would be predicted correctly.

Hidden in Table 4.3 are some numerical coincidences, which could be discovered only after many years of observation and recording. If you read across the table you will see that after 19 years eclipses often recur on the same dates. The reason for this is that 19 years is almost exactly equal to 235 months. The length of the year (the one we use in the calendar, and called the tropical year by astronomers) is 365·2422 days. The length of the month is 29·53059 days. So

$$19 \text{ tropical years} = 6939 \cdot 60 \text{ days, and}$$
$$235 \text{ lunar months} = 6939 \cdot 69 \text{ days.}$$

Thus after 19 years the phases of the moon repeat on the same day, though not at the same time. This regularity is called the Metonic cycle, because it was reputedly discovered by the Greek astronomer Meton in 433 BC. The Metonic cycle is not an eclipse cycle, and the nineteen-year coincidence of eclipse dates breaks down after two repetitions. The rotation of the lunar nodes is not in step with this cycle.

There is nevertheless a true cycle of eclipses called the Saros which was discovered in ancient times by Babylonian and Chaldean astronomers. Earlier in this chapter I explained that because the lunar nodes are rotating backwards, the sun takes 20 days less than a year to complete one revolution in the sky relative to the lunar nodes. To be accurate, the time it takes for the sun to travel from one ascending node to the next is 346·62 days. This period is called an eclipse year. Now.,

$$19 \text{ eclipse years} \quad = 6585 \cdot 78 \text{ days, and}$$
$$223 \text{ lunar months} = 6585 \cdot 32 \text{ days.}$$

After 223 months the sun, moon, and the lunar nodes return to almost exactly the same relative positions. If an eclipse occurred on a particular day, it will be repeated 6585·32 days later, that is, after 18 tropical years and $11\frac{1}{3}$ days. It will recur again after another 18 years $11\frac{1}{3}$ days, and so on. Eclipses can be grouped into families which may extend over hundreds of years. On Table 4·3 there are many examples: 8 January 1917, 19 January 1935, and 29 January 1953 are all total eclipses of the same family. Those of 3 March 1923, 13 March 1941, and 24 March 1959 belong to a family which has degenerated to partial eclipses. Successive eclipses in a particular family will not always be visible from the same point on earth, because of the odd 0·32 day in the cycle. This residue is equal to 7 hours 41 minutes, and eclipses will be that much later in the day for successive members in the cycle.

There are numerous other eclipse cycles, of which the most remarkable is 358 lunar months, corresponding to 28 years 345 days. The time error is just less than one hour, and the cycle repeats for about 15,000 years. Examples of two repetitions can be found in Table 4.3.

This is a suitable place to comment on Hawkins's and Hoyle's explanations for the Aubrey Holes at Stonehenge. Hawkins pointed out that three 18·61-year cycles have a duration of 55·83 years, and that on a particular calendar day, the direction of the line of nodes would be almost exactly the same as it was 56 years earlier. The moon would therefore rise with the same azimuth. Hawkins devised the rule that if the midwinter full moon rises over the Heel Stone, there will be an eclipse. The Heel Stone, as we know, approximately indicates the direction of the midsummer sunrise, and if the midwinter full moon rises over it, the moon must be half way between the major and minor standstills. If eclipses do occur that year, they will certainly be at midwinter and midsummer.

By moving tally stones around the 56 Aubrey Holes one step each year, it would be possible to keep a check on the moon's position in the 18·61-year cycle, and thereby know the most likely time of year for lunar eclipses. We can see from Table 4.3 that the 56-year cycle is correct for maximum declinations of the midwinter full moon, but for nothing else. It does not repeat the phases of the moon, which recur after 57 years (three Metonic cycles), nor does it apply to the repetitions of eclipses. In fact Hawkins's method has to be supplemented by carefully watching the phases of the moon, and can from time to time give an erroneous prediction. It has been criticized on the grounds that a large circle of holes is not needed simply for counting up to 56.

In Hoyle's suggested use of the Aubrey Holes, the circle of holes represents the ecliptic. He says markers can be placed beside the holes to indicate the positions of the sun, the moon, and the ascending and descending nodes. A typical arrange-

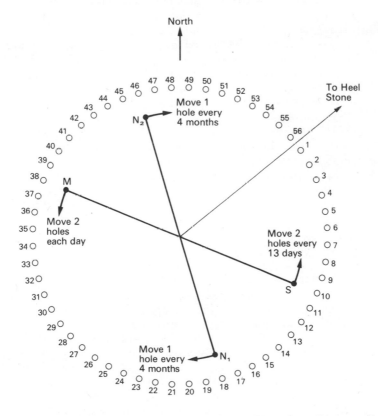

FIG. 4.11   Hoyle's method of using the Aubrey Holes as an eclipse predictor

ment is shown on Figure 4.11, where S and M are the sun and moon markers, N_1 and N_2 the nodal markers. S and M are directly opposite each other, because the figure shows how the markers would have been placed at full moon. The sun marker is moved anticlockwise by two holes every thirteen days, making one revolution in 364 days, very nearly a year. The moon marker is moved anti-clockwise two holes each day, making one revolution in 28 days. The nodal markers always keep on a diameter and they are moved clockwise one hole every four months, thus making a revolution in $18\frac{2}{3}$ years. These are reasonably good approximations to the three important periods. If the markers are initially set correctly, then every time S and M are opposite, *and* the nodal markers are within one hole, there will be an eclipse of the moon.

This is a better method than the one proposed by Hawkins, because it predicts every eclipse. It predicts solar eclipses equally well; they require the sun and moon markers to come together at the same hole and simultaneously be within one hole of either N_1 or N_2. It would not be difficult to set markers correctly for S and M, but it is far from obvious how the builders of Stonehenge could have positioned the nodal markers, or corrected them when they gradually drifted off the right setting. Hoyle suggested they would have observed precisely the time when the moon reached its maximum declination at the major standstill and then set one nodal marker on the hole that was occupied by S at the spring equinox. However, at the major standstill, the time of the highest maximum is hard to pick out—you could easily be a month wrong—and it would be more feasible to set or reset the nodal markers by the eclipses. The method, though elegant, is very subtle, and is regarded generally as being far too sophisticated for the Neolithic Period.

There are other ways of predicting eclipses which are more directly observational and do not require an extensive knowledge of eclipse cycles. The method propounded by Professor Thom is one of these. He believes that, by making very precise measurements indeed of the rising and setting azimuths of the moon, megalithic observers were able to discover a small irregularity in its movements which coincides with the eclipse seasons. We shall return to this method in Chapter 6.

The simplest method yet suggested, by R. Colton and R. L. Martin, is based on regular, yet easy, observations of the rising moon. A total eclipse happens only when the moon is exactly opposite the sun. If the horizon is horizontal, a regularly spaced circle of stones or other marks could be used as a protractor, to tell when the moon was rising opposite to the sun's setting position. The moon rises about an hour later each evening. It would be simple to watch successive moonrises and to observe how they approached the correct azimuth. For the eclipse to be visible on the night of the full moon, the moon must rise a short time, but not more than thirty minutes, before the sun sets. If it rises too early, the eclipse will not start until after the moon has set in the morning, and if it rises after the sunset, the eclipse is already over. The two conditions, of moonrise azimuth and time, make it possible to know in advance not only whether eclipses will take place, but also whether they will be visible from the observing point. The method does not require any particular number of stones or holes, though a large number of evenly spaced markers would be the best. The Aubrey Holes are well suited to this type of observation.

Prehistoric men must have been as familiar with the stars as with the sun and moon. The inhabitants of north-west Europe probably grouped the stars into patterns, or constellations, and invented stories to account for them, as did people in ancient civilizations in many parts of the world, from Babylonia to China. But the question is, did the early Europeans go beyond description and mythology and make systematic observations of the stars, as we believe they did with the sun and moon? We don't know, but the movements of the stars are very simple compared with the moon. They rise in the east and set in the west every night, and although their declinations are not absolutely fixed, they change so slowly as to make the stars appear to rise and set in the same directions from night to night. They do not of course always rise and set at the same times, but about four minutes earlier each evening. This is because we set our clocks in relation to the sun, not the stars. In a tropical year there are $365\frac{1}{4}$ days, but the earth actually makes $366\frac{1}{4}$ rotations relative to the stars. The sidereal day, as it is called, is therefore one part in $365\frac{1}{4}$ shorter than the solar day, or about four minutes less.

When we start to look for stone or other alignments that may have indicated stellar risings and settings in the Neolithic and Early Bronze Ages, we come across a problem that did not arise with the sun and moon. The tilt of the earth's axis, as well as diminishing slowly over the centuries, rotates, or precesses, making one revolution every 26,000 years. The motion of the earth can be compared to a spinning top: everyone will have noticed that a top wobbles—its axis precesses—as it slows down. The earth's precession, like the top's, is due to gravitational forces.

The effect of precession can be visualized by looking at Figure 4.3 and imagining the plane of the ecliptic to be motionless, while the polar axis of the earth precesses around a line perpendicular to the ecliptic. This moves the celestial equator round the ecliptic, causing it to change its direction in space. The positions of the stars remain static relative to the ecliptic, but since we measure declinations from the celestial equator, they must all change. In fact the declination of every star has a 47° oscillation (i.e. -2ε) with a period of 26,000 years. In the last 4,000 years the declinations of all stars have changed by amounts which are not less than 5° and may be as much as 20°. Searches for stellar alignments must begin by calculating the declinations of the bright stars for the date in question. The mathematics of this is beyond the scope of this book, and may be found in astronomical textbooks.

Although precession may not make much difference from night to night, it is certainly fast enough to make stellar alignments go out of date in the period of a man's lifetime. In 50 years the rising directions of the faster-changing stars will move by $\frac{1}{2}$°, and this fact alone might incline us to be doubtful about the value of indicating the rising and setting points of stars with permanent stone structures.

There is a serious observational problem when it comes to observing stars down to the horizon. Tangential rays are strongly absorbed by the atmosphere, which is why it is possible to look at the setting sun without hurting our eyes. As stars set they gradually get fainter and become quite invisible when they still have an elevation of a few degrees. According to Professor Hawkins's personal observations, even the brightest star, Sirius, can only just be seen when rising over a clear sea horizon. The lowest altitude at which a star can be seen is called its extinction angle and it depends on atmospheric conditions as well as the brightness of the star.

Professor Thom has listed about fifty sites where he finds sightlines corresponding to stellar risings or settings at dates between 2100 BC and 1500 BC. Without independent dating, these alignments are completely speculative; the declination-changes during the period he considered amount to several degrees, and it is possible to find coincidences of stellar alignments with a wide range of azimuths. In one of his statistical tests, he took a set of supposed alignments and then deduced the extinction angles at different dates in the Early Bronze Age. This procedure has too little external evidence to be convincing. The case for stellar alignments is further weakened by his more recent attribution of some of the alignments to declinations of the sun intermediate in date between the solstices and the equinoxes. It may also be significant that he finds no certain alignments for Sirius, in spite of its brilliance compared with other stars. If stellar alignments really exist, we should expect to find them for the very brightest stars, setting over high skylines.

None of these arguments precludes the use of stars at night for telling the time, or even as an aid to telling the seasons. The ancient Egyptians set their calendar by the heliacal rising of Sirius: that is, the first appearance of the star each year just before dawn in the eastern sky, after its period of invisibility when it was in conjunction with the sun. Their use of the star does not require the rising to be marked on the horizon, and therefore leaves no archaeological trace. We know about the technique through the written records. We shall never know if this idea had occurred to the Neolithic and Early Bronze Age inhabitants of north-west Europe.

5 The Solar Observatories

We do not know when men first began to speculate about the nature of the sun, moon, and stars. The food-gathering and hunting communities who preceded the neolithic farmers were dependent on the climate for their livelihood, though rather indirectly. Their standard of living would follow the natural variations in the abundance of wild animals and edible plants; they wandered round the country-side living in temporary encampments, always looking for the most plentiful supply of food. There is a great difference between winter and summer if one is living off the land. It would seem likely that they recognized the pattern of the seasons and associated the cold winter with the shortening of the days many thousands of years ago. They would have learnt to insure themselves against the lean times of the year by preserving food—storing nuts and drying meat, perhaps —and they would have known when to do this by keeping track of the annual movements of the sun. They would have been aware of the seasons in a casual, imprecise way, for nothing more was needed at the time.

With the introduction of farming at the start of the Neolithic Period, the way of life changed fundamentally. We might well expect that this was the beginning of astronomy, because an approximate calendar is almost essential for planning the farming year, whether one is growing crops or raising animals. We shall see that accurate observations were made and a calendar was developed at some stage in the Neolithic Period but the first signs of an interest in astronomy are seen in the burial chambers and mounds. Whatever the incentive, very early in the Neolithic Period the movements of the sun became associated with death and interment, and very possibly the rites of sun-worshipping ceremonies took place in the vicinity of houses for the dead.

One of the earliest sites which shows an astronomical alignment is the neolithic tomb at New Grange in Ireland, about 50 km north-west of Dublin. The mound of this passage grave is circular and enormous, being over 80 m across and 10 m high. The burial chamber, which is not quite in the centre of the mound, has a corbelled roof, formed by overlapping the stones with each successive layer, so that they gradually get closer together as the roof ascends. The height of the chamber is about 6 m and it has three recesses, each containing a large stone basin for the remains of the dead. The passage leading to the burial chamber is 19 m long. Its walls are slabs of stone, some of which are decorated with carved designs of spirals and lozenges. The entrance to the passage must originally have been very impressive. The mound was surrounded by a kerb of large stones, and on top of this was a dry-stone wall. For 30 m on either side of the entrance quartz had been used as the walling material, and when the tomb was first constructed it would have gleamed and sparkled in the morning sunlight.

The entrance to the passage is unexpectedly complicated in design. A roof slab is supported by the vertical slabs that form the walls of the passage, and this in turn supports more dry-stone walling, with a second roof slab on top, so that it forms a window 0·2 m high and 1 m wide. The front of the upper roof slab is decorated with a lozenge pattern, and the designer of the 'roof box', as it is generally called, incorporated drainage channels, presumably to take away rainwater. The back of the roof box is open to the passage and allows light to enter. It was not, however, kept permanently open, and when not in use was sealed by a removable block of quartz. The main passage was also closed. At the conclusion of the ceremonies when the tomb was first built, a large blocking stone was set up in front of the entrance. Just outside this is the decorated kerb-stone, which is now considered to be one of the finest examples of neolithic art in the whole of Europe. For later burials the blocking stone could be removed, and the corpses would have entered, like present-day visitors, over the top of the kerbstone.

When the site was investigated and restored in 1969, the excavator, Professor M. J. O'Kelly, noticed that at the winter solstice the sun's rays shone through the roof box, down the passage, and illuminated the rear wall of the burial chamber. The declination of the sun at the winter solstice has changed a little since New Grange was built about 3300 BC, but calculations have confirmed that the sun

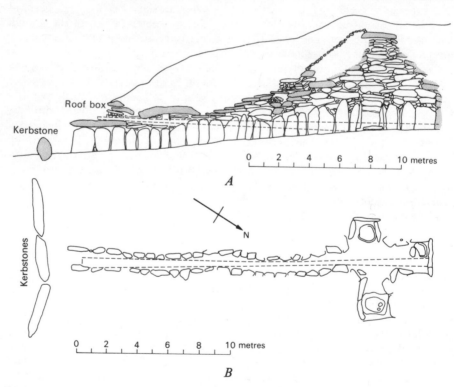

FIG. 5.1   Diagram of the internal structure of New Grange

A, Sectional elevation; *B*, Plan view. The dashed lines indicate the path of the sun's rays at the midwinter solstice. Based on a diagram in J. Patrick, 'Midwinter sunrise at Newgrange', *Nature*, **249** (1974).

would have shone to the end when the monument was new. In fact the box is a little larger than it need be, and the light reaches the burial chamber at sunrise for a few days before and after the winter solstice (Fig. 5.1).

Even before these discoveries, New Grange was reckoned to be an important archaeological site, mainly because of its lavish carvings which are unparalleled in the British Isles and can be compared with only a few sites in Brittany, such as the Tumulus de Gavrinis in the Golfe du Morbihan. New Grange can no longer be considered as a simple chambered tomb; it was also an astronomical clock for establishing the time of midwinter, for it is almost inconceivable that the elaborate roof box was constructed for any other purpose than to allow the sunlight to shine down the passage at the solstice. It would not have been accurate to the day, but it would at least have been accurate enough for regulating the farming.

In the eyes of its builders New Grange must have had more significance than this. The solstices can be marked more accurately by one or two standing stones, as indeed they were at other sites. There is no need to devise such a complicated arrangement, or to make it so large—there are 200,000 tonnes of stone in New Grange. It was built to be impressive, and it is a reasonable assumption that the forecourt of New Grange was the centre of midwinter ceremonies. Perhaps the monument was opened annually for ritual to encourage the return of the sun the following spring. And it is possible that the burial chamber received each year a sacrifice to ensure the lengthening of the days after the solstice.

We can speculate about the use of New Grange, but the one thing that seems reasonably certain is that as far back as 3300 BC the neolithic farmers were making observations of the sun. This is earlier by several hundred years than the first construction at Stonehenge, and about 1,000 years before the erection of the circle of sarsen stones. As far as is known, New Grange is unique amongst passage graves, but it would be unwise to rush to the conclusion that there were no other contemporary sites where the solstices were observed. The opposite is likely to be true. If the tribes who lived near New Grange found it necessary to have a rough-and-ready calendar, surely the same need arose in other places? We might expect that some of the other cairns, long barrows, chambered tombs, and passage graves of the period were similarly aligned, even though they did not have the theatrical device of the roof box. At Clava, for example, there are two graves with their passages in the same straight line, and both are orientated to the midwinter sunset. (The northern passage grave is enclosed in the Type I egg described in Chapter 3.) In the majority of cases intentional astronomical alignments are difficult to establish beyond doubt. There is always the possibility of an accidental astronomical alignment, especially if it was not of very high accuracy, as the early ones did not need to be. We can compare these ritual alignments to the east–west alignments of the majority of the Christian churches. They would approximately indicate the date of the Spring equinox, but certainly were not set up for this purpose.

Nevertheless, there is some evidence that some long barrows were associated with astronomical observations. If we look at the distribution of the orientations of the entrance end of earthen long barrows at Cranborne Chase in Dorset, it is far from uniform. The majority are orientated in the quadrant between east and south. Unfortunately it is not possible to deduce the orientations with very great accuracy from examining the external shape of the mounds. Erosion and farming have altered them in the last five thousand years. But there are hardly any with the entrances towards the west, and very many with entrances towards the south-east, in the approximate direction of the midwinter sunrise. By themselves the barrows would not give the direction accurately enough even for agriculture, but with the addition of standing posts, they might have served very well. A few long barrows have been found on excavation to be associated with postholes, and after the discovery of New Grange, it would seem prudent for excavators to consider the possibility of astronomical associations with long barrows during the course of their investigations.

One possible example of aligned earthen long barrows has already been reported on Cranborne Chase. This area is very rich in neolithic remains, showing that there must have been intensive occupation during that period. Two barrows (they are Gussage St Michael I and Gussage St Michael II, the custom being to number them in parishes) are only about 250 m apart. Both barrows appear to be orientated roughly to the south-east, but the interesting feature is that they also seem to be built on the same axis, and it is possible to make a reasonably accurate estimate of its orientation. Within $\frac{1}{2}°$ the line defines the azimuth of the midwinter sunrise in 3000 BC. This accuracy is not adequate for making a calendar, but when Gussage St Michael II was excavated in the nineteen-thirties, two very large postholes were discovered, large enough to take substantial posts. One of these was on the axis of the two barrows; the other was offset by 3 m. Viewed from just behind the other barrow, they would have had a gap about the same apparent size as the setting sun. It would have made a perfectly feasible sighting line, but of course there is no proof.

Cranborne Chase is famous for the mysterious earthwork called the Dorset Cursus, mentioned briefly in Chapter 2 (Fig. 6.2). Its main features are the two parallel earth banks about 80 m apart which run, though not straight, for 10 km across the Dorset countryside. The south-west end is very near the two barrows just mentioned, on Thickthorn Down, and the north-east end, on Bokerly Down, is also associated with long barrows. There is one barrow right in the middle of the cursus and another is incorporated into one of the banks. Since at this point it is clear that the cursus bank was built over the long barrow, it is safe to assume it was built later. The age of neolithic remains is very uncertain as yet, because the number of radiocarbon-dated samples is still small, but the likely period is 4000 BC to 3000 BC for the long barrows and 3000 BC to 2500 BC for the cursus. However, the strong association between the cursus and the barrows has led archaeologists to suppose that the cursus was a cult or ritual monument, perhaps a processional way for the dead. Rather curiously, there are no definite entrances, and to enter the enclosure at the terminals, the congregation would have had to clamber over the ditch and bank.

It is a very complex structure when examined in detail. For the moment we shall point out only that at about 3 km from the Thickthorn terminal it crosses Gussage Hill, and this is the place where the banks were built one on either side of an existing long barrow, Gussage St Michael III. There is quite a gap between the long barrow and the cursus banks, 20 m on one side and 40 m on the other. Over the top of Gussage Hill the cursus makes an S-shaped deviation, then crosses a shallow valley and climbs up Wyke Down. Here, half-way up the hill,

3 Avebury: the south-west quadrant of the henge, showing the bank, ditch, and ring of stones

4a Round-bottomed neolithic pottery

4b Beaker pottery

5a Neolithic grooved ware

5b Skara Brae: one of the neolithic houses, with 'dresser' and wall cupboards

6 Callanish: view looking to the north along the avenue, with the ruins of a chambered cairn in the foreground

7 Ring of Brodgar stone circle

8 Castle Rigg stone ring: a Type A flattened circle. View looking to the south

9 Penmaenmawr stone ellipse

10 Moel Ty Uchaf compound stone ring

11 Bryn Celli Ddu passage grave

12 Clach Mhic Leoid standing stone

This stone points to the Island of Boreray and indicates the position of sunset at the equinoxes

13 An Carra standing stone

From this stone the sun sets in the direction of Boreray at the start of the fourth and sixth months in the Bronze Age calendar

14 Standing stones at Ballochroy

At midsummer sunset in 1800 BC the sun would have set down the slope of the mountain above the right-hand stone. This slope is indi-

15 The solar observatory at Kintraw

At midwinter sunset in 1800 BC the sun would have set down the slope of the left-hand distant mountain. This photograph is taken from a point above the platform on the hillside (compare with Fig. 5.5)

16 Temple Wood standing stones: view towards the south-west, in the direction of the Bellanoch Hill alignment, which is hidden by the trees

17 Campbeltown standing stone

From this stone, at the major standstill, the moon just grazes the top of the mountain (compare with Fig. 6.7: the small irregularities of the horizon, 1 to $1\frac{1}{2}$ stone-widths to the left of the standing stone, are those on the diagram)

18 Cup and ring marks on the central stone at Temple Wood

19 Cup and ring marks on a rock at Achnabreck

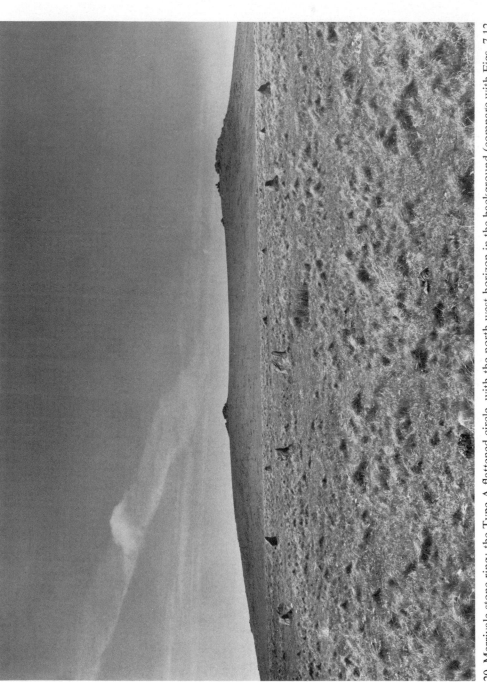

20 Merrivale stone ring: the Type A flattened circle, with the north-west horizon in the background (compare with Figs. 7.12 and 7.13)

21 Merrivale stone rows

Row II, looking to the west, with the blocking stone E in the foreground and stone R a short distance along the rows (compare with Fig. 7.10)

22 Mid Clyth stone rows: view from near the top of the ridge, looking approximately to the south-east

23 Le Menec stone rows

24 Le Grand Menhir Brisé

The menhir is lying in four parts, with its former base at the left. The megalithic tomb in the background is La Table des Marchands

there is a transverse bank, completely blocking the processional way, if it was one. The cursus continues for several kilometres beyond this, but the transverse bank looks so very like the two ends that it is known as the Wyke Down Terminal. From our point of view the interesting fact has emerged that if one stood at the Wyke Down Terminal in about 2500 BC and looked south-west towards Gussage Hill, the barrow on the top would have indicated the position of the setting midwinter sun. In fact, from near the centre of the Wyke Down Terminal the sun would have appeared to slip neatly down between the cursus bank and the end of the long barrow (Fig. 5.2). The Wyke Down Terminal has never been excavated and it is now badly eroded by the plough, but somewhere within the terminal enclosure one might expect to find a small area marked out, possibly by wooden posts, which would indicate to the user exactly where he had to stand to make the observation.

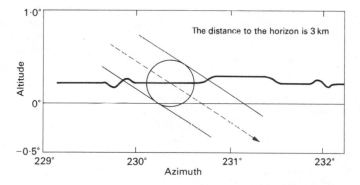

FIG. 5.2   Midwinter sunset over the Gussage St Michael III long barrow in 2500 BC, as seen from the Wyke Down Terminal of the Dorset Cursus

If the cursus was used for observations of the sun at the winter solstice, it shows an improvement in technique over New Grange. Much higher accuracy of observation is possible if a long sightline can be obtained. A good way of doing this is to use an indentation, or notch, in the skyline, and observe the sun rise or set behind it. Great precision can be obtained if the notch is sharp, and this would enable the observers to find the solstice to the nearest day. But if there is no notch, as on the smooth hills of Cranborne Chase, what better than to make use of an existing large and conspicuous barrow on the horizon? Because the barrow was built first, we might conclude that the first observations from Wyke Down were casual ones made by farmers tending the herds during the winter. The value of a distant object as a foresight would have eventually been appreciated, and from that time it would have become desirable to draw attention to it in some way. The cursus banks would have served this purpose. Originally they would have been gleaming white chalk, looking like polished railway lines as they climbed the hill towards the long barrow. Thinking of New Grange, we seem to have another instance of an over-elaborate solution to the problem;

surely a simple row of posts would have done just as well? But perhaps the cursus banks served to mark out the area of ground that had to be kept free of trees and scrub so that the observations were not impeded, and maybe it was also a site for a midwinter ceremony.

The cursus is an example of an observatory with a distant foresight which was indicated by something near the observer. This is a common combination, and when there is also a mark to show where the observer should stand, we have everything that is needed for the basic observations. Other features in the Dorset Cursus appear to have astronomical significance, but for observations of the moon, and will be described later.

The chambered tomb at New Grange, the Wyke Down part of the Dorset Cursus, and of course Stonehenge have all been built with some provision for making astronomical observations of the sun, though it is difficult to be sure if this was their primary function. They are all very complicated structures, and far more complex than is needed if they were simply for solar observations and nothing else. In principle, to find the date of the solstices the only equipment required is a distant post or stone which sticks up above the horizon, or better still a sharply defined irregularity on the horizon, and some way of marking the position where the observer should stand. There are some sites which are hardly more elaborate than this, though until quite recently they have not been recognized for what they are. Several of these are in Argyllshire and were studied by Professor Thom.

For instance, at Ballochroy on the western coast of the peninsular of Kintyre there are some standing stones (Pl. 14). The hillside here rises quite steeply from the shore, but about 200 m inland there is a level patch of ground with an elevation of 40 m. This is where the stones have been erected. There are three large stones and one rather despoiled cist, or small burial chamber, all in a straight line. The centre stone is a thin slab and one of its faces has the appearance of having been deliberately flattened and smoothed. Looking along this face towards the sea, beyond the Sound is the island of Jura, with the Paps of Jura on the horizon. The sightline directs the eye to Corra Beinn, the most northerly peak in the Paps, about 30 km away. This marks the position on the horizon where the midsummer sun would have set about 1800 BC, and quite precisely too, because the slope of the mountain side is almost the same as the apparent path of the setting sun, and even small differences in declination would be seen (Fig. 5.3).

In the twenty-four hours from either the winter or summer solstice the change in declination of the sun is very small. It makes a difference in the azimuth angle of the sunset of only 0·008°. So if the distant marker is, say, 100 m away, and the observer tries to line up the sunset each evening exactly behind the marker, a movement of his head of only $1\frac{1}{2}$ cm will be all that is required from the day of the solstice to the next day. But if the foresight is 30 km away, as with Corra Beinn, the movement from one evening to the next is 4 m, so there is no problem about getting the observer's head in exactly the right place. Distant foresights are much more accurate than near ones, and even the sightline used in the Dorset Cursus, which was 3 km long, though an improvement on New Grange, would not have been long enough to identify the exact day of the solstice with certainty.

Ballochroy, for all its apparent simplicity, represents another improvement in observational technique. It would take the setting sun about three minutes to

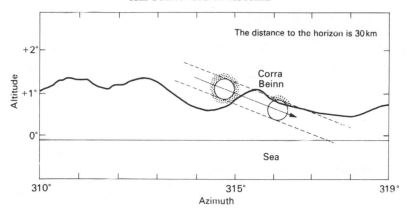

FIG. 5.3   Midsummer sunset at Ballochroy in 1800 BC

Compare with Plate 14; the photograph was, however, taken from a point off the line of the central stone, which is why it does not appear to be indicating the correct mountain top.

slide down the slope of Corra Beinn. The observer would station himself some-where along the line of the stones and the cist, in such a position that the sun would just vanish at the top of the slope. But the slope is slightly steeper than the path of the setting sun, so that the sun's edge would reappear lower down. He would then walk to the left, keeping the sun's edge just grazing the slope until it finally vanished, and he would put a marker on the extreme position. By repeating this from day to day, it would be possible to tell when the solstice had passed, because the marker furthest to the left indicates the day nearest to the solstice. Presumably when this had been repeated several times, and the solstitial setting position was well known, the large slab was erected, with its attendant stones on either side. The measurements would not, however, always be as easy as this. Refraction conditions would vary from time to time, and this could complicate the observations. Perhaps, after using this site over a long time, the observers got to know its vagaries and how they depended on the weather, and could make allowances.

Ballochroy also gives the midwinter sun's setting position. From the stones, looking towards the cist, we can see Cara Island, which is on the horizon at 12 km. The midwinter setting sun would have just grazed the end of the island. This sightline would also be fairly accurate, but it does not have the precision of the line over Corra Beinn.

About 50 km north of Ballochroy, near the hamlet of Kintraw, is another solar observatory (Pl. 15). It resembles Ballochroy in that the observers chose to make use of a level area in an otherwise hilly site, and also that the distant marker is Beinn Shiantaidh, one of the Paps of Jura at a distance of 43 km. On the level ground there is a large standing stone, about 4 m high but now leaning 25° out of the vertical. Near it is a stone cairn about 14 m in diameter, which has been badly robbed of material over the years (Fig. 5.4). Observing from this site, the sun at the winter solstice would set behind Beinn Shiantaidh, but again like Ballochroy, the slope of the mountain is steeper than the path of the setting sun, and its edge would reappear for a short space of time in the col formed by Beinn Shiantaidh and the neighbouring mountain Beinn a' Chaolais (Fig. 5.5). If the observer adopted the technique of moving to the side he could get himself into the position where the sun's edge momentarily appeared in the col, and he could record this with a marker. A repetition of the procedure on successive evenings gives him a row of markers, and in this case the one on the extreme right marks the day of the solstice.

When this site was first described by Professor Thom, it was not entirely clear how the observatory could have been set up. The elevation of the level area is just too low, by about two metres, to get a clear view of the col, because there is a small nearby ridge of land jutting out into Loch Craignish. The col can be seen by moving to the right, but then the observer is out of line for the midwinter

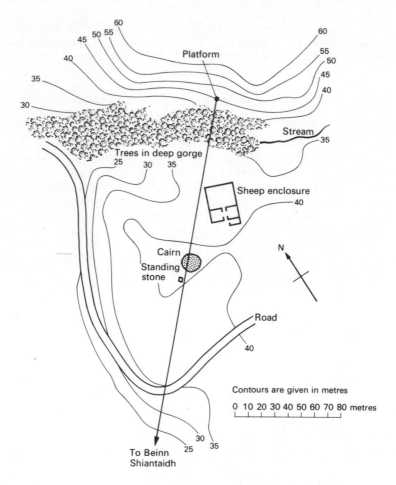

FIG. 5.4   Plan of the solar observatory at Kintraw

Based on a diagram in Hodson (ed.), *The Place of Astronomy in the Ancient World*.

sunset. If the cairn had been a little higher than it is now, which seems a reasonable assumption, the col would be in view when the observer stood on top of it. What is more, the cairn is in the correct place for making the observations, and it is wide enough for several evenings' viewing. It looks as though it was deliberately constructed for this purpose. The problem is: how could the builders of this observatory have known where to build the cairn when they could not see the col from this piece of ground?

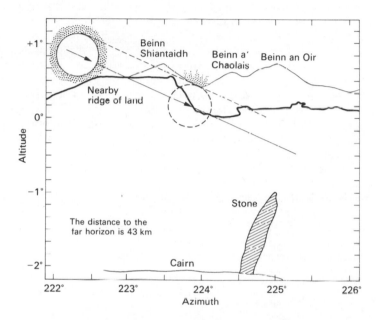

FIG. 5.5   Midwinter sunset at Kintraw as seen from the platform on the hillside in about 1800 BC

Based on a diagram in Hodson (ed.), *The Place of Astronomy in the Ancient World.*

To find the solution we must look at the hillside inland of the standing stone and the cairn. Here the slope is very steep, and between the cairn and the hill is a deep and dangerous gorge with a stream at its bottom. On the side of the hill there is a small level platform and on it are some large boulders. It is on the direct line of the standing stone and the distant col, and is just over 4 m higher than the ground level at the cairn. From this platform the col is clearly visible. It would not be possible to make all the measurements from the hillside, because it is far too steep for observers to move easily into position, and Professor Thom suggested that the platform was made by the constructors of the observatory to enable them to establish the correct line for building the cairn.

Dr Euan MacKie of Glasgow University realized that if excavation could show whether the platform was natural or man-made, it would help to resolve the astronomical interpretation of the site. He excavated in 1970 and 1971, and exposed an area of the platform immediately behind the boulders in line with the cairn and the distant mountain. He found that the boulders were pointed, as though forming a notch, and the level space behind them was covered with a compact layer of stones, which extended upstream but not downstream from the boulders.

There were no obvious signs of human interference, like pottery or worked tools, and evidence for or against a natural origin of the stone layer had to be sought from the arrangement of the stones themselves. Mr J. S. Bibby, a soil scientist, examined the stones, measuring the orientation and dip of a hundred adjacent ones. He plotted the results on a Schmitt net. In this representation, used by geologists, the angle of the stone is indicated by a point on a disc. The distance of the point from the centre gives the slope: i.e. if a stone has its axis vertical, the point is plotted at the centre of the disc; if its axis is horizontal, it is plotted on the circumference. Intermediate angles are somewhere between the centre and the perimeter. The position of the point round the disc gives the compass direction of the axis of the stone. A plot of naturally deposited stones gives a diagram like Figure 5.6, where the points are grouped in one part of the disc, showing that stones tend to become orientated down the slope. In the case of the platform at Kintraw, the diagram looks like Figure 5.7; the points are more evenly distributed round the circumference. It shows, in effect, that when men surface an area by laying stones flat, they do not orientate them down the slope. Mr Bibby's conclusion was that 'the available evidence supports the hypothesis that the Kintraw pavement was man-made'.

The location of the paved area is additional support. The downstream end of the stony surface, beside the notch formed by the pair of boulders, is the limiting position for observing the solstice, while the extension of the platform

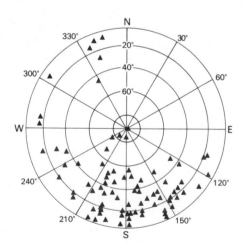

FIG. 5.6   Schmitt net plot for a layer of
naturally occurring stones

Based on a diagram in Hodson (ed.), *The Place
of Astronomy in the Ancient World.*

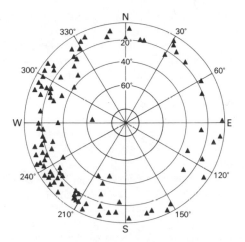

FIG. 5.7   Schmitt net plot for stones on
the platform at Kintraw

Based on a diagram in Hodson (ed.), *The Place
of Astronomy in the Ancient World.*

upstream is in the right place for observations on the days before and after the
solstice. The care that must have been taken in cobbling the area seems excessive
if its only purpose was to make once-for-all sightings of the sunset in order to
position the cairn. MacKie thinks it was the primary viewing point, because the
platform allows more room for movement than the restricted space on the top
of the cairn. This may well be so, but is it possible that, though the observations
were made from the hillside, the cairn was built as a focal point for annual
ceremonies at the solstice?

This excavation gives valuable support to the astronomical theories of
Professor Thom. At sites like Kintraw and Ballochroy conventional archaeological
techniques do not usually provide a lot of information. We would not expect
standing stones, usually separate from occupied sites, to be associated with
masses of household rubbish, like pottery, bones and other small finds, which are
invaluable for dating sites and putting them into their correct cultural context.
Standing stones are exceedingly difficult to date by excavation, unless it happened
that datable material was put, or fell, into the socket hole. Even if there are
several standing stones, or stones and other remains such as cists and cairns, it
is not easy to relate them to each other. For these reasons the precise dates of
standing stones are rarely found by the usual methods.

With Kintraw and Ballochroy we are thrown back on the astronomical dating
method devised by Lockyer and used by him unsuccessfully at Stonehenge.
Fortunately both these alignments have a long baseline and are extremely precise.
From the centre stone at Ballochroy the declination indicated by the slope of
Corra Beinn is $+24 \cdot 17°$ and if the sun set behind the mountain with its upper
limb just visible, the declination of its centre would be $+23 \cdot 90°$. At Kintraw the
indicated declination is $-23 \cdot 63°$; when the upper limb of the sun was just visible
behind Beinn Shiantaidh, its centre had a declination $-23 \cdot 90°$. From Table 4.1,

the sun's declination was 23·90° in 1750 BC, and this is the approximate date we would assign to both sites on astronomical grounds. They give the same date, are relatively close together, use the same observational technique and do not duplicate (since one is for midsummer, the other for midwinter), and these facts suggest strongly that they were intended for complementary observations and set up by the same group of people.

But who were the people who so carefully set up these precise observing stations? In 1750 BC the old neolithic culture characterized by large communal tombs had long since passed, and we were well into the Early Bronze Age. The cairn at Kintraw is Early Bronze Age in style, though when it was excavated in 1959 and 1960 no central burial was found, only the base hole for an upright wooden pole. Nevertheless, similar cairns in Strathclyde, for example at Ballymeanoch only 8 km away, contained Beaker pottery. The cist at Ballochroy is large and is likely to be neolithic. It poses a problem, for if it was once covered by a cairn, as most archaeologists believe, it would have blocked the midwinter sighting to Cara Island. This is not a serious objection to the interpretation of the site; the cairn could have been dismantled deliberately to permit the observations.

Although neither of these sites has been dated by independent material, the astronomical dates can be accepted archaeologically, and it is reasonable to attribute them to the Early Bronze Age and give the credit, until we know better, to the Beaker Folk.

It begins to look as though the Beaker Folk had special talents for geometry and astronomy. The sophistication of the observing techniques is intellectually consistent with the geometrical and numerical discoveries incorporated in the stone circles and rings. When the Beaker Folk arrived in the British Isles they must have found an established method of observing the solstices, practised by the neolithic tribes. It seems they took it over and perfected it, so that it was no longer a rough-and-ready indication of the approximate date of midwinter, it was a precise tool capable of timing the solstices to the nearest day. They increased the accuracy of the method by extending the foresight so that it was now as long as the atmospheric visibility would permit, and they actually selected foresights with special properties, such as sloping hillsides. They dispensed with the unnecessary construction work and all that remained were the bare essentials: the marker to show where the observer should stand, a pointer to indicate the foresight, and a foresight as far away as they could find. We shall see in the next chapter that there is strong evidence for their applying the same methods to precise observations of the moon. If all this is really true, the Early Bronze Age was a most imaginative and intellectual period in human history.

From Professor Thom's researches we think that one of their achievements was to devise a calendar. How could we do this if we had only the tools that were available in the Early Bronze Age? Let us suppose that we had watched the sun for many years and had come to be familiar with the annual cyclical movement of the rising and setting points between the midwinter and midsummer extremes. We could count the days from midwinter to midsummer and then, the following year, we could record in some way the point on the horizon where the sun appeared to set half-way between the two solstices. We might have to go a few miles from our original observing site to find a suitable horizon mark, or failing that, erect a large stone. This would give us, approximately but not accurately, the dates of the equinoxes. We could then divide the year still further with more markers, so that we had eight periods of about 46 days each, and if we so wished repeat the procedure to give sixteen periods of about 23 days. In essentials, this is how we think it was done in the Early Bronze Age. It sounds fairly easy, but there are several practical difficulties.

The first of these is that the time it takes for the earth to go round the sun is not a whole number of days: the year is 365¼ days long. We make allowances for this by introducing a leap year into our calendar once every four years. Of course, once they had established the foresights, the early astronomers could have ceased to count the exact number of days in each month, and they would not then have needed to bother about the extra day. It is doubtful, though, whether they could have set up all the foresights without taking account of the odd quarter-day in the year. Good distant sightlines have to be carefully selected and, because the conditions are stringent, are not very easy to find. Even to set up the calendar for a local area requires sites that are many miles apart. The sightlines must be co-ordinated and, bearing in mind that it may have taken years to make sufficient observations of the sun, try the approximate positions for the marker stones, readjust them where necessary, quarry, transport, and finally erect the large permanent stones at the backsights, it seems impossible without having a leap year once in four.

But we believe the calendar was not just local. There is some evidence that people as far apart as Wales and Caithness were using the same calendar at this period, and that these calendars were actually in synchronism. The calendars could have been brought into line by travellers 'taking the date' from one community to another. To do this they would have had to count the days as they went on their journey, and on reaching their destinations they might have had to wait for months before there was a clear sunset on one of the days when they wished to set up a foresight. This, too, argues for the introduction of the leap year in the megalithic period.

In our official calendar the year is divided into four seasons: spring and autumn which begin at the equinoxes (21 March and 22 September), and summer and winter which begin at the solstices (21 June and 21 December); the actual day varies slightly from year to year. The equinoxes are defined as the days when the sun crosses the celestial equator, i.e. has zero declination. They are the days when the lengths of day and night are equal all over the world, although the day is slightly longer than the night owing to refraction of light. We might expect the seasons to be exactly the same length but this is not so. This is because the earth's orbit is elliptical and the speed of the earth in its orbit is not constant. When the earth is in that part of its orbit nearest to the sun, it moves quicker than when it is furthest from the sun. It so happens that the earth is closest to the sun in January, and it takes a shorter time to move from the autumn equinox to the spring equinox (about 178 days) than from the spring equinox to the autumn equinox (about 187 days). So if we were to place markers to indicate the position of the setting sun on the horizon half-way between the two solstices, the dates would not coincide with the equinoxes, but could be as much as two days out. In fact the declination of the sun would not be zero, but about $+0.8°$. In the Early Bronze Age the earth was closest to the sun in November, not January, because the major axis of the earth's orbit is rotating slowly and had then a different orientation in space; this would have made the difference between the two halves of the year smaller than it is now. Nevertheless, when we look for astronomical sightlines for the equinoxes, we should expect to find them indicating not zero declination but a small positive value. They need not have been as accurate as the solstitial lines, because the sun changes its declination quite rapidly in spring and autumn (about 0·4° per day), and an indication to $\frac{1}{4}$° would have been good enough.

Sightlines for the equinoxes have been identified at several sites, including Stonehenge. At Callanish, on the Isle of Lewis, which we have already mentioned in connection with its stone rows, there is one of the most remarkable groups of stone settings in the British Isles. The main ring of standing stones (Callanish I), with its avenue and three radiating lines of megaliths, is spectacular enough to have gained the title of the 'Scottish Stonehenge'. Several investigators have claimed that astronomical alignments are incorporated in the stone rings of the Callanish area but these have not all been substantiated by recent research. The equinoctial sunset seems to have been marked at Callanish I by an east-west line of four standing stones. This line has geometric connections with the stone ring, which is not circular but is a Type A flattened circle with its axis also east–west. One of the secondary centres is on the line of the four stones and, as if to emphasize its significance, it is also on the centre line of the avenue and on another line of four stones which may mark a lunar alignment.

The western coast of Scotland seems especially rich in solar alignments, because of the investigations of Professor Thom and his colleagues. (Other areas have not been studied in such detail.) The Isle of Lewis has other sites besides Callanish, and one of them is on the Harris peninsula in the southern part of the island. A slab on the west coast of Harris, called Clach Mhic Leoid (Pl. 12), points to the rocky island of Boreray, nearly 90 km to the west in the Atlantic Ocean. Boreray is the most northerly of the islands in the St Kilda group. From Clach Mhic Leoid the summit of the island, which projects only 0·1° above the horizon, has an azimuth corresponding to a sunset with declination +0·23°; if the atmospheric conditions had allowed it to be seen at this great distance at the right time of the year, it would have made an accurate alignment for the equinoxes.

Another, on the north-east coast of Scotland, is at Learable Hill in the Kildonan valley in the county of Highland, 15 km up the river from Helmsdale. There are settings of stones which point almost due east and may be an equinoctial marker. There is a similar site called Eleven Shearers in the Borders County, 13 km east of Jedburgh. Yet another, and rather puzzling, site at Duntreath, 17 km north of Glasgow in the Strathblane valley, indicates equinoctial sunrise. We shall discuss this site in detail later, because it is one of the very few stone settings that has been excavated with a view to throwing light on its supposed astronomical significance.

A calendar of four periods of about 91 days each is not very practical, and once having started to divide the year it would seem logical to carry on to make a larger number of shorter periods. Dividing the intervals by two successively could result in a calendar of sixteen 'months' of about 23 days each. The months might be arranged into, say, thirteen months of 23 days and three months of 22 days, giving a total of 365 days for the year. The problem is: how do you distribute the shorter months throughout the year, especially if you want to make the monthly markers serve for two dates, one when the sun's declination is increasing and the other when it is decreasing? Professor Thom's studies of stone alignments, particularly in Scotland, have led him to the conclusion that this problem was successfully solved by the people who erected the megaliths in the Early Bronze Age.

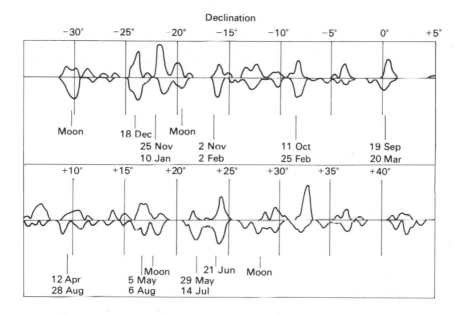

FIG. 5.8 Histogram of observed astronomical alignments, plotted as the number for different values of declination

The dates indicate the declinations of the sun on the sixteen days in the year which mark the start of the months in the suggested Bronze Age calendar. The four lines marked 'moon' indicate the limiting declinations at the major and minor standstills. Based on a diagram in Thom, *Megalithic Sites in Britain*.

His evidence is largely statistical, using data from more than 300 sites, most of which he has surveyed himself over a period of many years. Thom's information includes alignments of the many different types found at Neolithic and Bronze Age sites, such as rows of stones, two well separated stones, circles with outliers, distant foresights indicated by stones, and so on. He then calculated the declination of the astronomical object whose rising or setting was marked by the site. Plotting these declinations gives a very interesting result (Fig. 5.8). If the alignments were quite accidental we should expect to find that no direction was indicated more often than any other. What is actually found is that some declinations are very often indicated, and these include the midsummer and midwinter rising and setting positions of the sun. There are peaks on the graph corresponding to the equinoxes, and some which can be explained by the limiting values of the declinations of the moon. But there are other preferred declinations as well, around the values $-22°$, $-16°$, $-8°$, $+9°$, $+17°$, and $+22°$.

Thom next calculated the dates when the sun would have had these declinations in the year 1800 BC, making the assumption that the sightlines were intended to be used twice each year. The result of his analysis is given in Table 5.1. He found the declinations fitted very well with a sixteen-month year, providing the days were distributed in eleven months of 23 days, four months of 22 days, and one month of 24 days. He goes so far as to claim that there is no better solution than the one apparently used in the early Bronze Age, and that different arrangements of the months, for example a year made up of only 22- and 23-day months, is less accurate. If he is correct, the people of the Early Bronze Age had accomplished an intellectual feat that stands comparison with many of more recent times.

'Month' number	Number of days	Number of days from the spring equinox at the beginning of the 'month'	Declination of the sun at the beginning of the 'month'	Corresponding date in our calendar
1	23	0	$+0.44°$	20 March
2	23	23	$+9.16°$	12 April
3	24	46	$+16.67°$	5 May
4	23	70	$+22.06°$	29 May
5	23	93	$+23.91°$	21 June
6	23	116	$+22.06°$	14 July
7	23	139	$+16.67°$	6 August
8	22	161	$+9.16°$	28 August
9	22	183	$+0.44°$	19 September
10	22	205	$-8.46°$	11 October
11	22	227	$-16.26°$	2 November
12	23	250	$-21.86°$	25 November
13	23	273	$-23.91°$	18 December
14	23	296	$-21.86°$	10 January
15	23	319	$-16.26°$	2 February
16	23	342	$-8.46°$	25 February

Table 5.1   The sixteen-month Bronze Age calendar

We should not accept the result without looking at the evidence. All the monthly declinations are represented several times among the sites discovered by Professor Thom. Many of the known sites, like the equinoctial ones, are in Scotland, and some of the most interesting are exceedingly remote and difficult to visit. There is an interesting group of sites in the Outer Hebrides. These islands extend in an arc 200 km long off the north-west coast of Scotland. From north to south the largest islands are Lewis, North Uist, Benbecula, and South Uist. We have already seen that from the southern part of Lewis, the little island of Boreray marks the sunset at the solstices. It can be seen from the other islands, and on each there is an orientated slab of stone pointing to Boreray. On North Uist there is a stone called Clach ant Sagairt, and from this point the sun would appear to set over Boreray when it had a declination $+9\cdot06°$. It could have marked the beginning of the second and eighth months in the Bronze Age calendar. On Benbecula is a precisely orientated slab near Ben Rueval, giving a sunset marker for the first days of the third and seventh months; and on South Uist a huge standing stone, almost 5 m high, called An Carra (Pl. 13), gives the start of the fourth and sixth months. These three islands, North Uist, Benbecula, and South Uist, are separated by narrow straits and crossing from one to the other would not have been too difficult in good weather. With the Clach Mhic Leoid site, they form a composite observatory capable of giving sightings to fix half the months of the year.

If we pick out the sites giving an orientation for $+16°$, that is the sites which mark the beginnings of the third and seventh months, we find they include the stones at Learable Hill, already mentioned as an indicator for the equinoxes. Two other rows of stones nearby, but part of the same complex, are aligned on sunrise with declination $+16\cdot6°$. In England this same declination appears at the two Type B flattened circles in Cumbria, Long Meg and her Daughters and Castle Rigg.

Long Meg is a very large stone circle, one of the biggest in the country. Associated with it is a small and very despoiled stone circle, Little Meg, on a suitable line to give the sunrise with declination $+16\cdot7°$. Castle Rigg has several declination indications built in to the geometry. The diameter which passes through one of the secondary centres of the flattened circle gives a sunrise with declination $-16\cdot0°$. Looking along this diameter in the opposite direction gives the midsummer setting sun. (The declination is not reciprocal because of the effects of refraction and a hilly horizon.) Other stones in the perimeter of Castle Rigg show the midwinter sunrise and various lunar alignments. In Wales only one site is known where there is a sightline to mark the beginnings of the third and seventh months. This is the complicated compound ring, Moel Ty Uchaf. However, the existence of the same indicated declination at sites as far apart as Wales and the Western Isles is evidence for the use of an identical sixteen-month calendar over a large part of the British Isles. Similar lists of sites can be compiled for the other monthly declinations, spread over the same large area. It implies that not only were the same methods in use, but that the calendars were probably in phase, i.e. the new year started everywhere on the same day.

Professor Thom reached his conclusions by calculation and statistics. Of course the builders of these sites would not have been able to calculate the correct positions for the stones, but must have relied on many years' patient trial and error. Presumably the solstitial sightlines were established first, then the equinoctial ones, and then by progressive division of the periods by two until the year had been divided into sixteen more or less equal parts. Once the calendar had been finalized, there would no longer have been the need for the precise and difficult observations at the solstices. The months on either side of the solstices are the same length, 23 days, and the exact day of the solstice would be confirmed by observations on either side of it. Thus the operation of the calendar would become gradually easier, and it would not be a great inconvenience if bad weather inhibited an occasional observation.

Not all archaeologists have yet accepted the Bronze Age calendar, and their reservations ought to be mentioned. Of the people who have given serious thought to archaeo-astronomy, few if any doubt the validity of the midsummer and midwinter alignments. They are willing to concede that Neolithic and Early Bronze Age communities took a great interest in astronomical matters, and very likely held ceremonies at the solstices to mark the turning points in the year. Midsummer ritual is one thing; precise observation for timekeeping is quite another. Many archaeologists will say there is a lot of work to be done before the latter is proved. They point to the arbitrary nature of the sites: sometimes a slab of stone pointing to a distant hillside, or a notch on the horizon; sometimes a pair of stones to tell the observer in which direction to look; sometimes a stone ring, with or without outliers; and in a few cases rows of four or more stones. Is there a pattern, or are the investigators picking out whatever happens to be convenient to support their case?

These questions are extremely hard to answer. Like the controversy over the megalithic yard, they have to be tackled by statistical methods, and there is far too little precise information based on modern and comprehensive surveys of the sites, notwithstanding the prodigious amount of work by Professor Thom and his family. Archaeologists are more likely to be swayed by the results of excavations than by mathematics, and for this reason a lot of weight is attached to investigations like the one at Kintraw, which gave results in support of the astronomical hypothesis.

Dr Euan MacKie excavated another supposed observing site, at Duntreath near Glasgow. This is a small group of six boulders set on the side of a valley which runs from south-east to north-west. To the north-east there is a notch on the horizon at a distance of about $1\frac{1}{2}$ km and from the stones it marks the direction of the rising sun with a declination $+24 \cdot 00°$. Professor Thom included it in his list of solstitial sites. The baseline is too short for accurate observations to fix the date of the solstice, though this would not exclude a ceremonial, rather than an observational, use. The declination corresponds to about 2700 BC, so if it is genuine, it is much earlier than Kintraw and Ballochroy.

The notch to the north-east is not indicated in any way by the setting of the stones, but there is another notch on the skyline which is very precisely indicated. The only stone of the six still upright has one flat and even face which points directly towards a notch almost due east of the site. The declination of the sun when it rises with its upper edge in the notch would be $+1 \cdot 35°$, and it has been suggested that this is intended to be an equinoctial marker. If so, it is less accurate than we would expect, and will give a date three days after the spring equinox and three days before the autumn equinox.

The site was excavated by MacKie in 1972. Above the subsoil he found a layer of light orange-brown soil, containing no artifacts. On the upper surface of this layer were the remains of fires, wood ash and charcoal. The charcoal fragments, by the radiocarbon method, give a date corresponding to 3400 BC or 3500 BC in absolute chronology. On top of the orange-brown soil was a layer of darker soil, and this contained fragmentary prehistoric remains, such as flakes of jasper, flint, and quartz, which would not have appeared out of place at a mesolithic site. The uppermost layer was the modern topsoil, and it contained bits of recent glass and china as well as a little of the prehistoric material.

The socket for the base of the standing stone was cut into the orange-brown soil, according to MacKie, when the darker layer was accumulating. Unfortunately the excavation gave no clear-cut history of the site. One possibility is that there was a mesolithic camp at this place and the fires and small finds were there long before the stones, and that the location of the stones on the earlier site is just a coincidence. The second possibility, and the one favoured by MacKie, is that the fires were lit to clear the ground of scrub in preparation for erecting the stones. If this is the case, the stones were set up a thousand years before the likely date of Kintraw and Ballochroy. A third possible interpretation is that Duntreath is not an astronomical site at all and it is by chance that the smooth flat face of the standing stone points directly to the notch, and equally fortuitous that the notch is approximately in the right direction for the equinoxes.

Duntreath is apparently a simple, uncomplicated site, yet its excavation has not clarified the development of the solar observatories. The date of 3500 BC is too early to fit easily with the evidence from other sites, and is not consistent with the suggestion put forward earlier in this chapter that the *ceremonial* astronomy of the Neolithic Period was superseded by the *precision* astronomy of the Early Bronze Age. On the other hand, even if the Duntreath stones were much later than the radiocarbon date, the site would not fit comfortably into the Early Bronze Age; it has the functional style of construction, without the precision of other sites. The explanation of the Duntreath standing stone will have to wait for further work.

In spite of the difficulties with the site at Duntreath, we still have confidence that the other solar observatories were set up and used in the Early Bronze Age and that a calendar was established based on the movements of the sun. The solar calendar did not last. There is no evidence for solar observatories being put into use after 1500 BC, or for the existing ones being updated. The slow decrease in tilt of the earth's axis would have made the solstitial markers gradually less accurate and this would have been noticeable by 1500 BC. The calendar would have changed, too, and this has continued, so that if we tried to use the set of declinations given in Table 5.1 in our present century, we should find months varying from 19 to 26 days. Not that the changes would have invalidated the method; the monthly markers could have been readjusted to keep the calendar correct.

Much more likely reasons for the decrease of interest in observational astronomy were the climatic changes in the middle of the second millennium BC. By the end of the Early Bronze Age, as we shall see later, increasing cloudiness would have made the observations difficult, and knowledge of the techniques, which could no longer be practised, was eventually lost. The cultural changes after 1500 BC brought in a new lifestyle, when men were no longer interested in the precise movements of the heavenly bodies and had forgotten how to measure them. The age of solar observatories had come to an end.

6 The Lunar Observatories

We saw in Chapter 5 how the first ceremonial and approximate methods of finding the times of the seasons were developed, in the Early Bronze Age, into a polished technique for establishing a calendar based on the yearly motion of the sun. It is not surprising that the early farmers of north-west Europe needed a calendar for planning their year and regulating the sowing of their crops. What surprises modern archaeologists is how accurate their ways for doing this eventually became. It really doesn't matter to a week or two when you sow the corn; it is the condition of the soil, whether it is dry and workable or wet and sticky, which is more important than the exact date. So although the need for an agricultural calendar may have inspired observation of the sun's movements, other factors must have influenced these people or they would not have set out to improve their methods of observation to the state when they were able to find the times of the solstices and the equinoxes to the nearest day, or to fix the intermediate dates for the beginning of each of the sixteen months in the year.

Perhaps having discovered how to measure the position of the sun in the sky, by observing exactly where on the horizon it appeared to rise and set, they began to improve the method for the intellectual pleasure it gave them. Much the same spirit has stimulated mankind in later centuries, whether to develop engineering techniques for the refinement of cathedral architecture in the Middle Ages, or to study fundamental particles in our own time. The possibility that prehistoric men pursued knowledge for its own sake cannot be proved, yet it strikes us with great force when we see Early Bronze Age lunar observatories.

It is easy to understand how useful it would be for a primitive community to know the moon's phases in a rough-and-ready sort of way. The monthly cycle of lunar phases is conspicuous and convenient for defining a particular day if it is not too far ahead. As likely as not, from Paleolithic times, people would have made dates to meet and do things when the moon was at a certain phase, and especially when it was full. Around full moon there is a longer time for working out of doors without artificial illumination than at other times. Until the middle of this century farmers used to make good use of the 'Harvest Moon', the full moon nearest to the autumnal equinox. Because the moon at this time of the year is rapidly increasing in declination from night to night around full moon, it rises only a few minutes later each evening, and used to make it possible to cart and stack corn well into the night. The full moon provided light for ceremonies and social gatherings, and made it easier to find the way after nightfall. In Europe during the Second World War, when the street lamps were not lit because they would have revealed the position of towns to hostile aircraft, moonlight for a few years regained its old importance; people preferred to visit friends at full moon, if they expected to return home late at night. None of these activities requires a specially accurate knowledge of the moon's movements, yet the evidence points to the same precise and meticulous methods of observation being used for the moon as for the sun.

Bronze Age lunar observatories are as widespread as solar ones. They extend over much of north-west Europe from the Bay of Biscay to the Shetland Islands. Though the motions of the moon are much more complicated than those of the sun, men were able to track its movements through the heavens and also devise intricate and subtle methods for predicting the occurrence of lunar eclipses. They have left, in assemblies of standing stones, the remains of their 4,000-year-old computers. Their techniques must have demanded faithful observation for year after year, a means of keeping records, and patient trial and error, possibly for decades, until at last they solved the problem of eclipse prediction in a satisfactory way. Though their astronomy lacked theoretical understanding of the solar system, such as we have had since the days of Kepler and Newton, Bronze Age man's observational accuracy was not equalled again until the Renaissance. For several hundred years they must have devoted a considerable proportion of their communal labours to lunar astronomy, not just for making the actual measurements, but for hewing, moving, and erecting stones, or digging earthworks in stoneless areas, in order to construct equipment for observing the moon. In short, their interest in the moon amounted to an obsession and, whatever the original need, the technology that they developed far outstripped it.

Did they perhaps start by trying to set up a lunar calendar? Many civilizations, including our own, have based their calendars on the phases of the moon, dividing the year into months of about thirty days. By alternating months of twenty-nine and thirty days it is possible to make a lunar calendar which keeps well in step with the phases of the moon, because

$$12 \text{ lunar months} = 354 \cdot 3708 \text{ days and}$$
$$6 \text{ 29-day months} + 6 \text{ 30-day months} = 354 \text{ days.}$$

Unfortunately it is most difficult to keep the lunar calendar in step with the seasons, because there are 12·368 lunar months in a tropical year. Twelve lunar months are shorter than one year by $11\frac{1}{4}$ days. Before the time of Julius Caesar the Romans used a lunar calendar, and reconciled it with the seasons by stipulating an additional short month every other year. Apparently it was not always remembered, and in 46 BC, when Caesar reformed the calendar, he was forced to have one year of 445 days to correct the accumulated error. Since then we have retained twelve divisions of the year, but made them longer than the lunar month by introducing months of thirty-one days. Our present calendar has now only historical connections with the moon.

The Jewish calendar is still based on the lunar month and alternates months of twenty-nine and thirty days. In a period of nineteen years, twelve years have twelve months and seven years have thirteen months, making a total of 235 months. In fact, the lunar calendar is brought back into line with the solar year by making use of the Metonic cycle. The Muslim calendar is purely lunar, and the beginning of the year rotates round the seasons, making a complete revolution every thirty-three of our years.

If the original motivation for lunar observations in the Early Bronze Age had been to establish a lunar calendar, it would seem fairly certain that its inventors would not have allowed it to 'free-wheel' like the Muslim calendar, in view of the many sites set up for accurately observing the solstices. Once the solar calendar had been devised, they could have discovered the Metonic cycle simply by keeping records of the dates of the new moons, and from there it is a short step to the Jewish type of luni-solar calendar. We know that during the Early Bronze Age it was possible to count up to fairly large numbers, as is shown by the numerical sequence of the numbers of posts in the egg-shaped rings at Wood-henge, and this is borne out by the division of the year into sixteen nearly equal intervals. Providing they had some means of recording events in a semi-permanent form, it would have been consistent with their other achievements to devise a lunar calendar which kept reasonably in step with the solar one. The argument against this having been the motivation for the lunar observations is that, if we accept the evidence for the solar calendar, there was really no need for the lunar one. Furthermore, a lunar calendar does not require sites for accurately indicating the rising and setting points of the moon; all that is necessary is to count and record the appearances of the new moon. So even if their interest in the moon's movements included the idea of a calendar, this would not account for the lunar observatories. There must have been other reasons behind their observations.

The study of the moon seems to have begun later than the first ritual observa-tions of the sun. No one has so far discovered neolithic burial sites, like the long barrows or chambered tombs, which are orientated to the significant rising or setting points of the moon. There is no lunar equivalent to New Grange, with its 'window' to catch the light of the rising sun at the midwinter solstice, for example, nor of the passage graves at Clava which are aligned on the midwinter sunset. The majority of sites for lunar observations are much later than these and consist of standing stones, sometimes, but not always, associated with stone circles and other remains. The earliest sites where we think the moon was observed are untypical of the rest and both are in southern England: the Dorset Cursus and Stonehenge itself.

The early phases of Stonehenge are very enigmatic. There is the strange mystery of the Aubrey Holes, whose purpose is still obscure in spite of the many attempts to understand them. Even the very first construction, the bank and surrounding ditch, is puzzling. We are now accustomed to think of the axis of Stonehenge as being aligned with the midsummer sunrise, and this is certainly true for the Avenue and the Station Stones. But the entrance to the original enclosure, the causeway, is not quite on this alignment; it is several degrees to the north. When the Avenue was made, the short length of perimeter ditch within its two banks was deliberately filled in, presumably to make it easier to cross. This act establishes the sequence for archaeologists, so that there is no doubt that the original axis was not as we see it now.

At first sight we might be inclined to dismiss the misalignment of the original causeway and the Avenue as of little importance. Around the country there are many circular enclosures without astronomical significance, therefore why should not Stonehenge have begun as an ordinary henge, to have its solar alignment as a later addition? The difficulty in accepting this explanation appears when we look closely at the causeway. From the centre of Stonehenge the causeway subtends an angle of about 10°, just covering the arc of the horizon where the moon would appear to rise during one half of the 18·6-year cycle, 4½ years before and after the major standstill. When the ground around the causeway was excavated in 1922 by Colonel Hawley, he found about 40 postholes between the ends of the ditches. They are not evenly spaced and do not look like the foundations of a building (Fig. 6.1). Four of the holes are much larger than the others, and lie in a diagonal line across the causeway. The others are in six circumferential lines, with three in the inside line and up to nine in the others.

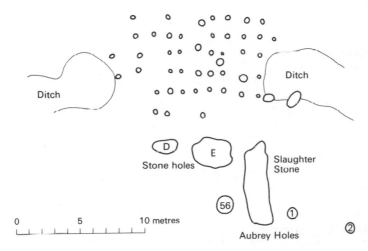

FIG. 6.1   Plan of the causeway postholes at Stonehenge

Peter Newham, in his booklet on Stonehenge, pointed out that this arrangement is just what one would expect if every year (apart from the cloudy ones) the users of Stonehenge had set up a post to mark the direction of rising of the midwinter full moon, as seen from the centre of the circular bank. Six lines would imply that these observations were continued for six cycles of the rotation of the lunar nodes, in all for about 110 years. If this interpretation of the causeway postholes is correct, it would explain how the 18·6-year cycle could have been discovered, and how the observations could have been recorded in a fairly permanent way. Archaeologists believe that the causeway postholes are contemporary with the ditch and bank, and therefore date to about 2800 BC. They are earlier than the midsummer sunrise alignment of the Avenue, and precede the majority of lunar observatories by almost a millennium. This may be difficult to accept, yet the four Station Stones, which undoubtedly include a lunar alignment for the major standstill, were erected quite early in the history of the site, and they must have followed some systematic study of the movements of the moon. The evidence on balance supports the view that Stonehenge was a lunar observatory from its earliest times, although another explanation for the causeway postholes has been put forward; there will be more about this in the chapter on Stonehenge.

Within a few hundred years of the first earthworks at Stonehenge, the neolithic tribesmen began to build the Dorset Cursus. I have already described how the central part of the cursus, from the terminal on Wyke Down to the earlier long

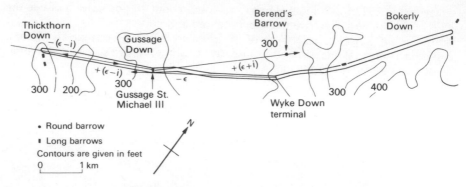

FIG. 6.2   Plan of the Dorset Cursus

The only alignments shown are those mentioned in the text.

barrow on Gussage Down, is orientated in the direction of the midwinter sunset. Other parts of the cursus are in suitable positions for making observations of the moon (Fig. 6.2).

The southern end of the cursus has a terminal on Thickthorn Down. This is probably the best-preserved part of the whole monument, and from the outside the terminal appears as a substantial bank with an external ditch; even today the bank is about 2 m above the ditch bottom. Inside, the terminal looks quite different, more like a carefully levelled platform than an enclosure, though its shape could have been modified over the years by weather and agriculture. Standing in the centre of the terminal and looking along the line of the banks towards the north-east, we can see the long barrow on Gussage Down just below the horizon. In about 2500 BC the rising moon at the minor standstill would have appeared above the skyline in the space between the long barrow and the right-hand bank of the cursus. The horizon here is smooth and level, and neither the long barrow nor the bank is quite high enough to make a visible 'notch'. Observations would nevertheless be quite feasible, for they could have lit bonfires on the top of the hill to show the expected position of the moonrise, a technique which is impossible with the much brighter sun. The Thickthorn–Gussage alignment works equally well in the opposite direction, viewing the moon with declination $-(\varepsilon-i)$ as it set over the terminal on Thickthorn Down. Perhaps the platform here was designed so support a beacon: only an area excavation of the terminal will tell us what, if any, hidden structures are there.

The Dorset Cursus also provides sightlines for the moon at the major stand-still, though they are not directly along sections of the cursus, as the two just described. Looking north-east from the long barrow on Gussage Down, you can see an extremely large conical barrow, called Berend's Barrow. It is the only barrow visible on the horizon, for though there are many Bronze Age barrows in the vicinity, they are all tucked away in hollows off the skyline. From Gussage Down, standing beside the long barrow, to Berend's Barrow gives an alignment for the moonrise with declination $+(\varepsilon+i)$. The visibility of the barrow would be much improved at night if it was the site of a beacon, and in this connection it is interesting to know that when Berend's Barrow was excavated by Colt Hoare in 1800, he found a large quantity of ashes and charred wood.

The Dorset Cursus has other possible alignments as well as these, but it is not necessary to enumerate them in detail. The point is that from about 2500 BC (although Berend's Barrow may be later than this date) the neolithic communities of southern England had already built structures which were adequate for observing the gross movements of the moon. With them they could have discovered the 18·6-year cycle, and if the lunar alignments in the Dorset Cursus are genuine, they show that the major and minor standstills had by then been discovered. Perhaps at this time neolithic people became aware of some of the simpler regularities in the patterns of lunar eclipses—that they occur at the equinoxes when the moon is at the standstills, for example—and this could have led to an early technique for lunar eclipse prediction.

In the earliest phase of Stonehenge, this would have been beyond the capabilities of the site. The sighting line is very short—only 50 m from the centre of the circle to the ditch—and this is not long enough to fix an accurate alignment. We can see from Table 4.3 that the difference in declination of the midwinter full moon from the year of the maximum to the next highest can be quite small, say 0·3° on average. The corresponding difference in azimuth of moonrise is about 0·5° which is equivalent to a movement of the observer's head of 40 cm. Since he could position himself more precisely than this, it would be quite practicable to see the annual change in declination and to detect the 18·6-year cycle. Finding the exact month of the major standstill is a much more difficult task. The difference in maximum declination of the moon from month to month around the standstills is very small, so it could not be detected with such a crude measuring method as sighting on posts set up in the causeway.

The Dorset Cursus improves on the causeway posts because the sighting lines are longer. For both major and minor standstills the foresights are about 3 km from the observers, roughly the same distance as for the solar observations. Were the observations to have been continued throughout the year, and at other phases of the moon as well as at the full, small changes in declination would have become apparent. It would have been necessary to put a permanent marker on the ground to ensure that the observer stood in exactly the same place each time, but if he had done this, declination changes smaller than 0·1° would have been easily seen.

Their first attempts to find the exact months when the major and minor standstills occurred would have led to very confusing results. The monthly maximum of the moon's declination does not increase smoothly to its highest value and then decline; rather it grows in a cyclical manner, with peaks 173 days apart, which we call the minor perturbation (Fig. 6.3). The cause is a gravitational interaction between the sun and the moon which puts an oscillation of $\pm0\cdot15°$ amplitude on the declination. We shall from now on use the symbol Δ, the Greek capital letter delta, for the minor perturbation.

There are very strong reasons for believing that the minor perturbation was discovered by men in the Neolithic or Early Bronze Ages, and certainly they had the technique to make this discovery when they learned how to use the horizon as a giant protractor. Some of the later lunar observatories have alignments corresponding to the declination of the moon at the maximum value of the minor

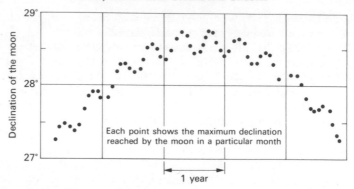

FIG. 6.3   Diagram showing how the maximum monthly declination of the moon increases in a cyclical fashion as the moon
approaches the major standstill

perturbation, for example moonrise indications for declinations $(\varepsilon+i+\varDelta)$ or
$(\varepsilon-i+\varDelta)$. For people without writing and astronomical instruments this was a
remarkable technical achievement. With all their astronomical and mathematical
sophistication, the Greeks in the classical period had no knowledge of the minor
perturbation. There is a possibility that it was discovered by the Arabs in the
tenth century, but it was not rediscovered in modern times until Tycho Brahe in
the sixteenth century noted it and measured its value.

The significance of the minor perturbation is that it acts as a warning signal
for the eclipse danger periods. Eclipses, both lunar and solar, can only occur
when the minor perturbation is at a maximum and adding to the lunar declination.
In principle it is easy to find out when the maximum occurs. We must go out
every month and observe the rising moon for the few days around its maximum
monthly declination. Suppose we have a convenient notch on the horizon a few
kilometres away and every moonrise we station ourselves in such a position as to
make the moon appear from behind the notch in exactly the same manner. We
must leave a marker on the ground to show where we stood each time.

Now as the declination of the moon increases, its rising point, if we always
stood in the same place, would move round the horizon to the left. We should
counteract this by moving to the right, and each night therefore we should place
our marker on the ground to the right of the previous one. After the moon had
passed its maximum declination we should find ourselves moving back again to
the left. The marker which was furthest to the right would tell us which day the
moon's declination was the maximum. If we were to repeat this every month, we
should find that the monthly maximum markers advanced to the right and
returned to the left. The furthest right of the monthly markers would give us the
maximum of the minor perturbation, and consequently the time when the lunar
eclipse would be likely to happen. Since the minor perturbation has a period of
173 days, it would have been possible, once we had found it, to predict ahead and
to know when the future eclipse danger periods would occur.

The above procedure was suggested by Professor Thom to account for the
remarkable precision inherent in the lunar observatories he has discovered,

particularly in western Scotland. The development of lunar observatories closely parallels the solar observatories. As the technique improved, the observatories became simpler and more effective. They were refined to the point where they consisted of a few carefully positioned standing stones, often indicating a notch on the distant horizon. In this way the techniques the men of the Early Bronze Age had been forced to invent in order to fix the exact date of the solstices were adapted to lunar observations and led finally to the construction of intricate devices for calculating eclipse phenomena, like the standing-stone rows at Carnac and Kermario.

The simplest lunar observatory is typified by the standing stone at Ballinaby on the west coast of the island of Islay in the Hebrides. The megalith is 5 m high and is a thin slab about 1 m by 0·25 m at its base. One side is flattened so that an observer sighting along the flat surface has his attention directed to a notch on the skyline 2 km away. At the major standstill the moon would have set directly behind this notch in the Early Bronze Age (Fig. 6.4). This site resembles the solstitial observatory at Ballochroy, because the slope of the hillside to the right of the notch is less than the angle of the path of the setting moon, and the upper limb of the moon, near the maximum of the major standstill, would sometimes reappear from behind the hilltop as it set. The position of the reappearance down the slope gives a sensitive indication of the declination, and would without doubt have revealed the minor perturbation. Professor Thom used the Lockyer astronomical method to date the site and concluded it was set up in 1650 ±70 BC.

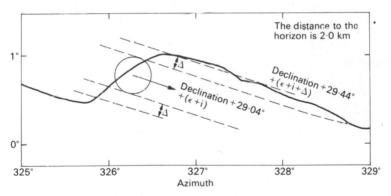

FIG. 6.4   The setting moon as seen from the standing stones at Ballinaby

We must digress temporarily to explain a difficulty in dating lunar sites that does not apply to solar ones. The principle of dating is the same: we find the declination corresponding to the alignment, and since the difference in lunar declination from the present-day value is due entirely to the decrease in the value of ε (i being constant), we can apply the data given in Table 4.1 to find the date. Unfortunately there is a snag. The calculation of lunar declination from the azimuth involves the parallax, which has been given in this book as 0·95°. However, the parallax depends on the distance of the moon from the earth, and because the moon's orbit is elliptical, its distance varies from 357,000 km to 405,000 km during the course of every month. The parallax in consequence varies from 0·90° to 1·00°, with a mean value 0·95°. This introduces an uncertainty into the calculated value of declination which depends on the latitude of the site and whether the alignment relates to the major or minor standstill. The resulting uncertainty in the date is about ±300 years. Professor Thom's more accurate estimates, such as the one given above for Ballinaby, are based on the assumption that the observatories continued in use for a period of 50 to 100 years and that the alignments were set up for a mean value of parallax, because this would be more convenient for the observers.

In Scotland, though distant foresights were quite commonly indicated by slab-sided stones like the one at Ballinaby, at some places the lunar alignment was shown in another way. Two or more standing stones were erected so that looking from one to another gives the direction of the notch on the horizon. There is a good example of this at Stillaig near the Kyles of Bute in the county of Strathclyde (Fig. 6.5). Here there are two large menhirs about 650 m apart. Standing beside the southern stone and looking towards the northern one, the viewer sees the summit of a hill called Cruach Breacain, 22 km away. The skyline immediately above the northern stone slopes down to the right. In the Early Bronze Age, at the moon's major standstill, it would have set with its lower limb appearing to slide neatly down the slope.

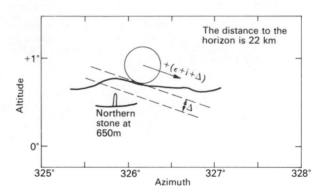

FIG. 6.5   The setting moon as seen from the standing
stones at Stillaig

Unfortunately not all suspected sites are as clearly indicated as Ballinaby and Stillaig. There are many sites with only a single megalith and where the shape of the stone provides no guide to the direction of the distant foresight. Professor Thom lists several large solitary stones as possible markers for lunar alignments. There is always doubt about isolated stones being for astronomical purposes, since they could have other uses such as boundary markers, but when they occur in areas having a number of reasonably authenticated astronomical sites, they do at least deserve serious consideration.

Some examples of isolated standing stones in an area rich in megalithic observatories occur in the long peninsula in south-west Scotland which extends from Inveraray southwards through Knapdale and Kintyre to Campbeltown. The solar observatories at Kintraw and Ballochroy are in this part of the country, and the lunar site at Stillaig is only just across the other side of Loch Fyne. Great attention was obviously paid around here to the movements of the sun and moon. Along the shores of the peninsula are several megalithic sites, such as the huge standing stone at Beacharr which stands on a ridge overlooking the west coast, 9 km south of Ballochroy. To the north-west is the profile of the Paps of Jura, giving almost the same view as from Ballochroy. There is a distinctive notch between the peaks of Beinn an Oir and Beinn Shiantaidh, 36 km away, making a good sightline for a moonset at the major standstill (Fig. 6.6). Behind the ridge there is a small hollow and beyond that the hill begins to rise towards the centre of the peninsula. At roughly the same elevation as the top of the ridge there is a stretch of flat level ground, and it has been suggested that this would be the natural position to stand for the observations, since it allows movement from side to side and the observer could find the exact spot to place markers. Although there are signs of disturbance on the small plateau, we should not jump to the conclusion that they are Bronze Age earthworks; they could be modern drainage ditches.

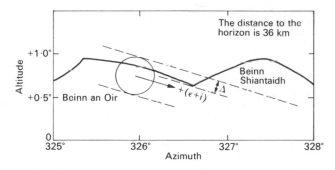

FIG. 6.6   The setting moon as seen from the standing stone at Beacharr

Another standing stone is at Muasdale, 4 km south of Beacharr. Its siting is very similar. This menhir is on the hillside overlooking the sea, and to the west are the mountains of the islands of Jura and Islay. The sightline here is probably to the slopes of Beinn Bheigeir 28 km to the north-west, which is in the direction for a minor standstill moonset. If genuine, Beacharr and Muasdale are complementary sites, together providing scope for observations over much of the 18·6-year cycle.

A single menhir, near Campbeltown towards the tip of the peninsula, gives a unique lunar alignment (Pl. 17). It also stands on level ground half-way up a hillside and overlooks the sea, in this case Campbeltown Loch. On the far side of the water the hill of Beinn Ghuilean is on the skyline and because it is fairly near, only 3 km away, the horizon has a high elevation of about 5°. In Scottish latitudes the moon at its very lowest declination only just reaches this elevation, and so when seen from the Campbeltown menhir in this extreme situation, the moon never totally rises. It skims the southern horizon and irregularities on the skyline give the usual sensitive indication of small changes in declination, making the minor perturbation visible even though the moon is on the meridian (Fig. 6.7).

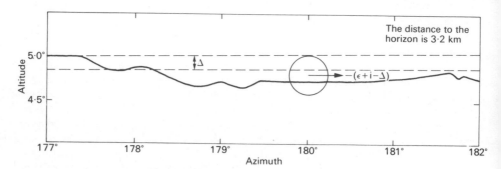

FIG. 6.7   The moon crossing the meridian as seen from the standing stone at Campbeltown

In the highland zone, the builders were able to exploit the mountainous nature of the landscape to provide distant foresights. In other parts of the country, where the horizon is much smoother, distant foresights had to be constructed. Artificial notches set a limit to the length of the sightline, because it is not practicable to build cairns or barrows that are large enough to be visible at distances of 10 km or more. Alignments were consequently less accurate and the observer had to position himself very carefully to use them.

Examples of observatories with artificial foresights are found on Dartmoor in England. Although the outcrops of granite on the moor make good notches in some places, the lunar observatory at Cholwichtown (now unfortunately buried under a heap of waste material from china-clay workings) made use of three hilltop cairns, $6\frac{1}{2}$ km to the south-east on Western Beacon. They were spaced so that the apparent distance between the two outer ones was almost as great as the diameter of the moon. When the moon rose at its minor standstill, with declination $-(\varepsilon-i)$, it would have appeared between the cairns and the position of its lower limb would have been shown by the right-hand cairn (Fig. 6.8). At the maximum of the minor perturbation, i.e. when the moon's declination was $-(\varepsilon-i+\Delta)$, the moon rose with its upper limb behind the left-hand cairn. The Cholwichtown backsight was not the usual standing stone but a small Type I egg based on a 3,4,5 triangle with sides $1\frac{1}{2}$, 2, and $2\frac{1}{2}$ MY. Fortunately the stones were surveyed and excavated in 1964 before the site was destroyed. The direction of the foresight is along the line of the minor axis of the egg, and although we might have expected an outlier to confirm the direction of sighting, none has ever been reported.

Another Dartmoor lunar observatory which is based on an egg-shaped ring of stones has definite indications of the direction in which to look. This is the

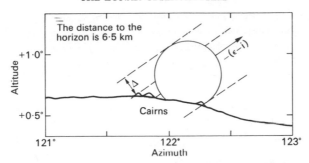

FIG. 6.8   The rising moon as seen from the stone egg-
shaped ring at Cholwichtown

small Type II egg at Lower Piles near the village of Harford. Its basic triangle is
not quite Pythagorean and its long axis points due north. There are several
standing stones and a cairn near the stone ring which together have some interesting geometrical relationships; for example the cairn, the secondary centre of the
egg, and one of the standing stones are all in a straight line. The foresight is the
distant (23 km) headland of Rame Head to the south-west, which accurately
defines a $-(\varepsilon-i)$ moonset by the natural notch between the land and the sea. The
direction of sighting is indicated by an outlying stone about 200 m from the egg,
in a precise line though in the opposite direction to the foresight. Lower Piles has
a second lunar sightline, for declination $+(\varepsilon-i)$, marked in the more usual
Dartmoor fashion by a cairn on the neighbouring hill of Penn Beacon at a
distance of 5 km.

   These sites, which are samples of many, show the variety of lunar observatories
which have been found in different parts of the British Isles. They are all rather
simple in concept, for they had no basis other than persistent and empirical
observations of moonrise or moonset, and they required no mathematical ability
other than the need for counting days.

   Faced with the difficulty of finding any other rational explanation for the
many standing stones in the British Isles, and the accumulation of results from
the investigations of Professor Thom and others interested in archaeo-astronomy,
archaeologists who previously doubted the plausibility of an astronomical interpretation are beginning to accept it for simple sites. However, not all sites are as
straightforward as those just described. There are several megalithic remains
which are much more complicated and seem to require explanations which
assume their builders were capable of far greater intellectual feats than merely the
observing and recording of moonsets, for example the standing stones at Temple
Wood (Pl. 16).

   The lunar observatory of Temple Wood is only 5 km south of the solar
observatory at Kintraw and is close to the village of Kilmartin. The locality is
famous for its numerous Neolithic and Early Bronze Age remains, particularly
the linear cemetery of burial cairns. The observatory, in the middle of this rich
area, has six large upright stones varying in height from 2 to almost 3 m, and
several smaller stones. They stand in a fairly level field in the middle of a valley,
with hills almost all the way round. Five of the tall menhirs are grouped together

in a narrow X-shaped pattern, with the tallest stone, which is dignified by deep cup marks, in the centre. Around the central stone are four of the smaller ones, and there is a little setting of small stones between the central stone and the two large menhirs at the southern end of the X (Fig. 6.9).

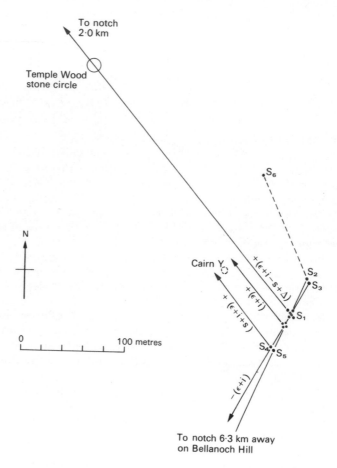

FIG. 6.9   The lunar observatory at Temple Wood

The arms of the X are quite straight, so that if one looks from any corner stone the opposite diagonal one is hidden by the large central block. One of the arms of the X points directly to a notch on Bellanoch Hill, 6·3 km to the south-west and in just the right direction to mark a major standstill moonset with declination $-(\varepsilon+i)$. Unfortunately this notch is not visible from the stones at the present time because of tall trees in that direction.

The five main stones, and several of the small ones, face more or less in the same direction, across the axis of the X. Sighting along the flat side of the central stone directs the eye to a very small notch in the hillside to the north-west, at a distance of 2 km. The two southern menhirs also point to and align with this notch, so that although, or perhaps because, it is inconspicuous, it is particularly well indicated. The little notch gives another astronomical alignment, for it shows the moonset at the major standstill with declination $+(\varepsilon+i)$. The similarity with the solar site at Ballochroy is striking; both have one alignment indicated by a row of stones and another by sighting along a flat slab. However, Temple Wood is more complicated than Ballochroy. The foresight to the north-west is not very distant, and relatively small movements across the sightline will alter the apparent setting position of the moon. Very careful surveys have shown that from the two southern slabs the upper limb of the moon sets in the notch, i.e. the notch indicates a declination $+(\varepsilon+i+s)$; from the setting of small stones the centre sets in the notch, i.e. the indicated declination is $+(\varepsilon+i)$; and from the central large stone the lower limb sets in the notch at the time of maximum minor perturbation, i.e. the indicated declination is $+(\varepsilon+i-s+\Delta)$.

There is a geometrical link between this astronomical alignment and one of the burial sites in the linear cemetery. Three hundred metres from the central stone, and directly in line with the stone and the notch, is the Temple Wood stone circle. The circle has a diameter of 12·2 m and 13 stones remain from the original 20. In the centre is a cist surrounded by upright stone slabs. Unless the position of the circle is accidental, and this would seem to be unlikely, we can deduce that it is of a later date than the standing stones. When the builders decided to mark two alignments with one group of stones, there was only one position that could meet the requirement. It would therefore have been impossible to achieve the existing geometry if the circle had been constructed first. However, we cannot from this evidence say how much later the circle is than the stones. Another feature of the Temple Wood site, to be described in the next chapter, leads to the conclusion that the circle was erected during the period of use of the stones. Clearly an independent date for the stone circle would be of great interest because of its temporal and cultural relationship to the astronomical observatory.

The standing stones at the northern end of the X are, like the others, colinear slabs. They do not, however, point to the notch, but to the sixth and isolated standing stone, 108 m away. This line has no obvious astronomical significance in either direction, nor does it point to any notch on the horizon. We can conclude only that it had some other purpose.

Temple Wood is a particularly interesting site because of the insight it gives on how lunar observations were made in the Early Bronze Age. We have said earlier in this chapter that in using these sites the method was almost certainly for the observers to position themselves night by night so that the moon set behind the notch, and to place stakes in a line roughly perpendicular to the direction of the notch, so that the moon's maximum declinations would be recorded by the furthermost stake. Usually there is only one permanent marker left at the observatories, but at Temple Wood we can still see three observing lines to the small notch. Two differ by the semi-diameter of the moon, and the third (from the central stone) gives the magnitude of the minor perturbation.

Before the alignments could be set up in a permanent form, many years of preliminary work would have been required. We would expect that temporary stakes were put in the ground along the line of the standing stones. Professor

Thom suggested that there might have been a marker just to the north of the central menhir, indicating where to stand to see the lower limb of the moon set in the notch, i.e. recording a declination $+(\varepsilon+i-s)$. If two separate observers had simultaneously observed the upper and lower limbs of the moon disappearing in the notch, and had placed two markers on the ground in the places where they were standing, they would have been able to put a third marker half-way between them to indicate the centre of the moon's disc setting in the notch. (This is of course impossible to fix accurately by one man trying to estimate where the centre of the moon is.) Hence, by studying the Temple Wood observatory, we see how the observers very probably overcame the problem of the variation in the apparent size of the moon. The middle position between two simultaneous observations eliminates the errors due to changes in lunar parallax, and automatically leads to an alignment for mean parallax.

Naturally this procedure could only be used at full moon, when the whole of its disc was illuminated. At other phases part of the disc is dark and the line between the light and dark parts of the moon, called the terminator, takes different apparent positions during the course of the year. Sometimes the crescent moon seems to be standing on one point like an archer's bow; at others it is almost horizontal like a bowl. In the latter case only the lower edge of the disc can be used for moonset observations, because the upper limb is in shadow and there is no sharp edge to the top of the disc. The crescent moon would have appeared bowl-like to observers using the nearer notch at Temple Wood. It is easy to see why. The moon would be at its maximum declination north of the celestial equator, and higher in declination than the sun. It would have seemed to be illuminated from beneath. The most commonly used alignment after the observatory had been set to work would therefore be when the lower limb set in the notch, and this is the one marked by the central stone.

Although there are no similar remains of multiple sightlines to the other notch on Bellanoch Hill, it is reasonable to assume that the same techniques were used for setting up both alignments, and that Bellanoch Hill also indicates a mean parallax position. Pairs of simultaneous observations would have been made, but only one sightline is shown by the standing stones. The Bellanoch Hill alignment marks the moonset at its lowest possible declination, when it would have had a lower declination that the sun and thus have appeared to be lit from above. It is not therefore surprising to find that the line of stones gives the sightline for the upper limb of the moon setting in the notch, because this would be usable not only at full moon but during the whole of the first half of the month.

The two declinations of the Temple Wood observatory have been compared by Professor Thom. The Bellanoch Hill notch gives $-29 \cdot 06°$ and the other notch gives $+29 \cdot 04°$. The difference is convincingly small and we can legitimately infer that our previous assumption that the users of Temple Wood were working to mean parallax indications is correct and also that both sightlines were in use at the same period. The declinations correspond to an ecliptic angle of $23 \cdot 90°$, and hence to a date of 1750 BC. Limits to the accuracy of measurement add an uncertainty of ± 100 years.

Temple Wood, though an important and revealing site which repays detailed study, is not the only observatory that has helped in unravelling Early Bronze Age observational techniques. There are others, such as the Ring of Brodgar in the

Orkneys and the Hill o' Many Stanes at Mid Clyth, 15 km south of Wick in the county of Highland (Pl. 7, 22). From these sites comes the answer to another practical problem, which so far has not been mentioned in this book. It creates a great difficulty for anyone trying to use the horizon for precise measurements of lunar declination.

The problem is simply this: the moon moves very quickly through the sky in comparison with all other astronomical bodies. It goes through its full cycle of declination, from the highest angle above the celestial equator to the furthest below, in a lunar month. Its rate of change of declination is smaller when it passes through the maximum than at other times; nevertheless, twelve hours before it reaches the maximum its declination is about 0·2° short of the peak, and twelve hours after the maximum it has declined to the same value. Moonsets can be observed only once every twenty-four hours, and if the observers were unlucky enough to find that the moon went through its maximum declination midway between the two moonsets, they would be in error in fixing the positions of the stakes. The Temple Wood observatory shows inherent accuracies of declination measurement to around one hundredth of a degree. How could the observers do this when individual measurements were liable to have errors as great as 0·2°? And how indeed did they follow the maxima of the minor perturbation which are only 0·15° deviation from the mean?

One method, we suppose, might have been by tedious and painstaking observation. This would have led to many abortive attempts to find the monthly maximum. Only when the moon happened to be nearly at its maximum declination at the time of setting would they have made valid observations. Duplicating the sightlines would have made it easier, by giving two chances for moonset observation each month, as at Temple Wood. They could have developed their technique further by observing moonrises as well as moonsets, but suitable sites for more than one alignment are not easy to find. If separate sites were used, they would have had to be close together, so that the observers could have exchanged the results of their work, and hence come to a common opinion on the time of the maximum declination.

The practical problem of finding the declination maximum seems formidable, yet we know it was solved because of the alignments perpetuated in stone at Temple Wood and other observatories. The evidence points to another, more subtle, approach than automatic and repetitive observation. The difficulties were overcome when either an individual or group of people, with inspiration and brilliant mental capability, found a geometrical method of working out, from observations made on either side of the maximum, where they would have had to stand to see the moon set at maximum declination. The achievement is the more amazing because the actual technique is simple, requiring only ropes and measuring rods. Its discovery was the intellectual peak of the Early Bronze Age in north-west Europe.

7 The Early Bronze Age Calculators

Scientists and archaeologists who write about lunar observatories use the word 'extrapolation' to describe the task of calculating the maximum declination of the moon from measurements made away from the maximum. It is applicable because, in the language of modern mathematics, to extrapolate is to estimate a quantity from, and beyond, the range of values already known. A familiar example of this is forecasting the future economic performance of an industry from regular returns of its trading figures.

Unlike economic predictions, which are always beset with imprecision, the future position of the moon can nowadays be very accurately predicted because the factors which control its motion are thoroughly understood. Each month the moon's changes of declination follow a curve called a cosine wave. This oscillating curve also describes the motion of the bob of a pendulum, the vibrations of a tuning fork, an alternating electric current, and many other things. In our particular problem of extrapolating from observations made very near the maximum declination, we are only interested in the small part of the cosine curve near its peak, and this can be represented accurately enough by a simpler mathematical curve, the parabola. This is the path traced out when someone throws a ball; it is also the shape of the boundary of an illuminated area when the cone of light from an electric torch shines at a grazing angle to a wall. In the remainder of this chapter, we shall use the parabola to represent the moon's movements in declination.

In the Early Bronze Age there was no reservoir of analytical mathematics to assist the astronomers with extrapolation. But they were not starting completely from scratch. As we know from studies of the geometry of stone circles and rings, they were able to measure distances accurately, to count to fairly large numbers, to set out right angles, and to draw quite complicated shapes. In arriving at their solution they would obviously build on their existing knowledge, and if we bear this in mind we might begin to understand how they could have solved the extrapolation problem. Of one thing we can be sure—they would not have used the modern mathematical approach.

How then would the problem have looked in the Early Bronze Age? Let us think of an observatory like Temple Wood, with a line laid out more or less perpendicular to the direction of the notch (it does not have to be precise) along which they would position themselves to observe the moonsets. Typical behaviour of the lunar declination on two successive months is plotted on Figure 7.1. Each month it rises to a peak and then declines. The dots on the curves show schematically what might have been the values of the declination at the moments of moonset. At the first maximum, moonsets were observed on days 1 to 4, and it happened that on the second and third days the moon had almost equal declinations. The observers would put stakes in the ground, as in Figure 7.2, marking the positions where they stood to see the lower limb of the moon set down the slope of the notch. The stakes on days 2 and 3 are very close together; somewhere to the left of them is the unknown position (A) marking where the observers would have had to stand if the moon had set with the maximum declination for the month.

No observations would be possible for 25 days, the moon being too far south for this alignment to be used. At the next maximum, suppose stakes were set up

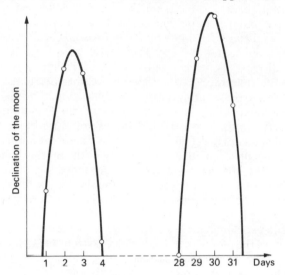

FIG. 7.1   The declination of the moon at two successive maxima

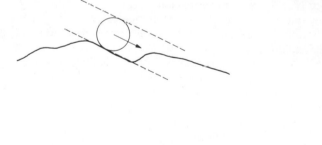

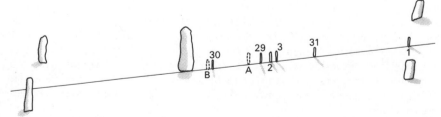

FIG. 7.2   How the stakes would be positioned at two maxima when the moon's declination was as in Fig. 7.1

on days 29, 30, and 31. In this case the two left-hand stakes are comparatively far apart, and the unknown position for the stake which would mark the maximum declination is only just to the left of the further one of this pair, at B. The extrapolation problem is, of course, to find the points A and B from the positions of the other stakes.

A regular series of observations would fairly quickly reveal some consistent patterns. From observations made on the three days nearest to the maximum, they would have found a simple rule connecting the positions of the stakes: *the distance from the furthest left stake to the mid-position of the other two is exactly the same every month*. It would no doubt have been regarded as a special or characteristic distance associated with a particular alignment, and would have been quite useful to know, because if cloudy weather prevented the observation on the day nearest to the monthly maximum declination, the missed stake position could be found by applying the rule. In addition, they would have noticed that the distance between the two left-hand stakes could never be greater than the characteristic distance of the alignment, though of course it was frequently smaller. By comparing results from one observatory with another's, they could have discovered that the characteristic distance depended on the proximity of the notch on the horizon. The nearer the notch, the shorter the distance would be.

The concept of characteristic distances associated with each lunar observatory would have become familiar to its users at an early stage. They would have found, when they made two simultaneous observations of the moonset, using the upper and lower limbs of the moon, that the distance apart of the two stakes, though not the same every time, kept within narrow limits. The average spacing of the two stakes would be large if the notch was on a distant horizon. In effect, for each observing line there is a ground equivalent of the lunar diameter. On relating this to the maximum stake separation on two successive nights, they would have discovered that the ground equivalent of the lunar diameter is just over half the maximum stake separation for an alignment at the major standstill, and about equal to it at the minor standstill. This rule applies to all lunar observatories.

Further qualitative information would come from studying the positions of the stakes which marked the maximum observed declination each month, that is the positions of the furthest left stakes each month at a moonset observatory like Temple Wood. The monthly stakes would gradually, but irregularly, advance to the left and then retreat again as the moon went through its major standstill. Every so often there would be a badly placed stake which did not follow the sequence, because it would be to the right of its expected location. A perspicacious observer would eventually realize that the furthest left stake for the month seemed to be in the best position when the next stake to it was some distance away. Conversely, when the next stake was close, the left-hand one did not fit well into the monthly sequence. It is but a short step to deduce that the correct position for the monthly stake is to the left of the furthest left stake found by direct observation, and that some extra distance to the left ought to be added. This distance is small if the nightly stakes were far apart, and large if they were close together.

We can see graphically what is happening from Figure 7.3. The curve represents the lunar declination, or its equivalent, the position on the ground where one would have had to stand to see the moon set behind the notch. Rather than have all the points superimposed on a line, as the stakes most likely were at the observatories, the figure has been opened out by showing the time in hours before and after the time of maximum declination. The curve is a parabola, and its apex is the maximum declination. We shall make an unimportant approximation in the explanation, and assume that moonsets are always twenty-four hours apart.

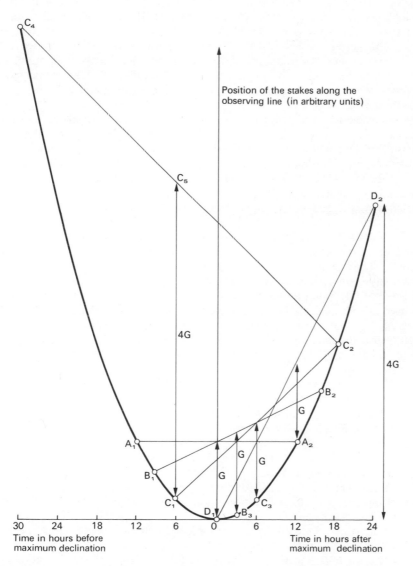

FIG. 7.3   How the stake positions would depend on the time of moonsets in relation to maximum declination

When moonset occurred twelve hours before and after the maximum, the stake positions at the two moonsets are represented by the points A_1 and A_2. To mark the maximum declination, a special stake should be put in at a point represented by D_1, the apex of the parabola. This would be a distance, G, which on the ground would be to the left of the two stakes A_1 and A_2.

If the moonsets occurred nine hours before and fifteen hours after the maximum, the stake positions correspond to B_1 and B_2. Putting the special stake a distance G from the midpoint of the pair brings it to B_3, which is a point on the parabola nearer to the apex than either of the two stakes B_1 and B_2. Trying out other pairs of points, e.g. C_1 and C_2, shows that the distance G from the midpoint of the pair always leads to a third point on the parabola. In other words, if the observers found the midpoint of the two stakes nearest the maximum, and then measured a distance G to the left and placed another stake there, they would have gone some, but not necessarily all, of the way to the correct position for the special stake.

It is particularly interesting to see what happens when one of the moonsets occurs at the exact moment of maximum declination. In that case the other moonset will be twenty-four hours later, and the two stake positions are represented by D_1 and D_2. This is the situation that gives maximum possible separation between the two stakes nearest to the peak of declination. Adding the distance G to the midpoint of the pair will bring us to A_2, a position still short of the required correction by the distance G. It is clear from the figure that the separation of stakes D_1 and D_2 is 4G.

We can bring in the characteristic distance of the sightline by plotting another point, for example C_4, which represents an observation twenty-four hours before C_1. The distance from the midpoint of C_2 and C_4 to C_1 (i.e. from C_5 to C_1) has already been defined as the characteristic distance, and from Fig. 7.3 this also is seen to be equal to 4G. The same result would have been obtained if we had used points corresponding to observations twenty-four hours before A_1, B_1, or D_1. The characteristic distance for the alignment is therefore the length 4G, which is also the maximum separation of the stakes on two consecutive nights near the time of maximum declination.

To summarize:

(a) Each observatory has a characteristic distance, 4G, for each sightline. The distance is readily found from observations on three successive moonsets, and it is also the maximum separation ever found between a pair of stakes set up at the two moonsets nearest the maximum declination.

(b) The pair of stakes will not give the maximum declination for the month; a third stake should be set up to the left of the left-hand one of the pair at a distance which depends on the separation of the two stakes.

(c) When the two stakes are coincident, the correct position for the third stake is found by extrapolating a distance equal to one quarter of the characteristic distance, i.e. G, to the left.

(d) When the two stakes are not coincident, extrapolating G from the midpoint of the two stakes is not far enough. The further apart the two stakes, the bigger the error in this method of extrapolation. When the stakes are 4G apart, the correct extrapolation is 2G.

(e) All the above statements apply directly to moonsets. The same general phenomena are observed at moonrises, but the observer's movements would all be in the opposite direction. To extrapolate to the maximum declination positions, he would have to move to the right.

Modern scientific knowledge enables us to calculate 4G from astronomical constants and the geometry of the site. The moon's declination decrease in the twenty-four hours from the maximum is 0·91° at the major standstill and 0·55° at the minor standstill. (Some authors give the decrement for twelve hours, which is one quarter of these values.) The change in azimuth corresponding to the declination decrease can be found from equation (1) of Chapter 4, and this has then to be related to an actual movement on the ground by multiplying the difference in azimuth angle (in radians) by the distance from the notch to the observing site. When the presumed line of stakes is perpendicular to the alignment, this gives the correct distance on the ground; but if the stake line and the alignment are not perpendicular, as is the case at Temple Wood, the answer has to be increased by dividing the result of the first calculation by the sine of the angle between the two lines. Other corrections are required if the ground is not level at the site.

Unfortunately there are no written records from the Early Bronze Age to tell us how the people who used the observatories set about solving the problem of extrapolation. We see only the end-products of their work in the archaeological remains from the period, which we have to study and analyse in the search for clues. By calculating the characteristic distances for various sites and comparing them with existing remains, archaeologists are coming to the conclusion that the Early Bronze Age people had discovered the significance of the characteristic distance, because at some sites it is actually recorded in the separation of standing stones or by the placing of other contemporary structures. At Temple Wood there are two alignments, and since their foresights are at different distances, 2·0 km and 6·3 km, there must be two values for 4G. These are calculated to be 83 m and 308 m respectively. When Professor Thom and colleagues first surveyed the site in 1939, they noticed a small cairn-like mound at Y on Figure 6.9, 81 m from the central menhir. This is very close to the correct distance for 4G for the alignment on the nearer of the two notches, and Thom has suggested that the purpose of the mound was to give a permanent reference for this important distance.

The other value of 4G is recorded in a rather more striking manner. We find on looking closely at the plan of Temple Wood that the distance from the largest menhir to the centre of the stone circle is 300 m, which is within 3 per cent of 4G for the Bellanoch Hill alignment, We have already commented that the stone circle and cairn are on the direct line to the nearer notch, and therefore must have been built after the lunar observatory. If we accept its distance as being a deliberate record of one of the characteristic distances, it implies that the circle and cairn were constructed whilst the observatory was in use, and probably not long after it was set to work. Temple Wood gives us a rare example of a direct association between a group of standing stones and another type of Early Bronze Age monument.

Now that we know the users of the lunar observatory at Temple Wood had discovered the distance 4G and perpetuated it at the site, the natural question is, 'How could they have used their discovery for extrapolation?' The evidence implies that their method of extrapolation was quite accurate, because the stone alignments themselves are correct to about one fiftieth of a degree. If the reason for the lunar observatory was to predict eclipses by looking for the maximum of the minor perturbation, a similar order of accuracy was essential in fixing the maximum of the lunar declination each month. One fiftieth of a degree is equivalent to a movement of less than 2 m on the ground when the nearer notch was in use. Without any extrapolation from the direct observations, the largest error would have been G, about 20 m, and ten times too big for effective use of the observatory.

To be wildly speculative for a moment, let us try to recapitulate the steps of logic that might have passed through the minds of the Early Bronze Age astronomers when they began to study their own observations. We start from the assumption that they had discovered the characteristic distance, had made a permanent record of it on the ground, and were aware of the relationship between the observations on three successive nights near the maximum monthly declination, namely that the position of the stake on the middle night of the three can be found by moving the characteristic distance to the left from the midpoint of the other two stakes.

The left-hand stake of the three is obviously much nearer the correct monthly position than the other two stakes, but it is certainly not in the right place. There must be an invisible (magical?) stake position further to the left, and since the left-hand one of the three can be located even on a cloudy night from the positions of the other two, perhaps the same ritual repeated will lead to the location of the invisible stake. Why not measure another distance to the left from the midpoint of the two furthest stakes? But what is this unknown distance? How they might have discovered it was a quarter of the characteristic distance we don't know. Presumably it was found by trial and error. Once they had found the right distance to move, a very simple rule greatly improves the performance of the observatory. It is: *add the distance G to the midpoint of the two stakes set up at successive moonsets nearest to the maximum declination, and use that as the indicator of the monthly maximum if it comes outside the pair. If not, use the left-hand stake as the monthly one.* The maximum error using this rule is $\frac{1}{4}$G, or about 5 m at Temple Wood. In the early days of the observatory, a crude method like this might well have been the start of progressive improvements in the technique of extrapolation.

With more experience, the rule would have been found to be inadequate. Now perhaps is the time to repeat the magic spell and measure yet another distance to the left, this time from the two left-hand stakes: one of the original pair and the stake set up as a result of extrapolating the distance G. If the number four had been found to have some special significance in the first stage of the extrapolation, what better choice of distance is there than dividing by four again and moving leftwards $\frac{1}{4}$G? This gives the position of a fourth stake a little to the left of the others, and although they would not, we suppose, have realized why, it is now getting very close to a position corresponding to the maximum declination for the month.

We can see the reason for this by looking at Figure 7.4, which is the same as Figure 7.3 but repeated to avoid confusion by having too many lines on one diagram. The stake positions for the two moonset observations are represented by P_1 and P_2; the point P_3 gives the position of the third stake, distance G from the midpoint of P_1 and P_2. When we extrapolate $\frac{1}{4}$G from the midpoint of P_1 and P_3, we come to P_4. It is a property of the parabola that P_4 also lies on the curve and is nearer the apex than either P_1 or P_3. At the end of this step the maximum error is $\frac{1}{4}$G. We could follow the procedure another time if we wished, and extrapolate $\frac{1}{16}$ G from the midpoint of P_1 and P_4 to find the location of a fifth stake P_5. If at any time the new stake position is not to the left of one of the others, we stop and use the stake which is furthest to the left for the monthly marker. Three steps would be sufficiently accurate at any site, for the largest error would not exceed $\frac{1}{16}$ G, which roughly equates to $\frac{1}{70}°$ in declination.

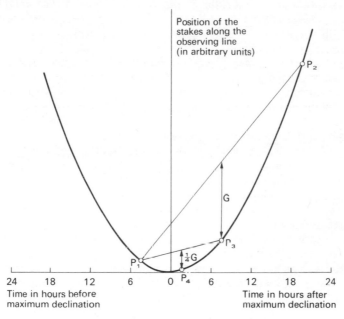

FIG. 7.4   The method of extrapolation by successive addition of G, $\frac{1}{4}$G, $\frac{1}{16}$G etc.

It must be stressed that although this method gives accurate extrapolation and requires no more sophisticated techniques than the ability to fold ropes and hammer stakes into the ground, we have no evidence for its use in the Early Bronze Age. Even when we find distances of G or 4G incorporated into the geometry of a site, it is no assurance that this method was followed because there are several other ways of extrapolating which would make use of these particular distances. Indeed some sites, especially in Caithness and on Dartmoor, have strange arrangements of stones with multiples of G in their layout. The evidence points to rather more complicated methods of extrapolation than the one just described. These other methods do not lead to the correct extrapolation distance by a series of progressively smaller steps but give the extrapolated position more directly, either as a distance from the midpoint of the two stakes, or as the distance from the further one of the pair.

To make it easier to follow the method, we shall use mathematical symbols. By common custom the letter p is applied to half the separation of the two stakes, their full separation being $2p$. It is possible to prove mathematically—and the proof is given in Appendix A—that the correct distance to extrapolate from the centre of the two left-hand stakes is $G+p^2/4G$. If we check our previous conclusions by putting $p = 0$ (the two stakes touching), we get G for the extrapolation, and if we put $p = 2G$ (the maximum possible separation of the two stakes), we find the extrapolation distance is $G+4G^2/4G$, which rearranges to 2G. These values are the ones found graphically in Figure 7.3. Measured from the left-hand stake of the pair, the extrapolation distance is $G+p^2/4G-p$. The Greek letter eta, η, is often used for $p^2/4G$, because it is convenient to have a single symbol for a quantity which appears very frequently in books and articles on this subject.

Neglecting for the moment the question of how Early Bronze Age people may have arrived at this solution, we naturally ask if there is any way that $G+\eta$ or $G+\eta-p$ could have been found on the ground without modern mathematics. Professor Thom showed in one of his books that it is quite possible to do this with strings and measuring rods. Look at the triangle in Figure 7.5. AB is the distance 4G for the alignment, which we assume is already known from previous observations. The two moonsets at the recent monthly declination maximum have given us the distance $2p$, and we next lay out a line, length p, in a perpendicular direction from B; this is the line BC. We now measure p from A to locate a point D, and from D lay out another line perpendicular to AB. The point at which this line intersects another rope joining A and C, we have called E. The distance $DE=\eta$, as can be seen from the proof on the diagram. It would be possible to use this method at any lunar observatory where 4G was known with reasonable accuracy, say to 10 per cent or better.

In practice there are neater ways of using this basic method of extrapolation, where the stakes set up during the observations can be part of the triangle. They make use of a variant of the scheme shown in Figure 7.5. By measuring p from B

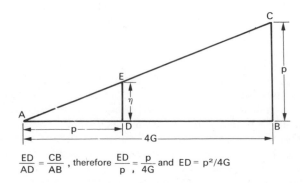

$$\frac{ED}{AD} = \frac{CB}{AB} \text{ , therefore } \frac{ED}{p} = \frac{p}{4G} \text{ and } ED = p^2/4G$$

FIG. 7.5   How to find $p^2/4G$ with strings and measuring rods

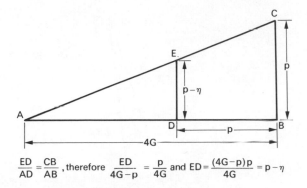

$$\frac{ED}{AD} = \frac{CB}{AB} \text{ , therefore } \frac{ED}{4G-p} = \frac{p}{4G} \text{ and } ED = \frac{(4G-p)p}{4G} = p - \eta$$

FIG. 7.6   An alternative use of a triangle in solving
for the extrapolation distance

instead of from A (Figure 7.6), the length DE becomes $p - \eta$, instead of η. It is very easy to apply this idea to an observatory like Temple Wood.

The relevant part of the Temple Wood observatory is shown on Figure 7.7, where the horizontal line is the $S_1 S_3$ alignment and the cairn Y is at the top of the page. P_1 and P_2 are two stake positions, the results of observations on two successive moonsets near the maximum declination. A rope of length $2p$ is folded to give the position of the middle stake, P_3. One end of the rope is now held at P_1, the other is swung round P_3, until it is on the line to the cairn. At its end another stake, E, is set in the ground. The next step is to locate a fifth stake, D, which is done by sighting in two directions: from P_1 to the cairn and from E to the notch on the horizon on Bellanoch Hill. (DE is therefore parallel to $P_1 P_2$.) The rope is moved, one end being placed at D, and the other taken around E and P_3 to the point F, on the line $P_2 P_1$. Since DE is $p - \eta$, from the proof on Figure 7.6, and the rope's length is $2p$, the section $P_3 F$ must be η. All that remains to be done to complete the extrapolation is to add the known distance G from F to the point A which now indicates where one would have had to stand to see the moon setting in the notch with the maximum declination for the month.

There are two interesting features of the application of this method of extrapolation at Temple Wood. The line from the main menhir S_1 to the cairn Y is not perpendicular to the line of stakes (Fig. 6.9). This does not matter at all, providing DE is parallel to it. Furthermore, since the stake P_3 will be in different places on the line from month to month, there will be a small variation in the distance, $P_3 Y$, being taken for 4G. The distance $P_3 Y$ is not very sensitive to movements of P_3, and P_3 can be sited almost anywhere from menhir S_3 to menhir S_4 without a change in $P_3 Y$ of more than 10 per cent. We have already pointed out that this is an acceptable accuracy for 4G.

The remains on the ground at Temple Wood give no indication which of these methods, or indeed whether some other method, of extrapolation was employed there. We have to go to Caithness in the very north-east corner of Scotland to find sites where the surviving stones give a lead as to the way the extrapolation could have been carried out. There are four rather strange sites in this remote part

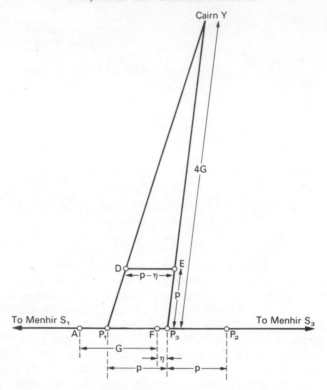

FIG. 7.7   A possible method of extrapolation at the
Temple Wood lunar observatory

of the British Isles, all in a small area between 10 and 25 km south-west of the
town of Wick, at Mid Clyth (Pl. 22), Dirlot, Loch of Yarrows, and Camster. They
all appear to be lunar observatories, with conventional backsights marked by
stones and horizon notches in directions corresponding to moonrise or moonset
at the standstills. The curious features which differentiate them from lunar
observatories in other parts of the country are the fan-shaped assemblies of small
stones nearby. The basic arrangement is a grid pattern, with stones set at the
intersections of rows and columns (Fig. 7.8). The rows converge, though not to
the point where they would meet. At all four sites the fan-shaped settings are
comparable in extent; the largest is Dirlot, 45 m across by 42 m long, and the
smallest is Loch of Yarrows, 15 m by 40 m, though it is very likely in the latter
case that cultivation has destroyed much of the site. The individual stones are in
general 2 to 2½ m apart, and at any site they have the same spacing in rows and
columns.

Unfortunately all these sites have been fairly badly affected by ground
clearance over the centuries, and the vegetation has grown up around the smaller
stones, hiding them from view. The best-preserved site, Mid Clyth, still has more
than 200 low slabs, all less than 1 m high and packed with small stones around

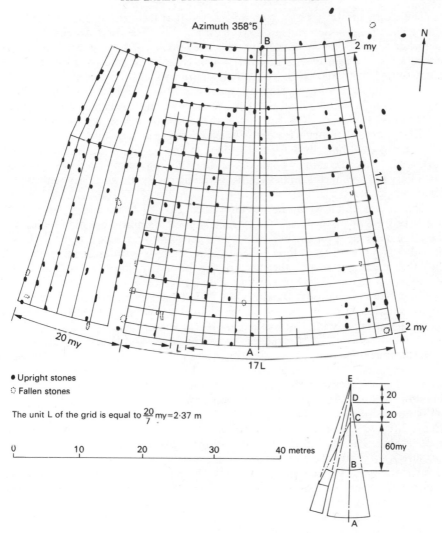

FIG. 7.8 Plan of the stone rows at Mid Clyth, with Thom's superimposed
geometrical interpretation

Based on a diagram in Thom, *Megalithic Lunar Observatories.*

their bases. The slabs themselves are orientated along the rows. Mid Clyth is a
more complex site than the other three, because it has a subsidiary fan to the west
of the main sector, and this has rows which are curiously bent in the middle.
From the scatter of stones to the east of the main sector, it seems there may have
been another subsidiary fan on the other side. The dimensions of the larger fan
are 40 m across its base, tapering to 24 m, with the rows 44 m in length. The
radius of the main fan is 110 m and of the subsidiary fan 126 m. The axis of the
main fan is within $1\frac{1}{2}°$ of true north.

The stones are set on a sloping hillside, so that the narrow end of the fan is almost on a ridge which runs east–west. Along this ridge there are more stones, including a large fallen menhir 2·7 m long, the remains of a small cairn, and other stones as well. Thom has suggested that this ridge is the line used by observers when setting their marks for two lunar alignments, a $-(\varepsilon+i)$ moonrise to the south-east and a $+(\varepsilon+i)$ moonrise to the north-east. There are small notches on the horizon in both directions, the $-(\varepsilon+i)$ moonrise being marked by a notch no less than 80 km away. The notch for the other moonrise is 2·9 km distant. Neither of these alignments is clearly indicated on the ground at the site, although the outer row of the subsidiary sector does in fact line up with the notch in the north-east, and Thom has pointed out that if there were originally another subsidiary fan arranged symmetrically, its outer row would similarly indicate the other alignment.

The distant notch would hardly have been a very practical lunar alignment, partly because of the necessity for extremely good visibility, but also because of the large movement on the ground—about 1,000 m—corresponding to 4G. On the other hand the ridge is long enough to accommodate observing positions for the other alignment when either limb of the moon is rising in the notch, and it would be usable for several years near the major standstill.

Thom's interpretation of the stone fans is that they were intended as calculators for the solution of the extrapolation problem. They would function in a similar way to the triangle with a side of length 4G, giving in one step a distance from which the users could derive the length η. The permanently set-out fans would have the advantage over the triangle method that they would not require stakes to be positioned by sighting from the further end of the 4G baseline. The observer would measure the distance p from the corner B of the fan, in two directions as shown in Figure 7.9, and then he would locate E, guided by the rows and columns of the standing stones. The distance ED is $p-\eta$, just as it was in Figure 7.6, and it would have to be measured with a length of rope in exactly the same fashion. The most direct way of finding the extrapolated position is then to measure $p-\eta$ along the line of nightly markers, from the most advanced one towards the next. Place a temporary stake here and from it measure G in the opposite direction, i.e. back towards the furthest marker. This is equivalent to measuring a total distance of $G+\eta-p$ from the stake set up at the observation with maximum declination.

When we come to consider how large the stone fans needed to be, an interesting possibility emerges. At first sight we would think that, since the maximum value for p is 2G, the rows and columns ought to be at least this long. However, this is not so, for if they are made exactly G in length, they will work when p is greater than the dimensions of the fan. The stones are used in virtually the same way: when p is greater than G, it is measured as before from the corner B of Figure 7.9, but the end of the rope is taken around the last stone of the row or column and folded back on itself. The end of the rope designates the distances BC and BD as before, but the amount now measured off the sides of the fan is $2G-p$. The geometrical proof on Figure 7.9 shows that the distance DE is now $G-\eta$, instead of $p-\eta$. The extrapolated position can then be found by measuring from the centre of the two nightly observation stakes the distance DE away from the most advanced stake, followed by measuring 2G in the opposite direction.

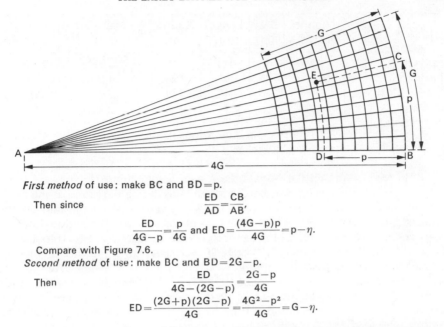

First method of use: make BC and BD = p.

Then since

$$\frac{ED}{AD} = \frac{CB}{AB},$$

$$\frac{ED}{4G-p} = \frac{p}{4G} \text{ and } ED = \frac{(4G-p)p}{4G} = p - \eta.$$

Compare with Figure 7.6.

Second method of use: make BC and BD = 2G − p.

Then

$$\frac{ED}{4G-(2G-p)} = \frac{2G-p}{4G}$$

$$ED = \frac{(2G+p)(2G-p)}{4G} = \frac{4G^2 - p^2}{4G} = G - \eta.$$

FIG. 7.9   The method of extrapolation using the stone fans

Using this rather subtle variation of the method saves an enormous amount of work in setting out the fans, by making them only one quarter of the area they would otherwise have to be.

Professor Thom's suggestion that the stone fans were designed as Early Bronze Age calculators for solving the extrapolation problem has far-reaching implications. If he is right, it gives solid support to the whole concept of Bronze Age astronomy, and in particular it makes the triangle method of extrapolation much more plausible. We ought therefore to consider carefully the parameters of the stone fans and weigh the evidence for and against Thom's idea.

What would we expect to find? First, of course, that they should be located near a site that could have been used as a lunar observatory. According to Thom, all four stone fans meet this criterion. The radius of the sector should be the same length as 4G for the associated alignment. The sector itself should have base and sides of about the same length, and these should be either exactly G or at least 2G, so that they will suffice for all values of p. The spacing of the stones does not matter, though it would obviously be more convenient if they were the same in rows and columns.

The dimensions of the four known stone fans are given in Table 7.1, the data having been taken from Thom's book *Megalithic Lunar Observatories*, Chapter 9. (The calculated values of 4G are a few per cent greater than the ones given there, to take account of a more accurate value of the moon's declination deficit in twenty-four hours than was available at the time he wrote the book.) The sites are arranged in order of the number of stones still existing and this is a guide to the weight of evidence we should attach to each.

Site	Number of stones	Base (m)	Length (m)	Radius (m)	4G (calculated) (m)	Radii as % of 4G
Mid Clyth	200	40	44	110	170	65
Dirlot	70–80	45	42	120	126	95
Loch of Yarrows	66	15	40	244	280	87
Camster	14	16	31	166	205	81

Table 7.1   Principal dimensions of the stone fans

Both Mid Clyth and Dirlot pass the test of having approximately the same base and length dimension; it is hardly worth considering the extent of the other two because so many stones are missing. Agreement between the radii of the sectors and the calculated values of 4G is satisfactory for Dirlot and Loch of Yarrows, and even at Camster the sector would be quite usable for extrapolation, in spite of its being too short by nearly 20 per cent. Earlier in this chapter, in connection with the triangle method of extrapolation, it was stated that ideally 4G should be known to within about 10 per cent. The same holds for the sector method, but an error of 20 per cent would not have caused insuperable difficulties for the observers. The magnitude of the error would depend on how exactly the sectors were used. When p was less than G, the value given by the sector for $p-\eta$ would be too small. If the observers located the extrapolated position by measuring $p-\eta$ from the further stake and then a distance G in the opposite direction, the two errors would tend to compensate for each other. For most values of p the error in the final extrapolated position would not exceed 0·1G, corresponding to an azimuthal error of $\frac{1}{40}°$.

Mid Clyth is the most difficult site to account for satisfactorily, yet it is the best preserved. The table shows the radius of the main sector is 65 per cent of the calculated value of 4G. This is almost certainly incorrect. 4G has been calculated on the assumption that the observers' line of markers was perpendicular to the alignment, but from the layout of the site this looks most improbable. Men at the site would have been working on an awkward slope, and it would have been far more convenient to have stayed on the top of the ridge on level ground. The line of markers would then have made an angle of 63° with the alignment, and the effective 4G distance along this line is 191 m. The radius of the main sector is only 58 per cent of 191 m.

In spite of these large errors in the radius of the main sector, the extrapolated position, for values of p up to $1\frac{1}{2}$G, is surprisingly near the correct place. The reader can easily check this, using a scale drawing of the sector, and assuming different values for p. If we do this, finding $p-\eta$ from the sector, but using 44 m for measuring G along the line of stakes (i.e. the base-length of the sector and not $\frac{1}{4}$ of its radius), we find that the largest error in locating the extrapolated position is again less than 0·1G for all values of p. This gives azimuthal accuracies which are quite good enough for using the observatory.

Although the Mid Clyth stone fans would have functioned satisfactorily as an extrapolation calculator, we should not ignore their inconsistencies. Since it is relatively easy to measure 4G from three nights' observations, it is strange that the radius should be inaccurate by such a large amount. One explanation might be found in the geography of the site. Beyond the ridge the ground slopes down to the north and it is impossible to see the centre from almost all of the stone rows. This would have complicated setting out the sector, but it is less difficult than many other geometrical feats of the Early Bronze Age.

The subsidiary fan to the west of the main one has a slightly greater radius, 126 m, but it still falls a long way short of 4G. The small sector is too narrow for effective use in extrapolation, and its purpose remains obscure. The bend in the middle gives it a superficial resemblance to the stone rows in Brittany at Le Menec and Kermario.

Many archaeologists have strong reservations about Thom's explanation for the stone fans. They could point out there are only four known, and that two of them are sadly mutilated. The fan-shapes at the two least damaged sites look convincing when the conjectural grid lines are superimposed on the layout, but less so when one sees a plan showing only the stones. Finally, the dimensions of the sector at Mid Clyth are not very close to the expected ones, and it may well be coincidence that they are nevertheless suitable for extrapolation. On the other hand, the stone fans are all apparently situated near lunar alignments, they are about the right size, and no other explanation for their existence has been put forward. Both sides would agree that our understanding of these sites would be greatly increased if one of them were excavated to provide a more comprehensive plan of the settings of the stones. Because they could have been used for extrapolation, it does not follow that they were; but until some more convincing hypothesis is proposed, it would seem reasonable to accept that this was their purpose, and to think about the consequences of this in our interpretation of the Early Bronze Age.

There are other places in the British Isles than north-east Scotland where stone rows are found. They can be seen in several parts of the country, but the largest concentration is to be found on Dartmoor in Devonshire, where there are about sixty known rows, single, double, and even a few triple ones. The shortest rows are about 30 m long and the longest more than 3 km. It is impossible to draw generalizations which apply to all the rows, but there are some statements which are more likely to be true than not. The orientations of the rows seem to be determined by the lie of the land, for they often follow the line of minimum slope. Many are associated with cairns, some being terminated by a cairn at one end, and one, Merrivale, has a cairn in the middle of a double row. The rows sometimes end with large transverse stones, and where the row is double, the transverse, or 'blocking', stone is set between the rows. Many rows are composed of very small stones, hardly $\frac{1}{2}$ m high, and they may be irregular in shape or flat slabs. The latter are always in line with the row. Most rows are fairly straight, though not accurately so, but some of the longer ones wander apparently aimlessly across the moor.

The stone rows on Dartmoor have been known to antiquarians since the eighteenth century and there has been much speculation as to their purpose. After the publication of Lockyer's book on the alignments of Stonehenge and other monuments it was inevitable that stone rows were studied to see if they, too, indicated astronomically significant directions. No definite indications were found, although solar and lunar alignments certainly exist on Dartmoor, in association with stone circles and cairns. Thom's work on stone sites opened up new possibilities, for it is now clear that the rows could be linked with astronomical observations without themselves being orientated to a particular moonrise or sunset, and it was with this in mind that Mr Alan Penny and I investigated the stone rows at Merrivale in 1974.

In the remainder of this chapter Merrivale will be described in detail as an example of a very diverse site with rows, cairns, megaliths, and stone circles. It illustrates how geometrical and astronomical aspects can be closely interlinked. Furthermore, it is one of the most important sites in the south of England and has long been recognized as such by archaeologists, though it is relatively little known to the general public. It is, however, the easiest of the Bronze Age sites on Dartmoor to visit, because it is just south of the main road from Ashburton to Tavistock, about 4 km west of Princetown.

The site itself is on the summit of a fairly flat-topped bluff covered with moorland vegetation. Its first use was probably as a Late Neolithic burial ground, because there are two cists to the south of the stone rows which are characteristic of this period. They have no connection with the other remains on the site. One of these is a ruined cairn, much despoiled, whose most prominent feature now is an ellipse-shaped kerb, 19 m by 16 m (eccentricity 0·086). This is also likely to belong to an early phase.

The stone rows (Fig. 7.10) are almost complete. There are two double rows, roughly east–west and almost parallel. Both have larger stones at their western ends and are terminated by 'blocking stones' at their eastern ends. The southern and longer row, Row II, has a cairn half-way along it, surrounded by a ring of stones in the form of a Type I egg (Pl. 21). Just to the west of this cairn is a single short row, Row III, which projects to the south-west from another cairn. There are several small cairns scattered about the site, all barely ¼ m high and less than 6 m in diameter. These are usually regarded as being Beaker graves and could have a date around 2300 BC. The stones at one end of Row III are actually set into a cairn, and therefore archaeologists know that the small row was not built earlier than the Beaker period.

As shown in Figure 7.10, there are stone rings to the north and south of the rows. The northern one is a true circle, 8·6 m in diameter, and the southern one is a Type B flattened circle (Pl. 20), diameter 20·55 m, with its short axis on the north–south line. Its stones alternate between pillars and slabs, as at some other monuments, notably the Kennet Avenue. Just over 40 m due south of the centre of the flattened circle is a large, 3·15 m high, standing stone, and because of its relation to the circle, Thom has suggested it was set up deliberately as a meridian marker. This was the first hint that Merrivale could have had an astronomical function. Precisely on the line between the menhir (I) and the eastern end of Row II there is a large stone slab (Slab I) set on edge with its long axis perpendicular to the line, and a few metres away is another (Slab II) with its axis parallel to the line. There are two other menhirs south of the stone rows and a fourth north of Row I.

The two double stone rows are very similar. The parallel lines of stones are very nearly, but not quite, straight and the separation between lines varies from 0·8 m to 1·3 m in Row I, 0·6 m to 1·2 m in Row II. They are much too close together to give substance to the idea, sometimes put forward, that they are

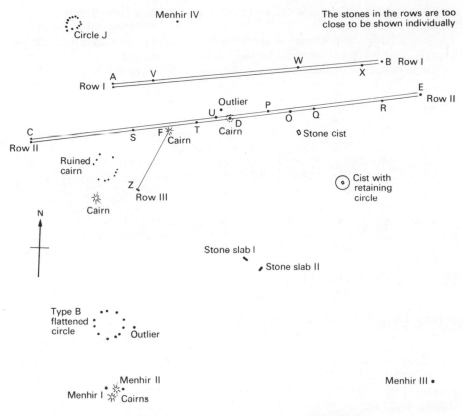

Circle J

Menhir IV

The stones in the rows are too
close to be shown individually

W   B   Row I

A   V   X

Row I

E

Row II

Outlier   P

U   O   Q   R

C   D

Row II   S   F   T   Cairn

Cairn   Stone cist

Ruined cairn

Z   Row III

Cist with retaining circle

N   Cairn

Stone slab I

Stone slab II

Type B flattened circle   Outlier

Menhir II

Menhir I   Cairns

Menhir III

FIG. 7.10   Plan of the stone rows at Merrivale

processional ways. Row I, on an orientation of 83·7°, is 181·7 m long and has 186 stones, though not all are visible because peat has covered some of the smaller and fallen stones. The majority of visible stones project less than 0·4 m above the peat—Merrivale is not a visually impressive site. The end stones, at A and B on Figure 7.10, are tall, about 1 m high, and three stones along the rows, at V, W, and X, are also much taller than their fellows. The spacing of the stones is uniform along the row, averaging 1·86 m.

Row II has an orientation of 81·7°, is 263·7 m long and has 266 stones, including those in the egg-shaped ring and a few buried ones. Again, most of the stones are small and the ends are marked by distinctively larger ones, and there are seven tall stones (lettered O to U) in the row. The stone spacings, whilst identical in the two lines, are not constant along Row II; they are wide in the central section between S and Q (2·24 m) and are small at the eastern end (1·12 m between R and E).

Row III is single, 42·3 m long, orientated to 23°, and has 41 stones with a mean spacing of 1·0 m. Only a few of these stones can be seen and we checked the positions of the others by lifting the surface of the peat to reveal their tops. The stones at the ends of the row are set transversely, so there is no doubt about its length.

At first sight the positions of the large stones in the rows seem to be quite irregular, but when the intervals between them are measured, certain distances are found to be repeated several times. They are listed in Table 7.2.

Row I		Row II			
XB	13·2	TU	12·7		
AV	26·9	DP	26·7,	RE	26·1
WX	43·3	ST	43·5		
WB	56·5	SU	56·1		
		TO	63·5,	OR	62·5
		SD	65·6,	UQ	66·8
		DR	103·8,	PE	103·3
AW	124·9	CU	124·1		
VX	141·3	UE	139·4		
VB	154·5	TE	152·1		
AX	168·2	SR	169·4		

Table 7.2   Distances between the large stones in Rows I and II (in metres)

The pattern is revealed when we realize that all the repeated distances are simple multiples of three basic lengths. I shall identify them by the Greek letters α (alpha), β (beta), and γ (gamma), and let these stand for 13·1 m, 15·6 m, and 43·4 m respectively. Putting the distances of Table 7.2 into the units α, β, and γ, gives the results in Table 7.3. The spacings are not absolutely precise as simple multiples of the three units, though they are remarkably accurate. Expressed as a percent-

Approximate Interval	Precise Interval			
	Row I		Row II	
α	XB	1·01	TU	0·97	
2α	AV	2·05	DP	2·04,	RE	1·99
5α			SD	5·01,	UQ	5·10
β			OQ	1·02	
3β			QR	2·98	
4β			TO	4·07,	OR	4·01
8β	AW	8·01	CU	7·96	
9β	VX	9·06	UE	8·94	
γ	WX	1·00	ST	1·00	

Table 7.3   Distances between the large stones in Rows I and II
(in units of $\alpha = 13\cdot1$ m, $\beta = 15\cdot6$ m, and $\gamma = 43\cdot4$ m)

age error, the least accurate is TU, which is 3 per cent short of α; eleven of the distances are within 1 per cent of simple multiples. The lengths are marked on a plan of the stone rows on Figure 7.11.

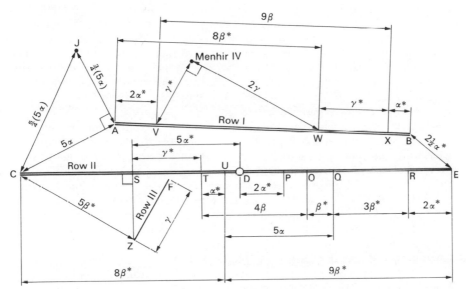

* Indicates the distances can be expressed in multiples of α, β, and γ to better than 1m.
Other distances are closer than $1\frac{1}{2}$m except for CJ and AJ

FIG. 7.11   Geometrical relationships in the Merrivale stone rows

The location of Row III relative to Row II also involves these units. The length of Row III is almost equal to γ (FZ = 0.97γ) and the separation of the western ends of Rows II and III, the distance CZ, is 5.01β. The direction and length of Row III are such that a right-angled triangle is formed with the stone S, i.e. CSZ is a right angle. The angle CZF is not a right angle, but is 93°. However, CZ and ZD are the same length to within 1 per cent, and so are ZF and FD. This distance, γ, occurs on the site no fewer than six times, for in addition to WX, ST, ZF, and FD, it is also the distance from the large menhir to the centre of the flattened circle and from stone V to Menhir IV. There could hardly be a more vivid demonstration than this that we are dealing with a site having some systematic basis for its design.

We have not yet exhausted the geometrical curiosities of Merrivale. Menhir IV makes a right-angled triangle with stones V and W of Row I. The two main rows are related by the distances between their ends, for the western ends C and A are 5α apart, and BE is $2\frac{1}{2}\alpha$. Circle J completes a 3,4,5 triangle with A and C. I have already mentioned that Slab I is on the direct line from Menhir I to E; Slab II is set so that a right angle is formed by the stones C-Slab-B and another by A-Slab-Menhir I. Both angles are right to within 1°.

These complex and strange geometrical relationships, incorporated many times into the stone-row site at Merrivale, are not accidental. Whether they are significant or not is another matter; it is arguable that they are the results of a large-scale doodle, laid out for the aesthetic pleasure of the geometry itself and with no more purpose than, say, the plan of an Elizabethan formal garden. Somehow one is loath to accept this explanation, partly because it is contrary to the way we would behave in the twentieth century. We like our civil engineering works to have a clear purpose and feel, possibly illogically, that prehistoric builders ought to have had a good reason for erecting stones, even though it may not always be obvious. But we also know that stones were set up at other sites for astronomical reasons, and therefore we can legitimately consider the observational potential of the site, to see if thereby some light can be shone on the mysteries hidden in the geometrical design.

The Dartmoor landscape is noted for the granite outcrops which are scattered about the moor like huge building bricks. Several are visible on the horizon from Merrivale and it would be natural to use them for distant foresights if astronomical observations were intended. The most interesting part of the horizon is to the north-west where there are two sharp notches (L and M on Figure 7.12) and, a little further north, the jumbled masses of Great Staple Tor (Pl. 20). There is little doubt that this sector of the skyline was important to the users of the site, since notch L is indicated very accurately by the line Menhir III-Slab II-Slab I (which itself points to the notch). As closely as can be judged, the centre of the ruined cairn is also on this line. Notch M is indicated by a small outlier north-west of cairn D. From the centre of the flattened circle, the solstitial sun would have set behind L in the Late Neolithic and Early Bronze Ages, and from the circle J, the moon would have set similarly behind notch M at the major standstill.

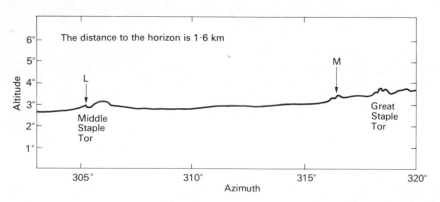

FIG. 7.12   Part of the north-west horizon as seen from the stone ring at Merrivale

These alignments would have been valuable for making visible the gross movements of the moon, but it would have been more accurate to have followed the procedure used at Temple Wood and made observations from a line permanently laid out on the ground. An additional and valuable refinement would have been to provide a fixed scale of distance so that in effect the line was a gigantic ruler marked out on the moor.

It would be difficult to specify a more suitable arrangement consistent with Early Bronze Age technology than the stone rows at Merrivale. From the end A of Row I, the moon would have appeared to set at major standstills around 1800 BC as shown in Figure 7.13. If the observers had stood elsewhere along the row the moon's apparent setting position would have been different, so that at 7 m from the end its lower limb would have disappeared in the angle of the notch. As the declination of the moon declined from the 18·6-year maximum, the observer would have had to move along the row to the west to keep the moonset in the direction of the notch. Row I is long enough for observations until the declination had decreased to 26·4°, making it usable over five successive years near the major standstill. Row II could have been used in an identical way. To see the moon at maximum declination set behind the notch, the observer would have had to stand near stone S. All other observations would have been made from positions between S and the eastern end E.

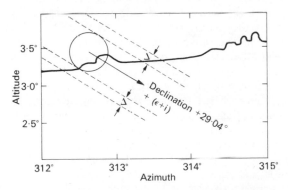

FIG. 7.13   The setting moon as seen from the
west end of Row I at Merrivale

The observing technique is very simple. Perhaps a number of observers were used, from the nearby Bronze Age village whose hut circles are still to be seen on the hillside less than 1 km from the stone rows. They may have been posted in between the lines of stones, one person to each pair. The people would have been told to notice carefully where the last glimpse of the moon was seen in relation to the notch. The nightly marker would have been placed beside the person who saw the moon disappear behind the preselected spot on the horizon. Just as at Temple Wood, observations would have been made on consecutive nights to find the day of the month when the moon was at maximum declination.

The observatory would not have been fully effective without some means of extrapolation. 4G can be calculated for both rows, and though it varies a little over their lengths, its mean value at the site is 61·2 m, equivalent to 15·3 m for G. This length is so close to that of the unit β, which is repeated many times in the rows, that it is very probable that spacings of multiples of β were set up to perpetuate the characteristic distance of the site.

Knowing the distance 4G, it would have been quite possible for the observers to have found the extrapolated position for the monthly maximum, using the method of successive approximations already described. No stone fans have been discovered on the site, but there are two right-angled triangles (CZF and VW-Menhir IV) and one naturally asks if these were suitable for the extrapolation methods of Figures 7.5 and 7.6. We know that extrapolated positions can be found sufficiently accurately even if the triangles are not quite the ideal dimensions. The triangle CZF, though oversize, would have been usable, but we doubt whether it was used in this fashion because the builders of the site knew 4G and could have constructed the correct triangle if they had wished. Instead they chose to make one side exactly 5G long, and this implies that, if it was used for extrapolation, the method was rather different from those we have seen at the Scottish observatories.

Following our survey of the stone rows at Merrivale, we worked out a possible way of using the short third row for extrapolating. Back in the Early Bronze Age, before they solved the problem, they would have already made many observations of the setting moon, and would have used stakes along the rows to record where they had to stand to see the moon set behind the notch. By this time they would have discovered that some extrapolation from the left-hand stake was necessary to find the position corresponding to maximum lunar declination. They would have found that when the two stakes were close together, the extrapolated distance must be at its largest. When they were far apart, i.e. separated by the characteristic distance 4G, no movement from the left-hand stake was required. In other, intermediate, situations, they would not have known how far to extrapolate, but they would have realized the distance was not related in a simple linear way to the stake separation, because when the stakes were half their maximum distance apart, the distance to be extrapolated from the left-hand one was not half *its* maximum. They were looking for a quantity that was large when the stake separation was zero, dropped very quickly when the stake separation first increased, and then tailed off when the stakes were still further apart. The men of the Early Bronze Age, familiar with geometrical shapes, would probably have tried to visualize this as a curve laid out on the ground.

Actually it can be closely represented by the distance from the tangent to the arc of a circle. On Figure 7.14 the distance to be extrapolated from the left-hand, or further, stake is shown by the curve LSM. The horizontal axis of the graph is half the stake separation, and the distance to be extrapolated is the height of the curve above the axis. Thus if half the distance between the stakes is OQ, the correct extrapolation distance is QS. Now the curve LSM is a parabola, and as far as we know the concept of a parabola was not known in the Early Bronze Age. However, they laid out a lot of circles, and the curve they pictured would have been an arc like LRM, which is part of a circle. Their problem would have been to find the dimensions of the circle which gave the best (most consistent) results, most likely using no other method than trial and error.

Our problem is to find mathematically what is the radius of the circle that lies closest to the parabola, so that we can compare it with what we find on the ground and see if there is any evidence for this approach to extrapolation. The calculation of the 'best fit' circle is given in Appendix A; it turns out there are several answers. If we laid off half the stake separation along OM, as on Figure

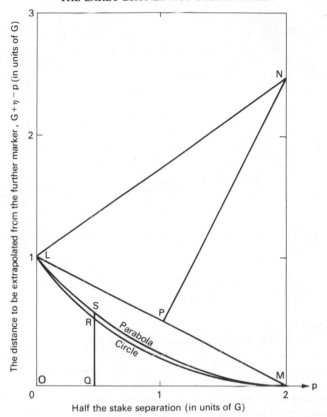

FIG. 7.14 Extrapolation from the further marker using
the arc of a circle

7.14, the radius is $2\frac{1}{2}G$. If we laid off the whole of the stake separation, the radius should be $8\frac{1}{2}G$; and with $\frac{3}{4}$ of the stake separation, the radius is 5G. This last solution is rather interesting, because it is the only one giving NM and OM as whole multiples of G, 5G and 3G respectively.

We find a 5G,3G triangle at Merrivale, associated with the geometry of Row III. I said (page 133) that CZF was 93° and not a right angle. Now, if we draw a right angle CZY, and put the point Y between the stones of Row II (see Fig. 7.15), we find that the distance CY is 46·4 m, which is only 1 per cent different from 3G. If the users of Merrivale had laid out a line ZY for Row III, the method of extrapolation would have been as follows:

(a) Lay off with a rope, from Y towards Z, $\frac{3}{4}$ of the separation of the stakes, putting down a marker Y_1 at the end of the rope.

(b) Take another rope, length 5G, put one end at C and swing it round to find the point Y_2, where the perpendicular Y_1Y_2 meets the rope.

(c) Measure on the distance Y_1Y_2 from the left-hand stake. This gives the extrapolated position.

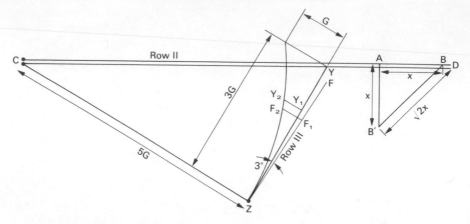

FIG. 7.15   The method of extrapolation using Row III at Merrivale

However, they did not do it quite this way. From the layout of the site, it looks as though that was how the extrapolation was first done, and then the method was modified empirically to increase its accuracy. When they used the arc of a circle instead of a parabola, they unwittingly introduced an error. This error can be very nearly eliminated by re-siting the short stone row to a position represented by ZF on Figure 7.15 and simultaneously changing the proportion of the stake separation to be laid off along the row. (Maybe excavation near Row III would reveal a set of earlier stone or post holes.) From the length of Row III we can deduce what proportion of the stake separation was actually laid off, because when it was 4G, they would have laid off the whole length of Row III. It turns out, rather unexpectedly, to be $\frac{1}{2}\sqrt{2}$. We should not be put off by the appearance of the square root of 2; it is easy to find geometrically, and the people of the Early Bronze Age would see it only as the length of the third side of a triangle. The method of extrapolation, using Row III as it is today, is:

(a) If the two stakes are at positions represented by A and B on Figure 7.15, take a rope of length AB and swing it round so that it lies along AB′.

(b) Now take another rope, length BB′, and fold it in two.

(c) Put one end of the folded rope at F, and lay it along the row so that the other end is at F_1.

(d) By swinging a third rope from C, obtain the distance F_1F_2, in the same way as Y_1Y_2. F_1F_2 is now the distance to be measured on from the left-hand stake to find the extrapolated point.

This modification to the first method reduces the extrapolation errors by about a factor of four. They are then quite negligible.

If this method of extrapolation was the one actually used at Merrivale, it would have been devised only after many years of patient, and sometimes frustrating, observation and experiment. Once found, the distances β and γ would have been of very great significance to the users of the site, and there is little wonder that they were preserved in the permanent layout of the stone rows, like data in the store of a modern computer.

This interpretation of the use of the stone rows at Merrivale has been criticized on the grounds that it is arbitrary and unique. There is no denying the fact that until an Early Bronze Age site is found with a similar method of extrapolation, Merrivale must remain an interesting, yet unproven, speculation. There are many things still unexplained; for example, why there should be two double rows apparently for the same purpose, and what is the significance of the distance a? Probably the interpretation is half right, and further work on this and other stone rows will clarify the situation eventually.

We should not be surprised at regional variations in the method of extrapolation. We have seen in the very north of Scotland how the evidence points to a permanent grid of stones being used as the extrapolation calculator, whilst in southern Scotland there seems to have been nothing more elaborate than a triangle with one side of length 4G. In the south of England, where there was a tradition of building stone rows, there are indications once more of a permanent setting of stones to facilitate the calculation. Although we may be puzzled at how they could have been devised in the Early Bronze Age, at least none of the calculators is complicated to operate, once the site is prepared. The stone rows in Brittany, which I shall describe in the next chapter, represent yet another variation on the basic ideas. It is in this area that the observation and interpretation of astronomical events reached its peak of sophistication and elaboration among the Early Bronze Age cultures of north-west Europe.

8 The Stone Rows of Carnac

The best-known of all the megalithic remains in France are undoubtedly the stone rows near the small seaside town of Carnac on the south coast of Brittany. The stones are so huge and so numerous that they deeply impress even the most casual of visitors, and hundreds of thousands of tourists go each year to see, climb on, and wonder at these strange relics from prehistoric times. Though Carnac is noted particularly for the stone rows, there are many other megalithic monuments nearby, and if it were not for the rows, this corner of Brittany would surely be famous for its burial chambers alone. Almost all the tombs were constructed on a grand scale, having large horizontal capstones like the chambers of Mané Lud and Table des Marchands, or covered with huge mounds like the Tumulus St Michel, which actually has a Christian chapel on its summit; or richly decorated with typical Late Neolithic carvings like the passage grave on the Ile de Gavrinis. The burial chambers of Brittany have fascinating variety and stupendous architecture, and are a most interesting subject for study. For the purposes of this book we have to leave them aside, except to point out that many of them appear to be roughly orientated towards the rising sun, reminiscent of New Grange and the long barrows of southern England. The orientations are ritual rather than observational, for there are no signs of accurate sightlines associated with them. They could, however, have been the first indications of a developing interest in the sun and the moon among the neolithic inhabitants of the region.

More important in the astronomical context are the many standing stones, or menhirs. This word has been borrowed from Breton. Another Breton word, dolmen, is also used, for the table-like structure formed by the uprights and horizontal slab of a megalithic tomb. Cromlech can also mean a tomb, but the word is best avoided because some writers (including Thom) call circles of stones cromlechs, and this can lead to some confusion.

The known astronomical sites in Brittany are all concentrated in a small area, 20 km or less from, and all south of, the town of Auray in the Département of Morbihan. The region is flat and low-lying, with hardly any land above 30 m elevation, and most of it undulates gently between 5 and 25 m. There is some woodland, and a little cultivated ground, and much of the remainder is covered with a thick and sometimes almost impenetrable scrub, with large patches of prickly gorse. The undergrowth quite seriously hampers investigators of these remains and hides some of them from all except the most determined sightseers.

According to the Thom family (and nearly all this chapter is based on their work) there are two lunar observatories in the region of Carnac (Fig. 8.1). Since there are no natural notches to exploit, the builders of these observatories were forced to set up menhirs as artificial foresights, which they did in two places, one near what is now the oyster-farming village of Locmariaquer, 9 km east of

Carnac, and the other at Le Manio, on the top of a low rise $2\frac{1}{2}$ km north-east of Carnac and quite close to the famous stone rows. Because the foresights had to be large to be visible at a distance, it was obviously economical to use them with many backsights, and the Thoms claim to have found several of these for each of the two large menhirs. Associated with the sightlines one would expect to find some arrangement for extrapolation and they have identified two stone fans, at Le Petit Menec and St Pierre-Quiberon, and one set of stone rows, at Keriaval, which could possibly have been used for this purpose. Perhaps their most dramatic claim is that a part of the great rows at Carnac was built as an extrapolation device, though we shall see that this interpretation leaves many of the features of the stone rows still unexplained. There are some reasons for thinking that the sightlines to Le Manio were the earliest, but in this chapter they will be discussed last.

The foresight near Locmariaquer is the remarkable Grand Menhir Brisé, the fallen and broken stone known as Er Grah, the Stone of the Fairies, in Breton (Pl. 24). I mentioned in Chapter 2 that this menhir, weighing an estimated 330 tonnes, was the largest one ever set up. Probably about 19 m of its total length of $22\frac{1}{2}$ m were above the ground when it was erect. It is sited at the southern end of a now almost flattened mound of the megalithic tomb known as the Table des Marchands. The stone is of a variety of granite the nearest outcrop of which is 80 km away in Finisterre. Evan Hadingham, in his book *Circles and Standing Stones*, speculates that there may have been a local source at some point now covered by the sea, which has risen several metres since the Early Bronze Age. Whether he is right or not, the erectors of the stone must have quarried it, moved it some distance, and set it upright. When we consider that their techniques were confined to ropes, levers, and the use of animal- and man-power, we must admit it to be a truly astonishing feat of engineering.

The stone itself is almost oval in cross-section, and has clearly been roughly shaped, with the intention, we assume, of producing a clean vertical line to make the sightings more precise. It now lies in four pieces, three of them in a line with the top towards the east, and these look as though they remain where they fell. The bottom part of the menhir has its top towards the north-west, and this has puzzled archaeologists for many years. Some have done experiments with piles of bricks, and have been unable to make them fall into similar positions to the parts of the Grand Menhir unless they were violently shaken. Monsieur Z. Le Rouzic, a French archaeologist who carried out many excavations in the Carnac area, concluded that the present state of the Grand Menhir was the result of a violent earth tremor, and this seems to be the explanation currently preferred. However, we should not totally discount the possibility that it was moved deliberately by human activity. There is some evidence that it fell about the end of the seventeenth century, and it captured the interest of at least one antiquarian, de Roubien, who sketched it, lying where it now is, in 1727. There is no record of an attempt to move the stone, but it could have reached its present position by being rolled over, using a team of horses.

The Grand Menhir is located on a small peninsula that juts out into the Baie de Quiberon at a ground elevation of 13 m. It is surrounded by water on all except the north side, and it is superbly sited for use as a universal foresight. To get the maximum value from the menhir, there should be clear sightlines in the eight

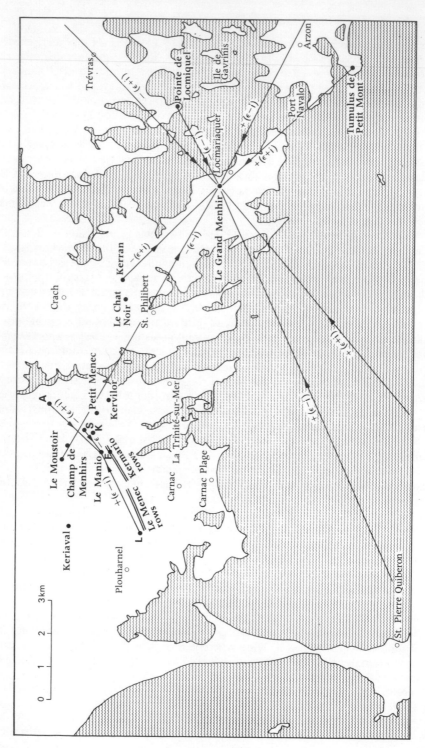

FIG. 8.1 Lunar observatories near Carnac

different directions, for moonrise and moonset, with high and low declinations at the major and minor standstills, as in Figure 1.3. The lines should be several kilometres long, so that accurate observations can be made, yet not so distant that the menhir has to be made impossibly large to project above the natural horizon when viewed from any direction. The first tasks undertaken by Professor Thom, in his study of the area, were to verify that clear sightlines did exist in the eight significant directions and to locate possible positions for the backsights.

Six of the eight sightlines view the Grand Menhir from the far side of a stretch of water, and two, to the north-west, across the land (Fig. 8.1). Thom and his colleagues made accurate profiles of these lines and established that there were places along the lines where the intervening ground was not high enough to obscure the Grand Menhir when it was upright. The profiles also showed where to look on the ground for backsights which would allow the menhir to be seen silhouetted against a sky horizon.

The results of their investigations are shown in Table 8.1. Along five of the lines they discovered no megalithic remains which could be interpreted as possible backsights. The other three azimuths produced more than one possibility, since the lines passed close to several groups of stones. For the $-(\varepsilon - i)$ moonrise there are potential backsights at three different distances, though of these the most likely one is the nearest to the Grand Menhir. From the two further suggested positions, only the very tip of the menhir would be visible, because of a small patch of elevated ground along the sight path.

The backsights at Kervilor and Kerran are small and unimpressive. For this reason little importance has been attached to them and the stones at Kervilor have been affected by recent building works. However, large stones are not required for the backsights; their purpose is to show the users where to position themselves for the nightly observations, and they need not be seen from a great distance. We must not assume that because they were important locations, they were necessarily marked by large stones.

The last column gives the 'expected' declination for the sightline, that is the calculated value of the declination of the moon when it was rising on the indicated line, using a value for the angle of the ecliptic appropriate to 1700 BC. On the whole there is substantial agreement between these values and the measured ones. Professor Thom has established a strong case that the Grand Menhir was ideally positioned for a universal lunar foresight, and he has demonstrated that it could have been seen from several important directions corresponding to declinations of the moon at the major and minor standstills. His interpretation provides a logical explanation for the existence, location, and size of the largest of all megaliths.

Nevertheless, his approach has been questioned by some scientists and archaeologists, including C. J. Butler and J. Patrick, who subjected his work to an intense critical analysis. They pointed out that the area around the Grand Menhir is particularly rich in remains from the megalithic period, and suspicious stones would probably be found on any line drawn from the menhir. There are eight basic azimuths, but by allowing lines with and without the moon's semi-diameter, s, and the minor perturbation, Δ, the Thoms are widening the choice to include far more possibilities. Butler and Patrick would have liked the suggestions for backsights to have been accompanied by a comment on the

Sightline	Possible backsight	Distance (km)	4G (m)	Declination corresponding to azimuth of sightline	'Expected' declination
$+(\varepsilon+i)$ moonrise	(a) Quiberon: menhir called Goulvarh	15·5	453	$+28·33°$	$+(\varepsilon+i-s-\Delta)=+28·63°$
	(b) Quiberon: stone near Goulvarh	15·5	453	$+28·72°$	$+(\varepsilon+i-s)=+28·78°$
$+(\varepsilon-i)$ moonrise	Not located: expected to be about 1 km south of St Pierre-Quiberon	about 15	228	—	—
$-(\varepsilon-i)$ moonrise	(a) Le Moustoir: menhir on top of tumulus	9·4	139	$-18·55°$	$-(\varepsilon-i-s)=-18·50°$
	(b) Le Moustoir: menhir near tumulus	9·4	139	$-18·30°$	$-(\varepsilon-i-s-\Delta)=-18·35°$
	(c) Champ de Menhirs	8·9	130	$-18·75°$	$-(\varepsilon-i)=-18·75°$
	(d) Kervilor: stone slab	7·45	115	$-18·46°$	$-(\varepsilon-i-s)=-18·50°$
$-(\varepsilon+i)$ moonrise	(a) Kerran: menhir near Le Chat Noir	4·1	124	$-28·77°$	$-(\varepsilon+i-s)=-28·78°$
	(b) Kerran: dolmen	4·1	124	$-28·90°$	$-(\varepsilon+i-s+\Delta)=-28·92°$
$+(\varepsilon+i)$ moonset	Not located: expected to be near Trévras	about 4½	about 130	—	—
$+(\varepsilon-i)$ moonset	Not located: expected to be near Pointe de Locmiquel	about 2½	about 40	—	—
$-(\varepsilon-i)$ moonset	Not located: expected to be near Arzon	about 5	about 80	—	—
$-(\varepsilon+i)$ moonset	Not located: expected to be near the Tumulus de Petit Mont	about 5½	about 160	—	—

Table 8.1   Possible lunar backsights for use with the Grand Menhir

statistical significance of the results. Although we have just stated that large stones are not essential for backsights, the inclusion of small stones increases the probability of adventitiously finding one in the right position. More recently, P. R. Freeman, a statistician who examined the evidence for the megalithic yard, has come to the conclusion that these sightlines could indeed have come about by chance.

Just over 1 km to the east of the east end of the stone rows at Kermario, there is a small group of about 100 stones in several irregular lines, known as Le Petit Menec (Fig. 8.2). Professor Thom considers these stones to be the remains of a stone fan, similar to the ones found in Caithness. By his interpretation the sector has a length of 92 m, a base 46 m and radius about 180 m. Now Le Petit Menec is quite close to the supposed backsights at Kervilor, and if it is associated with the alignment to the Grand Menhir, we would expect to find the radius of the sector to be equal to the characteristic distance for that alignment. However, 4G for Kervilor is only 115 m, and although satisfactory extrapolation does not require a precise radius, the difference between 115 m and 180 m is too large for it to be usable. Thom suggests it might have been constructed for use with a backsight at Le Moustoir, where 4G is 139 m, but even so the discrepancy is un-

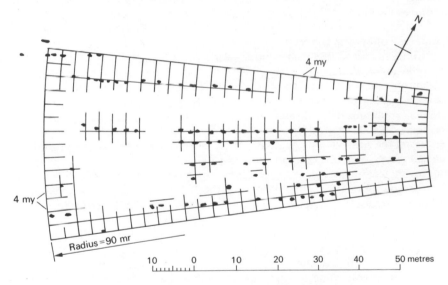

FIG. 8.2   The stone rows of Le Petit Menec

After Thom, showing his interpretation of the site as an extrapolation sector. Based on a diagram in the *Journal for the History of Astronomy*, **2**, by kind permission of Dr M. A. Hoskin.

comfortably large. Perhaps the explanation is that the line of nightly stakes or markers was not perpendicular to the alignment. If the two lines had been at an angle of about 50°, the stone fan would have sufficed well for Kervilor.

Le Petit Menec is a doubtful extrapolation sector for other reasons. It is far longer than is necessary, because we know that the sector need be only a distance

G in length, and the length of Le Petit Menec is half its radius. Furthermore this idea, too, has been dissected by Butler and Patrick, who are sceptical of Thom's interpretation of the stones as any sort of sector. They fitted a different set of lines to Thom's plan and claim that their eight lines make a better match than his fifteen. The Butler and Patrick lines do not fan out from a single point and their arrangement has no overall pattern. The disagreement between the two interpretations is being thrashed out on a statistical level, but it is not likely to be resolved unless the site is excavated, using modern techniques, and the holes of the missing stones are accurately located.

There is another group of stones which might have been a fan on the beach at St Pierre, near where we should expect to find the backsight for the $+(\varepsilon-i)$ alignment. This has far fewer remaining stones, less than twenty-five, and they cover an area only 30 m wide by 55 m long. The radius of the stone rows appears to be about 215 m, and this would agree very well with 225 m, the calculated radius of a stone fan for the St Pierre alignment. On the other hand, when the Revd W. C. Lukis visited this site in 1868, he recorded that the lines of stones could be traced out to sea when the tide was low for a distance of 193 m, and this would make the sector radius much larger than the required distance of 225 m.

Other small sets of alignments in the area include those at Kerlescan, a few hundred metres east of the east end of the Kermario rows, and at Keriaval, which is about $2\frac{1}{2}$ km north-west of the rows at Carnac. Whilst these sets may have some astronomical connections, they do not seem to be associated with the sightlines incorporating the Grand Menhir.

The great alignments of Kermario and Le Menec have received a lot of attention and have been surveyed by Professor Thom and his colleagues in several expeditions since 1970. We should not underestimate or undervalue the immense amount of work that has gone into producing accurate plans of these remains. In spite of the difficulties of the terrain and the size of the sites, the team surveyed the rows with meticulous attention to detail, checking their results with closed traverses accurate to one part in 1500. Without much more sophisticated surveying techniques (for example, laser ranging) it would be difficult to improve on the quality of their work. Whatever the historical outcome of research into archaeo-astronomy, archaeologists have reason to be grateful for Thom's thorough work and high standards of measurement.

Superficially the two sets of alignments are remarkably similar. They both consist of several nearly parallel rows of stones set up in the general direction of west-south-west to east-north-east. Both sets of rows are about 1 km long, and have their largest stones at the western ends, where huge rocks 4 m high and 50 tonnes in weight are not uncommon. In the centre sections of the rows the stones are much smaller, some no more than half a metre, and they are chosen so that there is a gradual decline in the sizes of the stones towards the east. Near the eastern ends of the rows the stones are larger again, though not as big as at the western ends. The rows are not straight, and both sets have distinct bends about half way along. The individual lines of stones wander about their mean positions, and some stones are even found between the lines.

Unfortunately both the Le Menec and Kermario alignments have been seriously disturbed in the past. Two hundred years ago hardly any of the stones were erect and the present appearance of the alignments owes nearly as much to the efforts of Le Rouzic and his gangs of French labourers as it does to the original builders. Le Rouzic marked stones that he had re-erected with a plug of red cement, but earlier restorers did not do this and it is impossible to be sure now that any stone is exactly in its true position. Most stones, in any case, have a red plug, and although Le Rouzic tried to set them up in their sockets, he was not always successful. The destruction and alteration of the alignments has made it difficult to deduce their initial geometry with certainty, but enough still exists to show that the layouts were quite complicated and incorporated geometric subtleties in keeping with the practices of the Early Bronze Age.

The geometry of the alignments at Le Menec is shown in Figure 8.3. There are twelve rows, in two distinct sections with a bend about half way along. The western section, which has the largest stones, is the more complete. The eastern section has been very severely robbed over part of its length, possibly because the stones were smaller and more easily moved but also because it passes over more fertile ground and there was a stronger incentive to clear it for agriculture. At the eastern end over a hundred stones still remain, though not all in their original positions.

The rows converge from west to east, so that the total width of the system is 101·3 m at the western end, 91·3 m at the knee, and 63·9 m at the eastern end. The rows are not equally spaced, Rows I, II, and III being closer together than average, as also are Rows X, XI, and XII. The change of direction at the knee has been achieved in a most curious way, since it does not take place, as we might expect, on a perpendicular line across the rows. Close examination shows that the builders made use of two near-Pythagorean triangles with a common hypotenuse (Fig. 8.3). They are a 4,8,9 triangle ($4^2 + 8^2 = 80$) and a 5,7½,9 triangle ($5^2 + 7\frac{1}{2}^2 = 81\frac{1}{4}$), arranged so that the total width of the rows shrinks across the bend in the ratio $8:7\frac{1}{2}$.

At the western end of the rows we find the last stones lie on a line at an angle of about 30° to the perpendicular to the rows. This arrangement makes Rows I to VII all the same length from the end to the knee, 456·6 m, and Rows VIII to XII would also be this length if it were not for the presence of a stone ring. The stones at the ends of the Menec alignments have been carelessly re-erected and many have been removed, but sufficient still remain to show that both ends were terminated with egg-shapes based on 3,4,5 triangles, a Type I egg at the western end and a Type II egg at the other. The existence of these two shapes in Brittany is rather surprising, for it implies closer links with the builders of the stone rings in the British Isles than might have been expected from the other remains of the period. However, they differ from the usual style of the British stone rings in the same way as the circles of Er Lannec: the stones were not spaced apart, but were flat slabs set together to make a crude wall. Even now, part of the western egg is used as a boundary wall, for a house at Le Menec was built inside it. Originally a farm, its present owners tend to the needs of the many tourists by selling picture postcards, soft drinks, and pancakes.

The two eggs are set opposite ways round with respect to the rows, i.e. the thin end of the eastern egg is near Row I and the thin end of the other one is near Row XII. The centres of the eggs are carefully related to the rows, because if Row IX were extended at each end, it would pass precisely the same distance, 2·1 m, from the centres of both eggs.

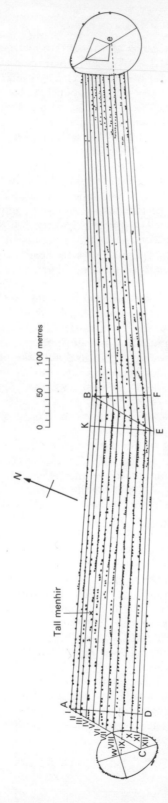

Triangle KBE has sides in the ratio 4,8,9 and triangle BEF has sides in the ratio 5,7½,9.

Triangle KBE has sides in the ratio 4,8,9 and triangle BEF has sides in the ratio 5,7½,9. In triangle ACD, AD = 2CD. Based on a diagram in the *Journal for the History of Astronomy*, **3**, by kind permission of Dr M. A. Hoskin

Fig. 8.3   The geometry of the stone rows at Le Menec

Much of Professor Thom's paper on the Carnac alignments is devoted to a statistical examination of the unit of length used in the construction of the rows. He concludes that they were based on a megalithic yard of length 0.8293 ± 0.0004 m which is exceedingly close to the yard he claims to have found at the stone circle sites in Scotland. In megalithic yards and megalithic rods (1 MR $= 2\frac{1}{2}$ MY) many of the dimensions given above in metres become round numbers. For example, the triangles inside the eggs have sides of 12, 16, and 20 MR, the perimeters of the eggs are 121.76 (an attempt at 122.0 ?) and 148.0 MR, and Row IX extended would pass just 1 MR from the centres of the two eggs. Thom's plans show the spacings between the stone rows as integral multiples of megalithic yards, at both ends and at the knee. These results are very impressive.

With rows as disturbed as the alignments at Le Menec, stastistical analysis is essential for recovering the unit of length (if any) used by the builders when setting out the stones along the rows. Professor Thom deduces that the spacing between the stones was exactly one megalithic rod and that this spacing was maintained all the way to the eastern end, more than one kilometre away. The stones were apparently laid out beginning on the slanting line at the western end, and the angle of this line was deliberately chosen to make the triangle at the end of the rows have a base equal to half its height (Fig. 8.3). A result of this is that the stones in any particular row are displaced relative to the stones in the adjacent rows by an amount equal to half the row separation.

These results have not been accepted by statisticians, for the reasons given in Chapter 3. Professor Thom assumes that a unit of length is present in the rows and that it is approximately 2.1 m; he then finds its precise value from the data given by the positions of the stones. He does not use the more searching statistical test which makes no assumptions about the existence of a unit but allows one to try a large number of possibilities and calculate their probabilities. On the latter test several other equally likely values are found for the unit of distance, and they are not the same from row to row. Thom's counter to this approach is that his work at other sites has shown that megalithic rods and yards were extensively used, therefore it is inherently more likely to be a unit of this approximate length than any arbitrary one, and so his statistical method is justified in the circumstances.

However, there is one mathematical peculiarity of the western section of the rows at Le Menec which does not depend on the unit of measurement. We know that the rows converge from west to east; if we take Row I as the baseline, it is obvious from even a casual glance at the plan that the larger the row number, the greater must be the distance it has converged towards Row I. We can find the convergence by measuring from Row I the perpendicular distances of each row at the west end and again at the knee of the alignments, and by subtracting one from the other. The actual distances (in metres) are set out in columns headed x_w and x_c in Table 8.2. The convergence (called z in the table) is the difference between x_w and x_c.

The interesting aspect of these numbers is that the convergence does not increase proportionately to the row number, as would be the case if each row got closer to its neighbour by the same amount. Instead the convergence increases by a parabolic law. This can be seen by comparing the numbers in the fourth and fifth columns of Table 8.2. The fourth column is the actual convergence of the rows and the fifth column is a calculated parabola whose constant of proportion-

Row number	Perpendicular distance of the row from Row I (metres)		Convergence (metres) $z = x_w - x_c$	Calculated value for z, assuming a perfect parabola
	At the west end x_w	At the knee x_c		
I	0	0	0	0
II	6·6	6·6	0	0·04
III	13·3	13·3	0	0·17
IV	21·6	21·6	0	0·50
V	31·5	30·7	0·8	1·00
VI	41·5	39·8	1·7	1·74
VII	51·5	49·0	2·5	2·74
VIII	63·1	59·0	4·1	4·07
IX	74·7	68·9	5·8	5·73
X	86·3	78·8	7·5	7·64
XI	94·6	85·5	9·1	9·13
XII	101·3	91·3	10·0	10·46

Table 8.2   The convergence of the western section of the Le Menec stone rows

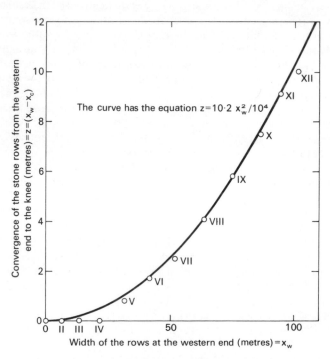

FIG. 8.4   The parabolic relationship built into the stone rows at Le Menec

ality has been chosen to make the best fit. We can see graphically how well the calculated numbers match the measured distance from Figure 8.4. The small circles represent the amounts of convergence for the individual rows and the curve is a plot of the numbers in the last column of the table. It has the equation $z = 10.2\, x_w^2/10^4$. The agreement is quite remarkable and inevitably gives rise to several questions. We are bound to wonder whether this is a chance result, or if it is intentional on the part of the builders of the rows. If it was intentional, why did they do it? Is there any significance in the value of the constant $10.2/10^4$?

Professor Thom has proposed that hidden in this unexpected property of the stone rows there may be clues to a method of extrapolation, based on three successive nights' viewing instead of the more usual two. I pointed out at the beginning of Chapter 7 that if stakes were planted to record the observing positions on three successive nights near the declination maximum, there was a simple relationship between their positions—the second night's stake is always a distance 4G from a point mid-way between the positions of the first and third stakes. We shall call the separation of the first and third stakes $2q$. The distance that has to be extrapolated from the second night's stake to give the maximum declination for the month has the symbol η' (eta dash) (Fig. 8.5). It can be found

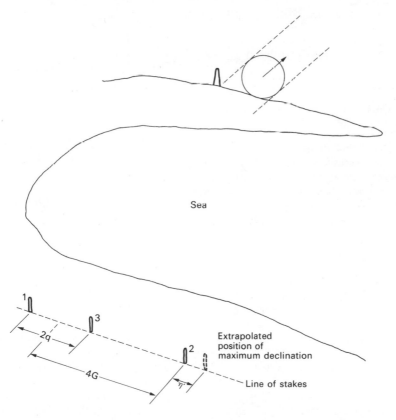

FIG. 8.5   Extrapolation from observations on three nights

quite simply from q, by the equation $\eta' = q^2/16G$. The proof of this will be found in Appendix A. The reader will notice how similar this is to the equation for extrapolation used in the case of two nights' viewing, $\eta = p^2/4G$.

If the users of the lunar sightlines to the Grand Menhir had attempted accurate observations of the positions of the moonset, as we think they did, they would have discovered the need for some method of extrapolation as inevitably as did the Early Bronze Age tribesmen in Scotland. Progress towards a practical solution to the extrapolation problem would have been empirical and slow as elsewhere, but it need not have led to exactly the same method. Extrapolation from three nights' observations is quite as feasible as extrapolation from two nights'. If they did it this way, we might expect to discover, somewhere near the sightlines, an arrangement of stones which could have been used for finding η' from a knowledge of q. To test for this we have to know the numerical quantities connecting η' and q in the relation $\eta' = q^2/16G$.

Table 8.3 gives the values of η' in terms of q for four of the alignments (all moonrises) listed in Table 8.1.

Sightline	Backsight	η' (metres)	4G (metres)	G (metres)
$-(\varepsilon-i)$	Kervilor	$21{\cdot}7q^2/10^4$	115	29
$-(\varepsilon+i)$	Kerran	$20{\cdot}2q^2/10^4$	124	31
$+(\varepsilon-i)$	St Pierre	$10{\cdot}9q^2/10^4$	228	57
$+(\varepsilon+i)$	Quiberon	$5{\cdot}5q^2/10^4$	453	112

Table 8.3   Values of η' for four lunar alignments to the Grand Menhir

Notice that the constant in the column headed η' for St Pierre is $10{\cdot}9/10^4$. This is very near to the constant built into the Le Menec rows, $10{\cdot}2/10^4$. It immediately suggests a close connection with the alignment and also a practical method of extrapolation, because the amount of convergence of the rows is exactly the distance needed for extrapolation at St Pierre. The Carnac astronomers could have extrapolated from the position of the second night's stake by the following procedure:

(a) Measure the distance between the stakes set up on the first and third nights with a rope.

(b) Take the rope to Le Menec, fold it in two, place one end at the corner A in Figure 8.3, and then note which row the other end reaches.

(c) Go to the knee of the alignments, and again place the folded rope across the rows, with one end on Row I. Put a tag on the rope where it crosses the same row that the end of the rope previously reached (estimating fractions of the row spacing where necessary).

(d) The extrapolation distance is given by the length from the tag to the far end of the folded rope.

This sounds very easy, but there are some snags. The most serious is that the rows, in spite of their size, are not wide enough to cope with the full range of q that will be needed in practice. The largest value of q ever measured will be 4G, which in the case of St Pierre is 228 m. The maximum width of the rows is only about half this, 103 m. Similarly the maximum amount requiring to be extrapolated is G, which is 57 m at St Pierre; by this method the alignments can give only up to 10 m.

But perhaps the alignments were primarily designed to be used with one of the other sightlines. The width of the rows is not far short of the maximum value of q for Kervilor, and Thom has suggested they could have been used with this alignment, in spite of the fact that the distance to be extrapolated could sometimes be three times the convergence of the rows. His idea is that q was laid off as measured, but the convergence was multiplied by $2\frac{1}{2}$ to get the final extrapolation distance. In other words, they measured the convergence in megalithic yards and then extrapolated that number of megalithic rods. The method will work for Kervilor (though it gives extrapolations which are about 18 per cent too large) and, by varying the fractions of q laid off across the rows, it can be adapted to other alignments as well. For example, to extrapolate for St Pierre, $\frac{1}{2}q$ should be set out perpendicular to the rows (i.e. the rope has to be folded twice) and the extrapolation distance is then given by five times the measured convergence (by extrapolating twice the number of megalithic rods as the measured convergence in megalithic yards). The rows can be used for the Quiberon alignment in exactly the same way, but this time laying off $\frac{1}{4}q$ and multiplying the convergence by 10. The reason the rows are so adaptable is found in Table 8.3: the ratios of 4G for the four alignments are within 10 per cent of 1:1:2:4. Were the locations of the backsights selected so that the Le Menec rows could be used as a universal extrapolator?

In this book so far, when extrapolation has been discussed, it has been assumed that the characteristic distance 4G was always constant for a particular alignment. Bronze Age observers who used the two-nights' method of finding the maximum declination for the month probably thought this was the case, but those observers who regularly used three nights' observations of the moonrise or moonset would sooner or later have found this was not true. It is easier to discover this with three nights' observations, because every month there is a new opportunity to find 4G.

This change in the characteristic distance is a direct consequence of the ellipticity of the moon's orbit. In Chapter 6 I mentioned that the distance of the moon from the earth went from a maximum to a minimum every month, in the context of its effect on the lunar parallax. The variation in moon's distance also causes its apparent diameter to change by ± 5 per cent from the mean, and for 4G to change by ± 22 per cent. At Kervilor the average value of 4G is 115 m, but it can be anything from 94 m to 140 m. For comparison, the ground equivalent of the lunar diameter (L), which is found by making two simultaneous observations of moonrise at Kervilor, with the upper and lower edges of the disc in line with a distant foresight, has an average value of 111 m and can vary from 102 m to 114 m.

From the known relationship connecting the extrapolation distance η', the characteristic distance 4G, and the separation of the stakes $2q$, summarized in the equation $\eta' = q^2/16G$, it follows that, for a particular value of q, when G is larger than average, η' is smaller. If the method of extrapolation is designed for an average value of 4G, it will make η' too big when 4G is above average and too small when 4G is below average. Unlikely as it may seem, the layout of the Le Menec stone rows makes it possible to adjust the extrapolation distance for variations in the value of 4G. The method makes use of the slanting ends of the western section. In effect it reduces the distance q when 4G is large by laying it off at an angle to the rows instead of perpendicularly.

The astronomers at Kervilor would have noticed that 4G and the ground equivalent of the lunar diameter increased and decreased together, and Professor Thom thinks they took the mean of the two, $\frac{1}{2}(4G+L)$, and used it for the basis of their improved method of extrapolation. The suggested procedure was to take a rope of length $\frac{1}{2}(4G+L)$, put one end of it at A on Figure 8.6, and swing the other end round until it lay on the line CD. Where it met CD, say at H, gave them the line AH along which q had to be laid off. They then followed the simpler method of extrapolation given above. If AP is the distance q, the point P designates the row whose convergence determines the extrapolation. This modification of the procedure clearly leads to a smaller value of convergence than if q had been laid off along AD. In fact it explains why there was an error of 18 per cent in η' when 4G had its average value and q was laid out perpendicularly to Row I.

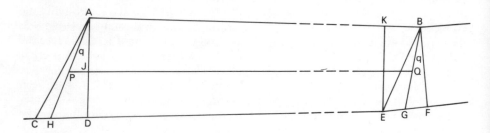

FIG. 8.6   A modified method of extrapolation at Le Menec

This procedure has no theoretical justification, and its plausibility rests in part on the fact that AD is close to the minimum value of $\frac{1}{2}(4G+L)$ and AC is near its maximum. If it was used in the Early Bronze Age, it was no more than an empirical and approximate solution that could only have been devised by many years of trial and error. Thom shows in a fairly lengthy mathematical analysis in one of his papers that using the slanting end of the rows leads to an improvement in the accuracy of extrapolation, reducing the errors from about 25 per cent at the worst to about 10 per cent.

The sightlines from Kervilor and St Pierre are both for moonrises at the minor standstill and the extrapolation makes use of the triangle at the western end of the rows. Kerran and Quiberon are major standstill sightlines and the western triangle is not in the right proportions; instead they would have had to use the triangle BFE at the knee of the alignments (Fig. 8.6). The way to extrapolate is just the same in principle. A rope of length $\frac{1}{2}(4G+L)$ is laid across the rows with one end at B and the rope is swung round until its other end G lies on the line EF. The direction BG is the line along which q has to be set off. The length of rope q indicates the stone row whose convergence gives the amount of extrapolation.

This interpretation of the stone rows at Le Menec accounts for many of the features of the site. It provides explanations for the parabolic law built into the western section of the rows, for the slanting end, and for the change of direction in the middle. The widths of the rows at the end and at the knee, AD, AC, BF, and BE, also fit into the picture. These are positive results, but notice that some of the most striking features of the rows are not included at all. Why are the rows so long? If their only function was to preserve the parabolic law in a permanent form on the ground, they could have been quite short. There is no need to go to the trouble of erecting this vast number of huge stones in order to make slowly convergent rows; the whole arrangement would have been more convenient if the rows had converged quicker. We must not forget also that no explanation has been put forward for the eastern section of the rows beyond the knee. And were the eggs at the ends part of the system, or simply ritual enclosures for the magical ceremonies which almost certainly would have accompanied the laying out of the ropes?

But perhaps the length of the rows was important and we have not yet recognized why. (It is worth noting that from the west end to the knee is 456 m, and this is only 3 m different from the value of 4G for Quiberon.) Possibly the method of extrapolation proposed by Professor Thom is right in some respects but wrong in others—he himself has doubts about some aspects of it. Maybe one of the readers of this book will be able to see a way of using the Carnac rows which accounts more completely for the arrangement of stones than any that has been suggested so far.

The least satisfactory aspect of the interpretation of the rows is undoubtedly the need to change from units of megalithic yard to megalithic rod to get the final value of the extrapolation distance. It is the only method of extrapolation so far proposed which requires the distance to be laid off in a particular unit of length. With other methods of extrapolation, such as those described in Chapter 7, it is possible to separate clearly the arguments for and against the megalithic yard from those relating to the astronomical function. Not so at Le Menec: we cannot accept this interpretation of the use of the rows without first being convinced that megalithic units of length were fundamental to their construction. Since the evidence for the existence of the megalithic rods and yards at Carnac has been doubted by professional statisticians, we have to reserve judgement for the time being. The stone rows of Carnac have not yet lost all their mystery.

There is a gap of only about 1 km between the two great alignments of Le Menec and Kermario. When you travel eastwards from Le Menec towards Kerlescan, the huge stones at the west end of Kermario suddenly appear at a sharp bend in the road. There is no sign here of any stone circle or enclosure; the area immediately west of the rows has been set aside as a car park, and if any stones existed there once, they have all been cleared away. Although the Kermario and Le Menec alignments look alike to the casual tourist, there are many differences in the details of their layouts.

The Kermario alignments were surveyed in 1972 and 1973 by a team of workers under Professor Thom. As always, they took the utmost care to ensure

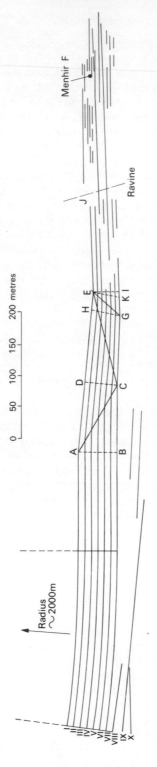

Fig. 8.7 The geometry of the Kermario alignments

Based on a diagram in the *Journal for the History of Astronomy*, **5**, by kind permission of Dr M. A. Hoskin.

the accuracy of the results, by duplicating traverses and by carefully checking every stage in the operation. There are special problems for archaeological field work at Kermario. Apart from the gorse, which is very thick in places, the stone rows cross a flooded ravine near their east end and disappear for nearly a hundred metres. Further east still, the rows become very fragmented and eventually peter out, so that the exact position of the far end of the alignments is open to question.

In their interpretation, the Thoms divided the rows into several distinct sectors (Fig. 8.7). Starting at the west end, the first sector is well defined. There are seven rows of stones, parallel but not straight; for 260 m they form arcs of a huge circle of radius about 2,000 m. The rows then become straight for about another 200 m, with the same separation, 10 m, as they have at the western end of the alignments. After this there is a series of complicated changes of direction in a number of short sections. The first takes place along the line AC of Figure 8.7, with a directional change of 5·3°. The builders used the same geometrical trick for changing direction as we have seen in the Le Menec rows. They set out two near-Pythagorean triangles with a common hypotenuse. In the figure the triangles are ABC and ADC and AC is the hypotenuse. The sides AB, BC, DC, and DA are in the ratios 12, 21, 10, and 22. The two triangles fit together well because $12^2+21^2 = 585$ and $10^2+22^2 = 584$.

The new alignment is retained for only a short distance and the rows change by 3·0° in the opposite direction along the line CE. Once more two near-Pythagorean triangles are involved, DCE and ECK, with DC, DE, EK, and KC in the ratios 10, 28, $8\frac{1}{2}$, and $28\frac{1}{2}$. This time we have $10^2+28^2 = 884$ and $8\frac{1}{2}^2+28\frac{1}{2}^2 = 884\frac{1}{2}$. The new section is very short indeed and the third change of direction, of 3·6°, occurs along the line EG. The two associated triangles are EHG and EGI, and their sides HG, HE, EI, and GI are in the ratios $8\frac{1}{2}$, $7\frac{1}{2}$, 8, and 8. The sums of the squares are $8\frac{1}{2}^2+7\frac{1}{2}^2 = 128\frac{1}{2}$ and $8^2+8^2 = 128$.

To the east of this last realignment the rows continue, with a break at the ravine, for about another 450 m, gradually becoming more and more indistinct and confused. East of the ravine there are indications of two row systems on slightly different alignments. Some of the rows are parallel to the section immediately west of the line AC, others are continuations of the lines in section EJ. This part of the Kermario alignments overlies a neolithic long barrow, which seems to have had associated with it a large menhir, F. The barrow was totally excavated in 1922, and no doubt this contributes to the general confusion of the eastern end of the alignments. Further east still, 600 m from E, there is another large menhir, which may mark the true end of the system, for it lies on the line of Row III of section EJ.

There are other rows, or fragments of rows, at the west end which do not fit into the overall pattern: Rows VIII, IX, and X on Figure 8.7. However, the survey showed that Row IX is parallel to the rows in section AH and Row X is actually a prolongation of Row VII in section EJ. Row VIII does not appear to have geometrical links with any other part of the Kermario alignments, but there is a possibility that the stones were moved during road widening.

There is one very curious result of the method used by the constructors of the alignments for changing the directions of the rows. The perpendicular distances across the alignments, at AB, DC, HG, and EI, are all in simple ratios, 12, 10, $8\frac{1}{2}$, and 8. Now the spacing of the rows at the west end is in fact 12 MY,

and therefore the directional changes are such that the row-spacing reduces in
steps from 12 to 10 to 8½ to 8 MY as one goes along the rows from west to east.
The total change of direction of the rows is only 1·3°, and if the builders' intention
was to reduce the spacing to two-thirds of its original distance, and simultaneously to have spacings which were easy measurements in megalithic yards and
avoid gross changes in the mean direction of the rows, they succeeded very well.
But there is no explanation as yet for the geometry of the Kermario alignments.
They are waiting for some scientist or archaeologist to provide the flash of
inspiration which will enable us to see the purpose of their underlying design.
Without the accurate surveys of Professor Thom and his colleagues, that day
would be a very long way ahead.

Whilst the Grand Menhir is the focal point of one lunar observatory in the
Carnac area, the menhir at Le Manio is the other. It is a tall, shapely stone,
standing nearly 6 m high, and if it were not for the other spectacular remains in
the area, it would be more famous than it is. Like many of the other megaliths,
it was re-erected by Le Rouzic, but there is no reason to suppose it was moved a
significant distance at the time. It stands near the summit of the highest hill in
the district, with an elevation of just over 25 m. The area is now densely wooded
and the menhir is not easy to locate without a large-scale map. Fifty metres to
the north and on the very top of the hill is a curious sub-rectangular enclosure.
It is believed to have been covered originally with a mound of earth, and if so
would be the kerbing of a neolithic long barrow.

The Thoms have identified several possible backsights for use with Le Manio
(Fig. 8.1). They searched the area thoroughly to locate all the prominent standing
stones. Ascertaining whether Le Manio was visible from each of these stones was

Letter assigned by Thom	Description	Distance from Le Manio (m)	Azimuth from Le Manio	Purpose
S	Menhir 3 m high	808	233·70°	Backsight for midwinter sunset
K	Menhir 3½ m high	380	246·62°	Backsight for sunset at Candlemas and Martinmas
F	Large menhir in the Kermario rows	about 250	180·00°	Meridian marker
A	Small stone	2,144	222·65°	Backsight for moonrise at the major standstill
L	Menhir 3 m high	2,652	62·32°	Backsight for moonrise at the minor standstill

Table 8.4

difficult, owing to the thick trees and scrub, but the final result was a short list of ten stones astronomically associated with Le Manio. The Thoms consider the purposes of five of these stones to be reasonably certain, though not all are lunar backsights (Table 8.4).

The sightline from the menhir L deserves special comment. Although the menhir at Le Manio would have been quite visible from L, accurate calculation shows that if Le Manio had been used as the lunar foresight it would have been inaccurate by almost a degree. But viewing from L, the moon would have appeared to rise directly over the long barrow at the minor standstill. Sighting on the north wall of the rectangular enclosure would have given a very accurate indication of the $+(\varepsilon-i)$ moonrise. It is interesting to note that the wall itself is orientated towards L, with an accuracy of $\frac{1}{4}°$, showing that the long barrow was seen exactly end on by the men watching the moonrise.

If the 'enclosure' was the kerb of a long barrow and the barrow's orientation was intentional, it implies that the sightline to the barrow was the beginning of the lunar observatories in the Carnac region. The menhir of Le Manio, sited less ideally off the summit of the hill, would have been erected later, and may have been the focus of observations during a second stage of the development of the observatories. Ultimately it would have been recognized that better accuracy of observation came with longer sightlines, and the consequence of this discovery could have been the construction of the large observatory centred on the Grand Menhir some time after 2000 BC. This sequence of events is plausible though as yet quite speculative. Much—very much—research remains to be done before we can write a comprehensive account of the Neolithic and Early Bronze Age monuments of southern Brittany.

9 Return to Stonehenge

No monument in the British Isles is as important to the study of prehistoric astronomy as Stonehenge. I began this book with a short description of its main features and an account of some of the theories about its astronomical function which have been advanced from time to time. This approach was intended to illustrate the development of ideas in archaeo-astronomy rather than to throw light on Stonehenge itself. There is much more to Stonehenge than has been touched on in Chapter 1. Considering that this is the most significant of all the British prehistoric solar and lunar observatories, it is necessary now to look in rather more detail at its layout and its alignments.

Stonehenge is unique in many respects. Not only is it very much more complex than any other site of the Late Neolithic and Early Bronze Ages, but also, owing to the many excavations that have taken place over the years, we have learned most about its long timespan of modification, change, and development. This complicates the astronomical interpretation as much as it does the archaeological one. Whilst it is reasonably certain that Stonehenge was some sort of astronomical observatory during part of its period of use, we should not assume that it was always used primarily for astronomical purposes; in our own time churches have been converted into museums and country railway stations into private houses. In the thousand years of activity at Stonehenge peoples came and went. The customs of agriculture, housing, and toolmaking all evolved, and, from evidence at other sites, so did the techniques of astronomical observation. Stonehenge is not just one celestial observatory, but several on the same site, at some times intended for tracking the movements of the moon, at others for watching the sun and perhaps establishing a calendar. Stonehenge is complicated, but when we can unravel the astronomical features and put them firmly into their true archaeological context, it will give an unrivalled opportunity for studying the development of observational methods and assessing their impact on the cultures of southern Britain in the second and third millennia BC.

Professor Richard Atkinson's book on Stonehenge is recognized as the most authoritative on the subject. His excavations and research have contributed a great deal to our present knowledge of the monument, and his work should be read by anyone wishing to obtain a comprehensive and ordered account of Stonehenge and its environment, the techniques used in its construction, and the sequence of building. Atkinson's division of the periods of construction of Stonehenge into three main phases, I, II, and III (with III subdivided into IIIa, IIIb, and IIIc), is now universally followed and must be the framework of any serious study of the remains. If we are to make sense of the confusion of astronomical orientations and geometrical relationships which have at one time or another been 'discovered' at Stonehenge, we have to take them phase by phase, hoping to ensure that they are considered in context and that characteristics are not supposed to be related when they really have nothing to do with each other.

The phases proposed by Atkinson cover a span of 1,000 years or more, beginning several hundred years before the end of the Neolithic Period and continuing until the end of the Early Bronze Age, about 1600 BC. It is not possible to give an accurate starting date for Stonehenge, and though 2800 BC is the middle of the range of estimates, it could be several hundred years in error. With one amendment, namely that the Station Stones are put in Phase II for reasons which will be given later, Atkinson's phases are:

(*a*) Phase I: the ditch and banks, the Aubrey Holes, the causeway postholes, the Heel Stone, the postholes near the Heel Stone, the two stone holes in the entrance of the circular bank, and possibly a wooden structure near the centre of the circle (though there is no archaeological evidence for this). See Figures 1.1 and 9.1.

(*b*) Phase II: the Avenue, the Station Stones, the Heel Stone ditch, a double circle of 82 bluestones (with radii about 1 and 3 m less than the existing Sarsen Circle, and later dismantled), and possibly the two stone holes on the axis of the Avenue.

(*c*) Phase IIIa: the Sarsen Circle, the horseshoe of sarsen trilithons, the Slaughter Stone and its missing companion.

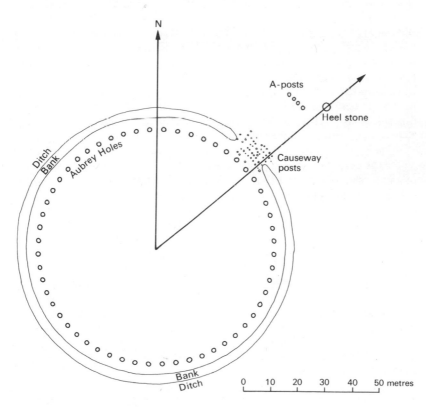

FIG. 9.1   Stonehenge I

(*d*) Phase IIIb: a setting of dressed bluestones (possibly erected inside the trilithon horseshoe and later dismantled) and the Y and Z holes.

(*e*) Phase IIIc: the existing setting of bluestones in the circle and the horseshoe.

In its first phase, during the Neolithic Period, Stonehenge looked very different from its appearance today. It began with nothing more than a simple bank and ditch, not unlike the small Class I henges which were fairly common in southern England. The only constructions there at that time, other than the ditch and banks, were sets of wooden posts. At this stage it was not aligned on the midsummer sunrise, for, as I have described in Chapter 6, the axis of the entrance was several degrees too far to the left. Instead it seems to have been in the right direction for observing the moon risings over half of the 18·6-year cycle. The causeway postholes (Fig. 6.1) may possibly be an incidental record of a series of systematic observations of the directions of rising of the midwinter full moon.

Twenty metres beyond the entrance are four large, evenly-spaced postholes, about 1 m diameter. There is no doubt that these belong to Phase I, because the most northerly hole was covered over when the Avenue was built in Phase II. Furthermore, a line drawn through the centre of these holes goes through the centre of the causeway. The most plausible explanation advanced so far is that they were permanent wooden markers, the A-posts, set up after the small posts in the causeway had done their work, to indicate the directions of moonrises at different times during its cycle of standstills. R. F. Brinckerhoff has pointed out that the moon's progress towards the major standstill could be followed by watching it rise through the gaps between the A-posts. When the moon rose between the two right-hand posts, i.e. between A3 and A4, it was one-quarter of the way in time from the midpoint of the cycle to the major standstill. When it rose in the next gap, between A2 and A3, it was one third of the way, and when it rose directly behind A1 it was half-way. Even in this early phase of Stonehenge, there appear to have been all the essentials for a simple lunar observatory.

During this phase the accuracy of the observations could not have been high. The gaps between the A-posts extend over an angle of about 1° from the centre of the circle, and if the observers had tried to estimate the moon's position by eye, it is doubtful if they could have done better than 0·1°. Indeed, this standard of accuracy requires the observer's head to be always in the same position at the centre of the circle to within about 10 cm, and it could not have been done without some structure, such as a vertical slot, to look through. High accuracy measurements, as were required for observing the minor perturbation, would have been out of the question.

In passing we ought to remember that some low-accuracy alignments were probably essential to the successful operations of Stonehenge. Whilst fairly careful observations would have been needed to find the moon's place in its cycle, presumably at certain times astronomical events would have been marked with ceremonies and ritual. On these occasions many people would want to see the moon rise through the gap between the posts, and the easy way to arrange this was to have the posts wide enough apart.

In spite of their limitations, the sightlines to the A-posts would have sufficed for discovering the 18·6-year cycle and for identifying where the moon was in its cycle at any time. Whether the megalithic astronomers could have gone on from this and found, by trial and error, a set of rules for predicting lunar eclipses has been the subject of much speculation in recent years. Most of the hypotheses have centred on the Aubrey Holes, and have been suggested by the numerical coincidence that the number of Aubrey Holes is very nearly equal to the period in years of three cycles of lunar standstills. These theories were described, and commented on, in Chapter 4. One can only add that if the Aubrey Holes were really intended for eclipse prediction, it shows a degree of sophistication for the Late Neolithic Period that is not paralleled at other sites. Perhaps lunar observations led to the choice of the number of Aubrey Holes, but merely in order to preserve 56 as a ritualistically important number, without any concept of a circle of holes as a calculating device. The exact purpose of the Aubrey Holes will probably always remain a mystery.

Professor Atkinson, on archaeological evidence, assigns the Heel Stone to Phase I. It fits in best with the astronomical interpretation of Stonehenge if its erection date was later than that of the causeway posts. It is easy to see from the plan of the site that the horizon in the direction of the right-hand postholes would have been hidden by the Heel Stone, and this would have impaired positioning the posts at the times of the rising moon. Similarly, the stones which were originally in holes D and E would have to be later than both the causeway posts and the A-posts, for they are in the direct line of sight. This does not rule out the possibility that they were late Phase I substitutes for the A-posts, which would ultimately have rotted and have had to be replaced.

It is fairly certain that the Heel Stone was a lunar marker and not, as is popularly supposed, an indicator for the midsummer sunrise. Viewed from the centre of Stonehenge, the solstitial sun rises to the left of the Heel Stone even at the present day, and the further back in time, the further left it would have risen, because of the change in ecliptic angle. At the time of Stonehenge I, the sun would have been well clear of the horizon before it reached the azimuth of the Heel Stone. Atkinson has calculated that the Heel Stone will not be in the correct line for the midsummer sunrise until about AD 3260. Therefore the stone's original purpose must have been to mark the moonrise at the midpoint of the 18·6-year cycle. (Although the declination of the moon at this time is ε, the same as the midsummer sunrise, the moon rises a little to the right of the sun, because of parallax.)

The geometry of Phase I of Stonehenge is very simple. The bank and the ring of Aubrey Holes are both accurately circular and the circles have a common centre, though this is not the same centre as the one used for the later circles of standing stones. The radius of the Aubrey circle is 43·2 m and its circumference is 271·6 m. The radial accuracy of the holes (standard deviation) is 0·17 m and the circumferential accuracy is 0·43 m, equivalent to 0·57°. The average angular spacing between the holes is 6·429°. Newham noticed that the chord of the angle made by three Aubrey Holes (19·286°) is 0·335 times the radius of the circle, which is only about ½ per cent more than one third. This gave him an idea of how the Aubrey Holes might have been set out. His method, which can be simulated on paper with nothing more than a pair of compasses, is:

(a) Mark out a circle on the ground using a rope of length equal to the radius of the Aubrey circle.

(b) Fold the rope into three and cut another rope equal to one third the radius of the circle.

(c) Put a stake on the ground where one of the Aubrey Holes is required.

(d) Starting at the stake, go round the circle, putting in stakes at intervals of the rope's length.

(e) Continue for three revolutions of the circle, by which time 56 stakes will have been planted and you will have returned to the starting point.

In Newham's method, the angle advanced round the circle each time is 19·188°, and the small difference between this and the required angle of 19·286° gradually accumulates as more stakes are put in, causing irregularities in the spacings. The accuracy of the Aubrey Holes is rather better than could have been achieved using the method just described, but quite possibly this is how they did the initial layout, to be followed by a more accurate attempt with a slightly longer piece of rope.

Newham came to the conclusion that the length of the chord spanning three Aubrey Holes was a significant unit in the early phases of Stonehenge. He found several other distances were simple multiples of this length, 14·5 m, and he called it the lunar measure (LM). For example, the distance from the Heel Stone to the centre of the Aubrey circle is, within 1 per cent, equal to $5\frac{1}{2}$ LM. Now according to Professor Thom and his family, the circumference of the Aubrey circle, 271·6 m, was intended to be a whole number, 131, of megalithic rods. Since the chord and arc of 19·286° differ by only $\frac{1}{3}$ per cent, it follows that the lunar measure must be equal to $131 \times 3/56 = 7$ MR, very nearly.

Before we finally leave Stonehenge I, Professor Thom's alternative suggestion for the causeway postholes should be mentioned, though he did not put it forward very strongly. He proposed that they were part of an extrapolation sector, of the type found in Caithness. The postholes radiate out from the centre of Stonehenge, giving a sector radius of 57 m, and this therefore is the characteristic distance 4G. From this we can calculate the distance to the foresight, obtaining about 1·8 km, which is the distance to the horizon in the north-west. Whilst it is quite possible, and even likely, that distant foresights were used at Stonehenge, there would be a real difficulty in accepting that the technique of extrapolation had been developed here more than half a millennium before it appeared at other sites. Another objection, pointed out by Professor Atkinson, is that the holes are very irregularly spaced, and do not constitute a good enough sector for extrapolation measurements. Newham's proposal, that they were moonrise direction markers, is far more convincing.

The reconstruction which led to Stonehenge II probably began when the Beaker Folk arrived in southern Britain about 2400 BC. They realigned the monument, rotating its axis about 5° to the east, by lowering the bank and filling in the ditch on the east side of the causeway (Fig. 9.2). With a pair of parallel banks and ditches, they constructed the Avenue leading up to this new, wider entrance, and from now on the axis of Stonehenge, as indicated by the centre-line of the Avenue, was the midsummer sunrise. The Heel Stone was enclosed by the new Avenue, though not symmetrically. For some reason they dug a ditch round the Heel Stone and filled it in again a few weeks later with rammed chalk, as can be deduced from the absence of weathering on the sides of the trench.

The major work of this phase was quarrying, transporting, shaping, and erecting the double circle of bluestones from Preseli. The project was never completed, but the intention seems to have been to set up 38 pairs of stones, in

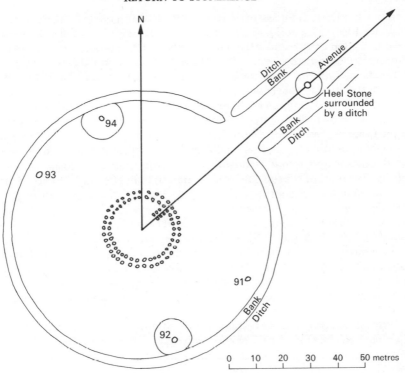

FIG. 9.2   Stonehenge II
The double circle of bluestones was never completed.

circles with radii 11·3 and 13·1 m. The axis of Stonehenge was indicated by additional stones, disposed so that there were three extra on either side, this axis being in line with the Avenue. The circles were set out from a new centre, 0·53 m to the north of the centre of the bank and Aubrey Holes. Presumably by this time the bank, already 400 years old, was getting worn down, and the Aubrey Holes were covered with grass, so it was difficult to recapture the original centre of the monument. Later stone circles were all laid out from the centre of the double bluestone circle of Stonehenge II.

From the point of view of the archaeo-astronomer, a real problem with Stonehenge II is the date of the Station Stones. There is good evidence that they were not set up in the earliest part of Phase I, because the ditches round the two missing stones are clearly later than the bank, ditch, and Aubrey Holes. Furthermore the intersection of their diagonals lies closer to the centre from which the stone circles were laid out than to the centre of the Aubrey Hole circle. Professor Atkinson, in his book *Stonehenge*, assigned them tentatively to Phase IIIa, making them contemporary with the other sarsen stones on the grounds of symmetry of design, and the fact that stone 93 shows signs of tooling like the stones in the sarsen circle. Not all authorities would place them as late as this. R. S. Newall, in the Stonehenge guidebook, puts them into Stonehenge II, because the sarsen circle obscures the view across the diagonal, and one of these alignments, as was seen in Chapter 1, is an astronomical sightline. Geometrically there is no reason to prefer Phase IIIa to Phase II, since the bluestone circle and the sarsen circle have the same centre and axis. The evidence of the ditches around two of the Station Stones, which resemble the Phase II ditch round the Heel Stone, seems to tilt the balance in favour of the Station Stones being in Phase II, or possibly towards the end of Stonehenge I.

The various astronomical alignments which have been claimed for the Station Stones are shown on Figures 1.4 and 1.5. Taken together with the alignments to the other stones or possible stones outside the main circle, they include six of the eight main directions of moonrise and moonset (only the southerly moonsets for the major and minor standstills are missing), all four solstitial rising and setting directions of the sun, and equinoctial sunrise. The diagonal 91–93 indicates a minor standstill moonrise and moonset, and serves also for an intermediate calendar date. These alignments are not in general particularly accurate, the average error being about 1° in azimuth. There are several reasons why this should be so: where the stones still stand they are irregular in outline, and some of them have obviously been mutilated in the past. Where the stones are missing, their exact positions in their holes can only be estimated, and not all the stone holes have been properly excavated. Station Stone 94, for instance, is assumed to have been in the centre of its ditch, but this has never been verified by the spade.

Professor Atkinson has studied the Station Stone alignments and has attempted to date them by Lockyer's method. There is no doubt that the line joining stones 91 and 93 is either a midsummer sunrise or a midwinter sunset, but which? Because of refraction, these directions are not reciprocal, and it should be possible to distinguish between the two alternatives. In a similar way, the line of stones 92 and 93 could be either a southerly moonrise or a northerly moonset at the major standstill. The interpretation which best fits the existing alignments of stones is that the one from 91 to 92 indicated the last flash of the midwinter sunset, and the one from 92 to 93 showed the northerly moonset, again for the last light before the moon disappeared. These two alignments are consistent with a date of about 2600 BC, which would put the Station Stones in the latter part of Stonehenge I.

But even if the Stonehenge alignments were originally more accurate than they seem to be at the present day, their baselines are too short for precise observations. This leads to the obvious question: if Stonehenge was used as an astronomical observatory, as well as a ritual temple, where were the accurate alignments associated with the observatory? The answer in part was found when the car park was extended in 1966. Three huge postholes came to light; their positions are now marked by concrete discs set in the road surface (Fig. 9.3). The associated posts must have been about $\frac{3}{4}$ m in diameter, and because the ground to the north-west of Stonehenge rises at first then falls away, they must have been at least 10 m high if they were to have been seen from the centre of the bank. Newham investigated the geometry and alignments of these holes and discovered that they could have served as foresights for several astronomical alignments when the observers had stood at either the Heel Stone or one of the Station Stones. His alignments include

(*a*) From stone 91 to posthole 1: last gleam at the summer solstice.

(*b*) From stone 92 to posthole 2: northerly moonset at the major standstill.

(*c*) From stone 94 to posthole 2: northerly moonset midway between the standstills (not indicated on Fig. 9.3).

(*d*) From the Heel Stone to posthole 3: northerly moonset at the minor standstill.

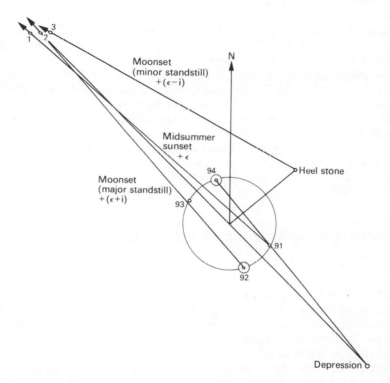

FIG. 9.3   Geometry and alignments connected with the car-park postholes

All of these alignments would have been more accurate than the sightings involving only the Station Stones, partly because the foresights would have been three times as far away, but also because the presumed smooth sides of the upright posts would have been better than the irregular outline of the stones. An accuracy of 0·05° would have been achievable. There is ample space around the Station Stones and the Heel Stone to set up nightly markers in the way that has been suggested for other megalithic observatories. No astronomical alignments to the car-park postholes have been found from the centre of the circle. Perhaps this is because the double bluestone circle would have impeded observations, not by obscuring the posts (the bluestones are too small for that) but by restricting the space available for nightly markers.

The astronomical links between the Station Stones and the car-park postholes suggest they are contemporary, though no direct dating evidence has been reported from the contents of the holes. There is a possible geometrical relationship connecting the postholes with Phase II, involving a small depression southeast of the centre of the circle. This depression is on the line of stones 94 and 91 (Fig. 9.3) and is 188·1 m from the centre of the circle. Another line projected from the depression through the centre meets posthole 2, 253·4 m on the other side of Stonehenge. The origin of the depression is not known, but from its appearance it could be a stone-hole and, if so, would have been a foresight for the southerly moonrise at the major standstill. The car-park postholes were discovered by a lucky accident, and there may well be more outlying foresights on all the significant alignments at Stonehenge.

The geometry of Stonehenge II has several points of interest. It has often been remarked that the Station Stones form a rectangle, though this is not necessarily true. The exact position of stone 94 is not known and the most we can say at the present is that the angle made by stones 91-92-93 is 89·42°. It is very close to a right angle, and many investigators of Stonehenge have assumed this was deliberate on the part of the builders. Now the Station Stone rectangle has one side (the short one) aligned approximately on the midsummer sunrise/ midwinter sunset line and the other side aligned on the moonrise/moonset line for the major standstill. Only at a latitude close to that of Stonehenge are these two alignments at right angles. At other latitudes the Station Stones would have formed a parallelogram, not a rectangle. Professor Hawkins and others have suggested that the site for Stonehenge was actually chosen so that the Station Stone setting would be rectangular.

This could only have happened if the sun and moon alignments had been accurately known over much of southern England before the first phase of Stonehenge was constructed. From the archaeological record there, this seems very unlikely. We have interpreted Stonehenge I as a lunar observatory, and the causeway postholes as the first attempts to find the accurate alignments of the rising moon. From the symmetry of the Station Stones in relation to the Avenue, the covering of the Aubrey Holes by the Station Stone mounds, and the two different geometrical centres, we infer that the Station Stones were erected later, perhaps several hundred years later, than the foundation of Stonehenge I. The Station Stones were set up in an existing henge and therefore its position cannot have been chosen to make the rectangle. However, there is one other possibility. There are many neolithic sites in southern England, and any one of them might have been picked out for development into a major observatory. Perhaps Stonehenge was selected for special treatment when it was discovered that these important alignments were very nearly at right angles.

When the builders decided to make the Station Stone rectangle indicate the midwinter sunset and the major standstill moonset, they could have chosen any one of an infinity of rectangles, from square to long and thin. Why did they choose the one we find there today? There are at least four possible answers, two astronomical and two geometrical. By altering the dimensions of the rectangle, the orientation of its diagonal can be changed. The diagonal of the Station Stone rectangle, according to Professor Hawkins, indicates the moonrise and moonset lines at a minor standstill (Fig. 1.5). It would be aesthetically pleasing to have an accurate minor standstill alignment incorporated into the Station Stone rectangle, but the errors in azimuth are rather large, 1·8° and 5·1°, and this alignment does not therefore stand up to scrutiny.

The alternative astronomical hypothesis is that the diagonal gives the sunrises and sunsets at times of the year approximately midway between the solstices and the equinoxes, on 5 February, 6 May, 8 August, and 8 November (Fig. 1.4). These dates can be compared with those given in Table 5.1 for the 'ideal' division of the Bronze Age year into eight parts, 2 February, 5 May, 6 August, and 2 November. Whether intentional or not, this alignment could have served as the basis for a solar calendar.

One of the geometrical proposals, by Professor William E. Dibble of Brigham Young University, USA, was that the Station Stone rectangle was chosen to incorporate the Pythagorean 5,12,13 triangle. The dimensions of the sides of the triangle of stones 91, 92, and 93 are 34·3 m, 79·5 m, and 86·2 m. The ratios of the sides are 5·18:12·00:13·01. Since the error in the length of the short side is only 1·1 m, which is less than the size of the hole that stone 92 was set in, it is quite possible that the builders were aiming for the Pythagorean triangle. The other geometric relationship (pointed out by Alan Penny) is that the length of the long side of the Station Stone rectangle is within a quarter of a metre of the distance from the Aubrey centre to the Heel Stone. Since the Heel Stone is believed to have been set up before the Station Stones, this implies that when the builders decided to erect the Station Stones, they tried to link the new construction with the geometry of the existing monument. Of course, only one of these geometrical relationships could have been the original intention. The fact that both conditions are closely met is a consequence of a geometrical feature incorporated in Stonehenge I: the diameter of the Aubrey circle and the distance from the Aubrey centre to the Heel Stone are in the ratio 12:13 to a high order of accuracy (better than 0·2 per cent). Whether this was intentional or accidental, it is impossible to say.

There is little sign of the megalithic units of length in Stonehenge II. Newham claimed that the long side and the diagonal of the Station Stone rectangle were both simple multiples of his lunar measure (5½ and 6 respectively, giving an incorrect ratio 11:12), but these are not sufficiently accurate to produce round numbers in the smaller units of megalithic yards and rods. Indeed we would not expect the sides of the rectangle to be whole numbers of megalithic units, because the Station Stones are sited on the perimeter of the Aubrey circle, whose diameter must be non-integral because its perimeter is almost exactly 131 MR. Unfortunately we do not know the dimensions of the double bluestone circle to the same degree of accuracy, and therefore cannot tell if the builders of the second phase of Stonehenge were as keen as they were elsewhere to make the perimeters of their circles equal to whole numbers of megalithic rods. The published radii of the bluestone circles, 11·3 m and 13·1 m, are within a few centimetres of suitable dimensions, for if the radii were actually 11·23 m and 13·21 m, the perimeters would have been just 34 and 40 MR.

The next stage of activity at Stonehenge was the most ambitious civil engineering of all. In Phase IIIa, perhaps about 2100 BC, the massive sarsen stone circle and the trilithons were erected. The stones came from the Marlborough Downs, 30 km north of Stonehenge, where they occur as irregular boulders lying on the chalk surface. They were pounded into shape, hauled south on sledges up and down the hills, and finally set up on Salisbury Plain inside the circular bank that was already a thousand years old.

From a detailed study of the stones, some of the techniques of construction have been made clear. The ground was prepared by dismantling the double bluestone circle and ramming chalk into the holes to provide a firm working area. (We know from radiocarbon dating that the bluestone circle was destroyed and the sarsen circle built at about the same time.) After accurately marking out the places for the sarsen stones, using the same centre for the new circle as for the old one, they dug out the holes to take the uprights. Each hole is roughly rectangular, with three vertical sides and one side sloping to form a ramp. The side opposite the ramp was protected by vertical stakes, so that when the base of the stone was slid down the slope into the hole, the soft chalk would not crumble under pressure. The depths of the holes were not all the same, but were dug according to the lengths of the individual stones, to ensure that, when upright, their tops would all be at about the same height.

The stones were raised by a combination of levers and ropes, and were finally manœuvred into their exact positions by swivelling them on their bases, which had been shaped to a point to assist this operation. The holes were then packed with small stones and rammed chalk to give the sarsens a firm foundation, and presumably they were left awhile to bed solidly into place.

The lintels were shaped on the ground beside their uprights. Sockets for the tenons were carved out on what were to become the undersides, and these sockets served as patterns for the precise shapes of the tenons on the standing stones. At this stage the heights of the flat surfaces on the uprights were finally adjusted with great care to be exactly level. Although the ground slopes by 0·4 m from one side of the sarsen circle to the other, the ring of lintels is horizontal to within a few centimetres.

We believe the lintels were lifted into their positions on the tops of the uprights with the aid of a timber crib (Fig. 9.4). Using levers, the lintel was first raised a small amount, say ½ m, and temporarily supported on wooden blocks. Around it was built a decking of squared planks, set like floorboards, with the planks in alternate layers at right angles to give a firm structure. When the crib reached the height of the stone, the latter was slid, or moved on rollers, on to the planking. The stone was then levered up another half metre, temporarily supported on blocks, and once more the crib was built up to meet it. By repeating this operation several times, the lintel was eventually raised to the level of the tops of the sarsen uprights. Finally it was moved sideways and lowered gently on to its permanent resting place.

The order of erection of the stones is not known for certain, but the central trilithons must have been set in position before the sarsen circle was completed. From excavations around the bases of the stones, which have given the locations of the ramps, we know that most of the trilithons were erected from inside the horseshoe. Stones 56, 57, and 58 were exceptions; 57 and 58 were put up from the outside, and 56, the standing megalith of the great trilithon, was put up sideways, possibly being slid down the ramp on its narrow edge. The stones in the sarsen circle were raised from the outside, with the exception of 21, which was raised from within the circle. All these departures from normal practice occurred in a narrow sector in the north-west quadrant, but we do not know why.

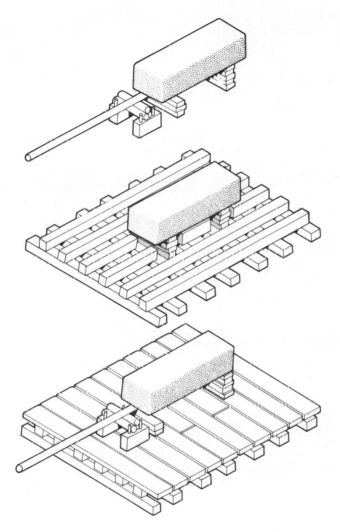

FIG. 9.4   Timber crib for raising the lintels

Based on a diagram in *Stonehenge* by R. J. C. Atkinson (Hamish Hamilton).

Until recently no one had thought to ask if the trilithons had been set up in any precise geometrical pattern. Following the Thom family's re-survey of the site in 1973, they discovered that four of the five trilithons were set so that their inner faces lay on the perimeter of an ellipse of eccentricity 0·78. The axis of the ellipse coincides with the axis of the whole monument, but its centre is 1·24 m towards the Heel Stone from the centre of the sarsen circle. The major and minor axes are 22·4 m and 14·1 m, which they interpret as 27 MY and 17 MY. This ellipse, like others described in Chapter 3, is based on a near-Pythagorean triangle.

In this case its sides are in the ratios 17, 21, and 27 ($17^2 + 21^2 = 730$, $27^2 = 729$) and its perimeter, 58·1 m, seems to be a very close approximation to 28 MR (Fig. 9.5).

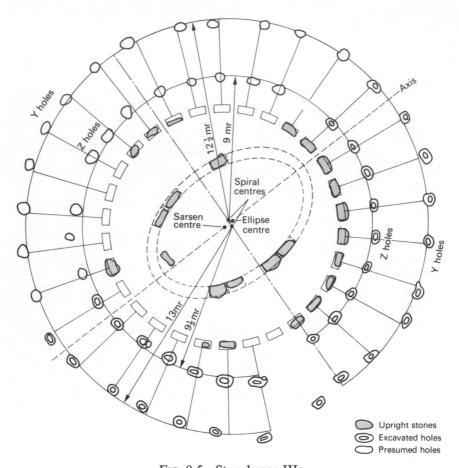

FIG. 9.5   Stonehenge IIIa

Thom's geometrical constructions for the sarsen circle, the trilithons, and the Y and Z holes are superimposed. Based on diagrams in the *Journal for the History of Astronomy*, 5, by kind permission of Dr M. A. Hoskin.

The stones of the great trilithon were not set on the ellipse; they are too close to the centre. Stone 56 is dished on its inner side, and possibly was intended to follow some other geometric curve. It fell before records of Stonehenge began and was re-erected in 1901, but presumably not in its original place, since it is not now perpendicular to the axis.

The sarsen circle is truly circular. The thirty upright stones were not all the same width, but they were spaced so that their centres were at equal intervals around the circumference, and irregularities in the sizes of the stones were compensated for by variations in the gaps between them. From their study of the dimensions, the Thoms concluded that the builders' intention was to make the stones average 1 MR wide, and the spaces ½ MR. This makes the circumference of the circle of the inner faces of the sarsens exactly 45 MR, or 93·3 m long. The theoretical radius is 14·85 m, which certainly does not differ by more than a few centimetres from the actual radius on the ground.

These discoveries concerning the layout of the sarsen circle and the trilithons give strong support to Professor Thom's ideas about the geometry of megalithic stone settings. Stonehenge IIIa is now seen to have more in common with other sites of the Early Bronze Age than had been previously recognized. The new information also adds to the evidence for the megalithic yard and rod, and seems to confirm the suggestion that the builders of these structures liked to make the perimeters of their designs equal to a whole number of megalithic rods. Paradoxically, the results from Stonehenge may cause some archaeologists to have further doubts. It is one thing to accept that there could have been a group of people in the Early Bronze Age who were obsessed with geometrical shapes and dimensions and who imposed mathematical relationships on their civil engineering projects. It is another matter to believe that the same geometrical designs and the same units of measurement were in use for nearly one thousand years, outlasting thirty generations and several cultural changes. Nevertheless, this would be the case if the men who laid out the Aubrey Holes in the first phase of Stonehenge had intended the circumference of the circle to be exactly 131 MR.

To put the issue into perspective, the only piece of evidence for the use of the megalithic rod in Stonehenge I is that when the perimeter of the Aubrey circle is divided by an arbitrary whole number, the result is extremely close (within 0·05 per cent) to the length used as a unit in setting out later constructions at Stonehenge. The agreement is not as impressive as it appears at first sight. When there are a large number of units in the perimeter, as there are in the Aubrey circle, and we select the number to give the best agreement for the length of the unit, the biggest discrepancy we can get is only one part in 262, i.e. 0·4 per cent. We would expect the error to be less than this and therefore 0·05 per cent is not especially surprising.

The number 131 has no significance as far as we know. If we seriously thought that the neolithic people who dug the Aubrey Holes wanted the circumference of the circle to be a whole number of their units, it is at least reasonable to speculate that, in the megalithic rods of the period, they were aiming for 132 round the perimeter, thereby giving themselves a radius of almost precisely 21 MR. But that megalithic rod would have been ¾ per cent shorter than the one used in Stonehenge IIIa. In summary, the evidence for the same unit of length in Stonehenge I and IIIa is very weak.

Superficially, the construction of the trilithons and the sarsen circle seems to contribute little to the astronomical features at Stonehenge. We deduce that there was a continuing interest in the movements of the sun and moon, because the builders maintained the orientation of the axis to be in line with the midsummer sunrise. The azimuth was remeasured by Professor Thom in his survey of 1973, and found to be 49·95°. After taking into account refraction and the elevation of the horizon in the Early Bronze Age, this is calculated to be the direction of the half-risen midsummer sun in the second millennium BC. The astronomically estimated date for the alignment is 1600 ± 450 BC, which is a little later than the archaeological date, but it is confirmation that Stonehenge IIIa was much later than the early phases of the site.

Another significant indication of the continuity of astronomical interest is that the size of the sarsen circle was chosen so that it did not obstruct the main sight-lines of the Station Stone rectangle. The diagonal sightlines were obscured, but the others are all clear. When you stand at Stonehenge and look along the long sides of the rectangle, it is very evident that the sarsen circle was made as large as possible, within the boundary of the sightlines. There is only one reasonable explanation of this: the Station Stones must have been still in use, even though they were erected long before. Professor Hawkins, during his comprehensive search for alignments, discovered yet another indication of astronomical interest. No fewer than eight astronomical orientations are built into the arrangement of the sarsen circle and the trilithons (Fig. 9.6). These alignments must be ritual and not observational. The baselines are very short and the spaces between the uprights are fairly wide, so there is no question of making accurate observations

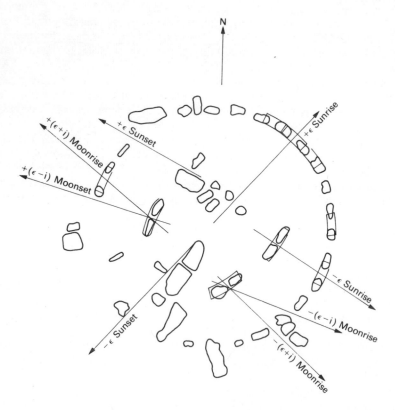

FIG. 9.6   Alignments built into the sarsen circle and the trilithons, according to Hawkins

of the sun and moon by sighting through the gaps. Until quite recently it looked as though the sarsen structures were either a product of architectural exuberance or had some inscrutable ritual significance, and that any astronomical function was incidental and of little importance in the eyes of the architects of Stonehenge IIIa.

Perhaps we shall have to revise this interpretation. A new suggestion has been put forward by R. F. Brinckerhoff, who persuaded the custodians of the monument to let him climb up to examine and photograph the upper surfaces of the lintels. I have already mentioned how the lintel circle is more level than the ground, and Brinckerhoff argued that if this was intentional, it implied the lintels were some sort of elevated walkway or observation platform. He found several holes on their upper surfaces, particularly on the three contiguous lintels still in position on the Heel Stone side of the circle, numbers 130, 101, and 102 (Fig. 9.7). Most of these pits are circular, and he thinks they are artificial. They range in size from 25 cm diameter and 8 cm deep, down to 4 cm diameter and 5 cm deep. Brinckerhoff suggested that the pits could have held small wands, and an observer standing in the correct place could have used them as foresights for astronomical observations.

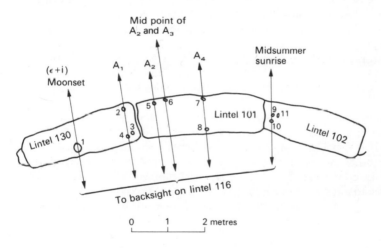

FIG. 9.7   The lintel-top alignments

Based on a diagram in R. F. Brinckerhoff, 'Astronomically orientated markings at Stonehenge', *Nature*, **263** (1976).

The only position for the backsight which gives any astronomically significant alignments is on the opposite side of the sarsen circle, on the top of the missing lintel 116. This position is not on the axis of Stonehenge, but above the fallen stone 15. From this point all but two of the eleven pits can be aligned with something of interest. The alignments he gives are:

—to hole 1, the $(\varepsilon+i)$ moonset, about 2000 BC;
—to holes 2 and 4, the A1 posthole;

—to hole 5, the A2 posthole;

—to hole 6, mid-way between the A2 and A3 postholes;

—to holes 7 and 8, the A4 posthole; and

—to holes 9 and 10, the midsummer sunrise, about 2000 BC.

The sightings do not in fact go exactly to the A postholes. There is a small difference of about 0·2° in every case, with the A postholes to the left of the lintel pit alignments.

Brinckerhoff's interpretation of these results is that when Stonehenge IIIa was set up, its builders wanted to make observations of the moon at different times in its 18·6-year cycle, just as the early users of the site had done with the A-holes in the Neolithic Period. They set up wands in almost the same set of directions; the 0·2° discrepancy can be accounted for by the change in ecliptic angle during the span of time from Stonehenge I to Stonehenge IIIa.

Some archaeologists have doubted whether the holes are man-made and think they could have been the results of natural weathering. Nevertheless, Brinckerhoff's explanation seems very plausible, until it is realized that one of the stones of the great trilithon, number 55, when upright would have been directly in the way of the sightlines. Moving the backsight only 1·5 m westward, to be on the axis of the monument and therefore in line with the gap in the trilithon, destroys the alignments. As with so many features of Stonehenge, there appears to be a direct conflict of evidence. Perhaps stone 55 of the great trilithon was thrown down in antiquity to permit the observations, Brinckerhoff suggested, but Professor Atkinson pointed out that the differential weathering of its lintel, stone 156, is consistent with a later collapse than the Early Bronze Age. Furthermore, there is evidence from excavation that it was not deliberately undermined.

Penny has suggested another possibility. The great trilithon is not on the same ellipse as the other four, and from excavations around the base of 56, we know it was put up from the side. Was this because space was restricted owing to the other stones already having been erected, and is the explanation to be found in a later erection of the great trilithon, after the observations with the wands had filled their purpose?

During the reconstruction project of Phase IIIa, the bluestones must have been put aside for safety and kept well clear of the building operations. When the sarsen circle and the trilithons were finished, they were re-used, in a quite different arrangement from that of Phase II. Although comparatively little is known about the bluestone setting of Phase IIIb, it seems they were set up in an ellipse, more or less in the same place as the present bluestone horseshoe but with a different spacing of stones. The new setting had at least two bluestone lintels, for among the fallen stones of the existing bluestone circle, two have mortices on their undersides. There was also a very curious pair of stones, one with a groove carved all the way down its side (still visible as 68 on the official plan), and its buried mate, number 66, with a matching tongue. The purpose of these two is completely unknown.

Contemporary with the bluestone ellipse, two rings of holes were dug outside the sarsen circle, the Y and Z holes. They appear on the plan of Stonehenge to be rather irregular, but this could be accentuated by the fact that only half of them have been excavated and the others have been located by the relatively inaccurate method of probing. The arrangement of holes is not quite as haphazard as it seems. Each Y and Z hole lies on a radial line passing through a sarsen upright, and each sarsen has its associated Y and Z holes, except for number 8. Circumferentially, the holes lie on two spirals, each spiral being made up of two semicircles (Fig. 9.5). Similar spirals have been found on carved stones, among the cup and ring marks of Bronze Age Britain, but so far this is the only known site where they are laid out on the ground.

Dimensionally the spirals fit in with the megalithic units of Stonehenge IIIa. The radii of the semicircles are 9 and $9\frac{1}{2}$ MR for the inner spiral and $12\frac{1}{2}$ and 13 MR for the outer one. They are set out from two centres, $\frac{1}{2}$ MR apart, neither centre coinciding with the centre of the sarsen circle.

The purpose of these holes and their strange layout is not known. They were thought to be stone holes, dug for taking the surplus bluestones which were not put in the ellipse of Phase IIIb. However, no stones were ever set in them, and they were not deliberately filled in like the Aubrey Holes, for excavations have shown that they slowly silted up over a number of years. Professor Atkinson has suggested that the project involving the Y and Z holes might have been abandoned before it was completed, in favour of the final stage of construction at Stonehenge, Phase IIIc.

About 1600 BC the bluestone setting of Phase IIIb was dismantled and the stones were re-used for a second time in the construction of the bluestone settings whose remains are visible to the present day. About sixty of the stones were set in a circle of radius 11·4 m, between the trilithons and the sarsen circle. The remaining stones were inside the horseshoe of trilithons, though not on any obvious geometrical curve. The Thoms interpreted their layout as a composite figure, some of them being set on an ellipse and some on an intersecting circle, but the correspondence between the stone holes and these curves is not particularly good. For the time being, the geometry of Phase IIIc remains in doubt.

As far as we know, the bluestone settings of the last two phases of Stonehenge have no astronomical significance whatsoever. I have mentioned all the known astronomical features of Stonehenge itself, phase by phase, but the story does not end at this point. The most dramatic outcome of the work of Professor Thom and family at Stonehenge is the possibility of its being the central point of a huge solar and lunar observatory with foresights on the distant hills. As we know, the longer the sightline, the more accurate the observations. The short sightlines at Stonehenge are rather poor for precise astronomy. If they were all that ever existed, it would seem very odd that Stonehenge should be architecturally so sophisticated, especially in its later phases, and yet not be capable of giving the accuracy of observation that could have been obtained from relatively crude sites like Ballochroy. From what we now know about other stone circles of the Early Bronze Age, we might expect to find distant markers at the appropriate points on the horizon as seen from the centre of Stonehenge.

Stonehenge is situated on a sloping hillside, in the middle of an undulating plain quite devoid of prominent natural features, such as the tors on Dartmoor. The distant foresights would therefore have been man-made, but the first problem to confront the builders was how to find where they should be positioned. One way would be to construct a temporary foresight which could have been taken down and re-erected in another place. A wattle structure, for example, could have been made large enough to be seen at a distance and light enough to be moved about. Once found, the exact spot for the foresight would have had to be marked permanently on the ground—it would have taken a lot of trouble to locate. The marker need not have been very large, because another temporary foresight could have been built beside it when the time came for the next round of observations.

It is interesting to compare this idea with the observatory near Carnac. The Grand Menhir was used as a universal foresight and the backsights were moved to suit it. Stonehenge on this hypothesis is a Carnac-type observatory, but inside out, with a universal backsight and several foresights. It is a more difficult way of setting up an observatory, and one which may not have left very prominent remains on the surrounding hills. Clearly the region around Stonehenge must be studied with great care if the suggestion is to be either proved or disproved.

The Thoms have identified several sites in the Stonehenge area where foresights might have been set up. They are listed in Table 9.1 and shown in Figure 9.8. The top one in the table is a suggested sighting for the midsummer sunrise. Peter's Mound is a small bump in the ground to the north-east of Stonehenge; it is called after Newham, who was the first person to point out its existence. The mound is on the top of a ridge which forms the horizon when viewed from the centre of the circle. At the present day there are trees in the direct line of sight, but in any case it is far too small to be visible from Stonehenge. It could not have been a foresight, but only a marker for the position of one.

In fact Peter's Mound is not more than 30 cm high and is quite difficult to find.

Locality of presumed foresight	Grid Reference	Azimuth from Stonehenge	Distance from Stonehenge (km)	Alignment	Declination corresponding to azimuth
Peter's Mound	SU14334397	47·79°	2·73	$+\varepsilon$ sunrise	$+24\cdot00°$
Coneybury Barrow	SU13554138	122·3°	1·54	$-(\varepsilon-i)$ moonrise	$-18\cdot8°$
Mound in Figsbury Rings	SU18833384	141·90°	10·64	$-(\varepsilon+i)$ moonrise	$-29\cdot00°$
Chain Hill	SU087373	216·27°	6·0	$-(\varepsilon+i)$ moonset	$-29\cdot40°$
Mound in Hanging Langford Camp	SU01313527	237·78°	12·95	$-(\varepsilon-i)$ moonset	$-18\cdot87°$
Gibbet Knoll	SU02735340	319·93°	14·70	$+(\varepsilon+i+s)$ moonset	$+29\cdot35°$

Table 9.1   Possible distant foresights associated with Stonehenge

It is at Larkhill, in a small plantation about 12 m to the east of Wood Road and 90 m south of the junction with Packway Road. It is oval in shape, roughly 3 m by 1 m, with its long axis pointing to the south-west. From its external appearance it is just as likely to be modern as megalithic, and in all fairness it has to be stated that the area around it has been disturbed in the recent past, not only for planting the trees but also for pipelaying earlier this century.

The azimuth of Peter's Mound has been very accurately determined, and this

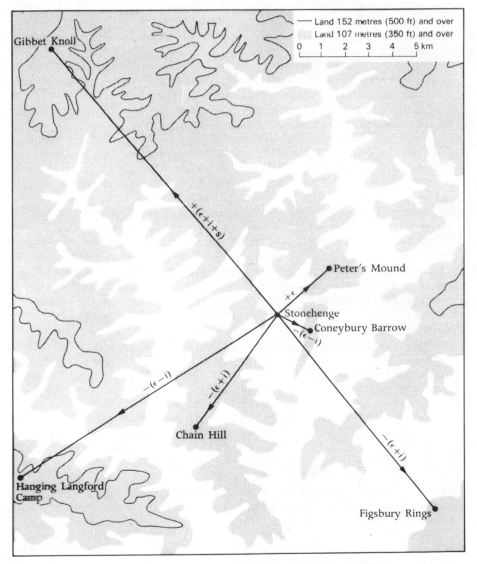

FIG. 9.8   Possible distant foresights for Stonehenge

allows the date of the alignment to be calculated. When seen from the Aubrey centre, the middle of the sun's disc would have been on the horizon in the direction of Peter's Mound at midsummer in 2700 ±400 BC. This date may be several hundred years in error, but nevertheless it is very early indeed for a distant foresight, judging by the results from other places. Professor Thom suggests that Stonehenge was actually located where it is, half-way down the hill, in order to establish the sightline to the ridge of Peter's Mound. From a position a few metres higher up the slope, very distant hills come into view, and it would have been impracticable to erect an artificial foresight on them because of its size. Moving down the hill only a few metres brings a nearby ridge to the horizon, and the sightline would have been too short for accurate observations.

This suggestion is difficult to reconcile with the archaeology. If Stonehenge had been sited on the hillside for these reasons, then the midsummer sunrise alignment would presumably have been the most important feature of the monument. But why then was the orientation of the bank not symmetrical about the line of the solstice in the first phase? The evidence from Phase I points to its having started as a lunar observatory and not a solar one.

The three lunar alignments to Gibbet Knoll, Figsbury Rings and Hanging Langford Camp have sightlines about 12 km long, and in each case there is an intervening ridge of high ground between Stonehenge and the suggested foresight position, preventing a direct sightline to the distant hilltop. But the ridges only just obscure the hills, and if the artificial foresights had been no more than four to six metres high, they would have been visible at ground level from the interior of the sarsen circle. Even the slight increase of refraction at night, caused by the cooling of the atmosphere, would be sufficient to make the hilltops appear over the ridges. From the height of the sarsen lintels, they would have been visible in the daytime as well. There are no similar problems with the remaining alignments, to Chain Hill and Coneybury Barrow, which are in direct view from ground level at Stonehenge.

One thing has to be made clear about the list of foresights in Table 9.1. None of them is a validated marker for a lunar alignment; they are simply the positions near where the foresights would have had to be set up to give the correct alignments in 2000 BC. They all have visible earthworks at the present day, but these are not necessarily contemporary with Stonehenge IIIa. Hanging Langford Camp and Figsbury Rings, for example, are Iron Age hill forts, and would not have been built before, say, the third century BC. We do not know enough about the mounds in the hill forts, whose grid references are given, to say if they mark the positions of the foresights, although the one in Figsbury Rings could well belong to the Bronze Age. There is a lot of work still to be done before we can be sure about the use of Stonehenge as a universal backsight, and this must include serious field archaeology followed by excavation. If the remains of Early Bronze Age structures are found near the predicted positions, it will enhance even further our respect for the intellectual achievements of the prehistoric inhabitants of southern England.

Very few of the many people who have studied the astronomy and geometry of Stonehenge have looked upon it as a three-dimensional object. Archaeologists are usually forced to work from ground plans because the standing parts of prehistoric and Roman antiquities have been destroyed, and deducing the missing upperworks of a building from the details of its foundations can lead to several equally plausible, but completely different, reconstructions. With Stonehenge we are in a happier situation. We know the main features of its above-ground construction, and taking them into account may lead to a deeper understanding of the function and purpose of the monument.

One of the many features which distinguishes Stonehenge from other megalithic stone circles is the ring of lintels. They may, of course, have been set on the sarsens merely for architectural effect, but the additional amount of work in constructing the ring was so huge that we are bound to ask if there was any practical purpose it could have served. If any, it may have had no connection with astronomical observations, but in the context of this book, and in the light of known astronomical activity at Stonehenge, we can't help wondering if the elevated ring could have been a help in observing the sun and the moon.

I have already mentioned as one of the possibilities the use of wands in the tops of certain lintels. This does not require, or explain, the complete circle of horizontal stones. If the distant foresights are verified by future archaeological research, a second possibility can be put forward. The distant lunar foresights would all have been in sight from a walkway 4·9 m above the ground, and a circular one has the advantage of being equally useful for alignments in any direction. The circle is not, however, large enough for all observations to be made from the lintel tops. This requires a space of 4G, or 350 m for the alignment to Figsbury Rings.

The heights of the trilithons, to the tops of the lintels, are 6·1 m, 6·6 m, and 7·3 m. These massive stones have an architectural bravado, and without doubt were meant to impress, yet it is easy to imagine them as a gargantuan staircase, connected by wooden catwalks to allow access to the top of the great trilithon. Perhaps this is how it was during Phase IIIa. It would have been most useful to station a man several metres up in the air when the group was watching for sunrise or moonrise, for he would see the first flash of light before the people on the ground and he would be able to give them ten seconds or more warning of the event. He would also be able to say where on the horizon the disc was going to appear, and they would have had ample time to get into the right position for making observations.

As research at Stonehenge has proceeded, more and more of its technical complexity and sophistication becomes apparent. But we must not let ourselves be seduced into thinking of the monument as a prehistoric prototype of the Greenwich observatory. Until a few centuries ago, there was no scientific astronomy as we know it, and the peoples of the Late Neolithic and Early Bronze Ages, notwithstanding their careful and systematic observations of the sun and moon, were practising a religion, not studying celestial mechanics. Thus we find cremated remains in the ditch and human bones in the Aubrey Holes, the relics perhaps of rituals which once marked the moon's arrival at the major standstill. With the construction of the sarsen circle and the trilithons in Stonehenge III, the scope for dramatic effects in the lunar and solstitial ceremonies was enormously widened, and, for all we know, that might have been the main reason why they were built.

10 Towards a New Understanding

If you go outside on a fine evening with the intention of watching the sun set, the chances are it will have disappeared behind cloud before it sinks down to the horizon. Apart from infrequent spells of prolonged good weather, such as the summer of 1976, it is rare in north-west Europe to see the sun or moon clearly when it is low in the sky. If we tried to repeat the regular astronomical observations of the Neolithic or Early Bronze Ages, we should find it a very frustrating experience. With patience and perseverance over a number of years, we could fix the solstitial sunrise and sunset positions; but we should probably conclude that deducing the regularities in the movements of the moon was a hopeless task owing to the generally poor visibility. How then was it done in prehistoric times?

The answer to this question seems to be that the climate of the British Isles was not the same as it is now. There is some evidence for a period of particularly favourable weather during a few centuries centred on 2000 BC, when the mean temperature was 2° to 3° higher than it has been during the last few hundred years, and calm, settled, and presumably clearer weather was more common. Scientific research supports this idea, and it is consistent with casual study of the upland areas of Britain. The Bronze Age hut circles and field systems on Dartmoor or the North Yorkshire moors, for example, are sited where arable farming is quite impossible today, and where it would be exceedingly unpleasant to live. As we tramp across the peat bogs of the moor, with the drizzle insinuating itself into our belongings, we inevitably conclude that it could not have been like this in the Early Bronze Age.

Many and varied scientific techniques have been called upon to give information on prehistoric climate. One of the most valuable has been the study of the distributions of different species of animals and plants. Snails, shellfish, freshwater tortoises, and beetles are some of the creatures that have contributed to research in climatology, but probably the best-known and most used technique is pollen analysis. Pollen grains are very small, usually about one-hundredth mm in diameter, and are easily blown by the wind. Each family of plants produces a characteristic shape of pollen grain and they can be readily recognized under the microscope. Pollen is very resistant to decay, and grains are identifiable even when they have lain in the earth for thousands of years. They are produced in vast numbers, and many can be found in a small sample of soil, so that by counting grains an accurate picture can be obtained of the vegetation at the time the deposits were laid down. From the analysis of many samples collected from different depths and at different sites, the overall pattern of vegetation is compiled. Thus the gradual improvement in the climate following the last Ice Age has been revealed by the sequences of different trees.

Archaeologists have divided the time since the end of the Ice Age into several periods, the five most recent being Pre-boreal (9500 BC to 8500 BC), Boreal

(8500 BC to 6500 BC), Atlantic (6500 BC to 4000 BC), Sub-boreal (4000 BC to 1400 BC), and Sub-atlantic (1400 BC to the present day). The dates are very approximate, partly because climatic periods do not have sharp beginnings and endings, and partly because they are based on carbon-14 measurements, which are still uncalibrated for the earlier periods. Furthermore, they are primarily pollen-zone periods, and there must be some time lag between the climatic shifts and the consequential changes in vegetation. Forests do not die and become replaced overnight.

The ice sheet began to retreat northwards from about 12000 BC and a ground cover of mosses and lichen appeared in its wake. In the Pre-boreal period the climate had warmed to the point where forests of birch and pine could flourish, and the first bands of mesolithic hunters and food gatherers arrived in the British Isles. The climatic improvement continued through the Boreal period, which got warmer and drier, allowing oak and hazel to establish themselves in the forests. The Atlantic period is believed to have been the climatic optimum. The temperature was high, but so was the rainfall. With the melting of the ice, the sea-level had been rising steadily for several thousand years, and by the start of the Atlantic period it was high enough to breach the area of the Straits of Dover and flood what is now the North Sea, thus cutting Britain off from the continent of Europe. Forests in this period were mixed, with oak, alder, and elm, and by its end deciduous trees grew at elevations up to 750 m above sea-level, far higher than they will do today.

The Sub-boreal period is the one that interests us most. It spans the Neolithic and Early Bronze Ages, and was the time when megalithic astronomy developed and reached its peak. Overall the climate was less good than in the preceding period, and it got worse towards the end. The beginning of the Sub-boreal is marked in the pollen record by a rapid decline in the number of elm trees, which is taken as a sign of forest clearance by the neolithic farming communities. There is evidence to show that on the lighter soils the deforestation was permanent. The prehistoric ground surface is preserved under the banks and mounds of barrows, henges, and other earthworks. Studies of snail shells in the trapped soil show that about this time shade-loving species declined in numbers, to be replaced by others whose habitat was open pasture land.

The final period, the Sub-atlantic, is one of deteriorating weather. The temperature decreased and the rainfall increased, giving conditions which favoured the growth of peat bogs on elevated ground. Birch and pine trees tended to increase again, though by now the dominant influence on the vegetation of the landscape was the activities of men, not the vagaries of the climate.

From historical records we know that the climate in the Sub-atlantic, though remaining generally cool and wet, has had several periods when it has been either colder or warmer than average. The best-known fluctuation is the warm spell around AD 1000, which permitted the Vikings to populate southern Greenland. Similarly the Sub-boreal period had its variations, and more detailed studies have indicated when these actually occurred. The growth of peat in raised bogs is one source of information, and this has shown that there were particularly wet periods around 2900 BC and 1400 BC, with a drier than average time in between. Other evidence comes from work on the size of particles in soil. Wind-blown deposits, such as would be favoured in dry periods, have a very different distribution of particle size from other soils; the finer grains, being lighter, are more easily transported. Early Bronze Age soil samples, including the fill from one of the Y-holes at Stonehenge, have the characteristics of wind-blown material, and this is generally interpreted as indicating an unusually dry period at this time.

Professor H. H. Lamb has collected climatic evidence from the whole northern hemisphere. As well as the peat bog and sea-level data, he took into account such varied research as the heights of the Nile floods, the water-level in Lake Chad, and even the frequency of discovery of comets in Chinese records (which is influenced by the cloudiness of the sky). He concluded that around 2000 BC the circulating weather pattern was much weaker than it is now, and this would give rise to a high frequency of anticyclones, with clear skies and calm seas in latitudes as far north as 60°N. These conditions would have been very favourable for the early astronomers, and would have made it a far more practical proposition to watch the movements of the sun and moon than it is in the present century.

Environmental studies point to another factor which has a bearing on the beginnings of astronomy. At the start of the Neolithic Period, when the British Isles were covered with thick forest up to a considerable elevation, from most places the distant horizon could not have been seen. As the farming communities grew, land was cleared for ploughing and pasture, and the grazing of domestic animals prevented the trees from re-establishing themselves. By the Early Bronze Age, much of upland Britain was deforested and covered with grassland and scrub, and for the first time the horizons could easily be seen. The result was that even small notches on the skyline would have been well-defined and permanently visible. The combination of an open landscape with clear skies was ideal for astronomy without instruments, but we should remember that, except in a few areas where the neolithic population was densest, it would not have been possible to make accurate horizon observations before the start of the Early Bronze Age.

That observations could have been made easily, plus the need for a calendar to aid agriculture, accounts satisfactorily for the solar observations, but does not explain why the early inhabitants of north-west Europe took such an obsessive interest in the moon and went to such lengths to track its complicated movements through the sky. From mythology, and from studies of primitive peoples by anthropologists, we know that it has been almost universal for non-literate societies to worship the sun and the moon as supernatural beings. It is likely that the moon was a goddess (or god) to the Early Bronze Age people of Britain, and if they believed it could be an influence for good or bad fortune in their daily lives, it would have been quite natural to watch this wayward creature and to try to find patterns in its behaviour. To establish the calendar, they devised the technique of tracking the sun by watching where on the horizon it rose and set. Applying this technique to the motions of the moon would have been an obvious step. I suggested in Chapter 6 that the very difficulty of the problem may have been a challenge to the observers which they felt they had to solve, but were there any practical benefits which might have been an extra spur to their night-time observations?

Several people have speculated about this and come to the conclusion that the tides may have been the motivation for studying the moon. The human race took to travelling by water at a surprisingly early date. The oar from the mesolithic settlement at Star Carr shows they had boats, probably coracles or canoes, about 8000 BC. In the Later Mesolithic, before 4000 BC, settlers had ventured as far as the island of Oronsay in the Inner Hebrides, a crossing of 15 km of open ocean. The distribution of megalithic tombs in western Europe is an indication of the use of sea routes in the Neolithic Period, for they reveal cultural links between the peoples of Brittany, Ireland, and the western regions of Britain which are not found in the eastern areas of the British Isles. During the Neolithic Period the distant islands of Britain, the Outer Hebrides, the Orkneys and the Shetlands, were settled with substantially the same culture as that of the mainland, and one type of pottery, grooved ware, is found from Orkney to southern Britain. In the Early Bronze Age sea travel had progressed to the point when it was possible to transport the Preseli bluestones along the coast from Milford Haven and up the Severn Estuary.

The sea around the British Isles can be extremely dangerous and one of its hazards is the strength of tidal streams, which in some places can reach four or five knots. Unlike the Mediterranean, where tides are barely perceptible, the daily range of tidal rise and fall on the coasts of Britain is several metres, and can sometimes reach 12 m in confined waters. Apart from considerations of safety, a working knowledge of the tides would have been essential to navigators whose boats were very slow and propelled by oarsmen. (If they had had sails they would have been primitive and useful only for going before the wind.)

Tidal phenomena are quite complicated when studied in detail, but even the most casual acquaintance with coastal waters is sufficient to show that the tides rise and fall twice every twenty-four hours, and that each day the time of high water is a little later than it was the day before. The tides are not always the same height; at certain times the rise and fall is twice what it is at others. There is never any doubt about how the tidal range on a particular day compares with the average; you have only to glance at the lines of high-water mark on the rocks to see how high the sea is in relation to its absolute maximum.

It is widely known nowadays that the moon is largely responsible for the tides. The connection is so obvious to someone who lives by the sea that it must have been discovered many thousands of years ago. High tides do not occur at the same time at all points along the coast, but at any particular place the time of high tide is always very nearly the same at a certain phase of the moon. Thus at Weymouth, the seaside town where I lived for several years, I soon got to know that at new or full moon the high tide could be expected about seven in the morning. The other obvious connection between the tides and the moon is that in the week following the new and full moons the tides are greatest, and that in the weeks after the first and last quarters the tides are smallest.

The cause of the tides has been known since Sir Isaac Newton formulated his theory of gravity. The earth keeps the moon in its orbit by exerting a gravitational pull on it, but of course the moon also exerts a gravitational pull on the earth. One effect of the moon's pull is to distort the sea surface by raising a pile of water in the direction of the moon. For reasons which are too complicated to go into in this book, there is another pile of water on the side of the earth facing away from the moon. As the earth rotates, these waters in effect remain still; thus to a person on the earth's surface, the sea rises and falls twice each day. If the pile on the moon's side of the earth were exactly in the direction of the moon, high water would occur when the moon was due south. However, the flow of water is much influenced by the coastline, and the time of high water depends mainly on local conditions.

In addition to the moon's gravitational pull, the pull of the sun also affects the tides, although at about half the strength. When the directions of the sun and the moon are in a straight line, as at new or full moon, the two gravitational pulls add together, and produce higher-than-average tides. When the directions of the sun and the moon are at right angles, as when the moon's phase is first and last quarter, the gravitational pulls oppose each other, and the tides are weaker than average. Higher-than-average tides are called spring tides (nothing to do with the season) and lower-than-average tides are called neap tides. In practice there is a time-lag in the build-up of the tides, and the spring and neap tides are a few days later than the moon's four phases.

There are other factors which influence the height of the spring tides, of which the most significant is the distance of the moon from the earth. When the moon is closest to the earth, its gravitational pull is greatest, and if this happens to be at full moon, the full-moon spring tides will be higher than normal. Equally, if the moon is near the earth at new moon, the new-moon spring tides will be higher than normal. The lunar month (page 71) is 29·53059 days and the time between two successive closest approaches to the earth (called the anomalistic month) is 27·55455 days. Now

$$14 \text{ lunar months} = 413 \cdot 428 \text{ days, and}$$
$$15 \text{ anomalistic months} = 413 \cdot 318 \text{ days,}$$

which is almost exactly the same. Thus every 14 lunar months the moon comes back to the same relationship between its phases and its distance from the earth. The effect of this is to put a cyclical variation on the height of the spring tides. The full-moon springs have their maximum rise and fall every 14 lunar months, and so do the new-moon springs. The maximum new- and full-moon tides occur alternately. There is a similar variation in the height of the neap tides.

All these tidal phenomena would have been known to the neolithic inhabitants of Britain. Even the last described, though less obvious than the others, is quite easy to see on a gently shelving beach because small changes in the height of the tide make a great difference to the line of maximum water. The connection between the tides and the moon could have stimulated interest in tracking its celestial movements. (If the sky goddess could have such a remarkable effect on the powerful sea, who would deny her influence over puny men?)

It is quite impossible to deduce how far an interest in the tides would have led Neolithic and Early Bronze Age men into the intricacies of lunar motion. A. D. Beach has gone so far as to propose that Stonehenge I was a tidal predictor. He has pointed out yet another way in which the Aubrey Holes could have been used —in this case for keeping track of the 14-lunation cycle in the heights of the spring tides. His method of using the Aubrey Holes is similar to that proposed by Hoyle (page 75), in which the Aubrey circle is seen as a large protractor indicating the positions of the sun and moon in the sky. Since there are 56 Aubrey Holes, and $56 = 4 \times 14$, it only requires a marker moved relative to the sun marker by four holes anticlockwise each month to keep in step with the rotation of the lunar orbit.

There is no doubt that this scheme would work, but several objections can be put forward. The 14-lunation effect, though large enough to be observable, is really quite small, being only about 10 per cent of the tidal rise and fall at the most. Knowledge of it would make little practical difference to either the ease or safety of voyages; meteorological conditions, such as wind direction and barometric pressure, can have a greater influence on the tides. If the 14-lunation effect was investigated by neolithic men as Beach supposes, the stimulus was curiosity, not seafaring. Furthermore, Stonehenge is two or three days' journey on foot from the nearest coast. It does not seem very probable that a tidal predictor would be built so far from the sea, for the purpose of making tidal predictions which were unnecessary and which could not have been conveniently checked by visual reference to the height of the water. The theory of the Aubrey Holes as lunar eclipse predictors can be objected to as well, but the forecasts could at least have been verified on site.

Whilst we can on balance reject the hypothesis of Stonehenge being a sophisticated tidal predictor, this is no reason to doubt that tides could have influenced the ideas of the early astronomers in north-west Europe. Indeed we may have here part of the explanation for one of the puzzles of megalithic astronomy, the lack of comparable interest in the movements of the moon in the more advanced civilizations of the Mediterranean region. The Egyptians had very little inclination towards observational astronomy. They devised a lunar calendar before 3000 BC and kept it in step with the year by annual observations of the heliacal risings of Sirius (page 78). They named the stars and the planets and used the stars for telling the time at night. But although they had a passion for covering the walls of buildings with inscriptions about every aspect of life, they apparently kept no astronomical records. From about 2150 BC diagrams of stars appear on coffin lids, and apart from those the only early astronomical 'texts' are decorated ceilings of tombs dating from the fifteenth century BC. In contrast the Babylonians maintained extremely detailed records of astronomical events, beginning in the sixteenth century BC, though they are very sparse before 651 BC. They recorded the length of each month, eclipses, the movements of the planets, the appearances of Sirius, and even bad weather. From their records they deduced the Metonic cycle of lunar months (page 74) and an eclipse cycle of 135 lunar months. Nowhere, however, is there any indication of the use of the horizon as a graduated circle, nor of observational techniques which remotely resemble the extrapolation method of finding the monthly declination maximum of the moon.

There are several factors which may have contributed to the different courses of development of observational astronomy in the Near East and in north-west Europe. The first is the climate, for in spite of the clear skies and good weather in the Early Bronze Age, visibility near the horizon would still not have been as good in northern Europe as in the more arid areas of the eastern Mediterranean. This may account for the different method of setting the calendar used by the Egyptians. By using the heliacal rising of Sirius they had no need of accurate alignments, since the essence of the observation was whether or not the star was visible on a particular day. The method is reliable only if a clear atmosphere down to the horizon is a certainty at the right time of year (mid-July), and whilst this may be so in desert regions, it would not have been the case on the Atlantic coast. Setting the calendar by the position of the sunrise at the solstice, on the other hand, demands accurate alignments but not such a clear atmosphere, because the sun is so very much brighter than a star.

The second difference between north-west Europe and the Mediterranean is, of course, the tides, which were unknown to the majority of ancient civilizations. They did not experience the direct influence of the moon on their fishing and sea communications. They would not have held the moon in quite the same awe as did the peoples living on the shores of the large oceans, and they would have had correspondingly less interest in the lunar cycles.

But probably the most important factor is the geographical latitude of the two areas. The further north one goes, the more noticeable the movements of the sun and moon appear. At the equator the sun rises within a sector of less than 50° of the eastern horizon, and at all seasons it is high in the sky at noon. At latitude 55°N, the azimuth of sunrise changes by nearly 90° from summer to winter, and the sun's height at midday varies from $58\frac{1}{2}°$ to $11\frac{1}{2}°$. For the moon the movements are even more dramatic, so that in the Shetland Islands the moon sometimes only just clears the southern skyline at the major standstill (page 68). Its rising and setting azimuths can be over nearly all the circumference of the horizon. The most likely reason why measurements using the horizon circle were exploited so fully in north-west Europe and not round the Mediterranean is that in the former area the movements of the sun and moon were much more conspicuous than in the latter.

In comparing the two astronomical traditions we have to bear in mind that the earliest northern observations of the sun, for example the construction of the passage grave at New Grange in 3300 BC, are more or less contemporary with the first Egyptian calendar, and the lunar observations, as revealed by the causeway postholes at Stonehenge, predate the Babylonian inscriptions by about 1,000 years. The heyday of the Early Bronze Age astronomy was over long before Babylonian astronomy reached its peak. Megalithic astronomy was an independent development; it owes nothing to ideas from the old civilizations of the east. Many archaeologists have found this very disconcerting, and have been reluctant to accept that agricultural tribes, living in small pastoral communities in mud huts, with no grand public buildings, artistic traditions, or even writing, would have been capable of the sophisticated observational astronomy claimed by Professor Thom and others. Surely these illiterate savages, with their limited resources and their disgusting practice of leaving bodies to decompose before interring them, could not be intellectually capable of predicting lunar eclipses?

It is a fallacy to suppose that the intellectual ability of the human race has changed much over the last 5,000 years. As a species, man is between one and two million years old and presumably intelligence has been developing, though not necessarily at a constant rate, over the whole of this period. Five thousand years is less than 1 per cent of the time the human race has existed; changes since then would be barely perceptible. When we consider the achievements of societies contemporary with the Later Neolithic farming communities of Britain, we can have little doubt about the abilities of the cleverest men of that period. The construction of the Egyptian pyramids around 2500 BC, for example, demanded a considerable understanding of civil engineering, of organization of labour, of planning and integrating diverse activities, such as quarrying, transport, and tool-making, and of logistics, such as the provision of food supplies for the huge work force. It could only have been undertaken by men of high ability.

Of course there is nothing as spectacular as the pyramids in Neolithic or Early Bronze Age Britain, but there is no reason to suppose the general level of intelligence was any lower, or that there was a smaller proportion of geniuses in the population. Many of the feats of communal engineering, from 3500 BC onwards, demanded courage, organization, and skill. Whether we think of the huge stones built into the megalithic tombs, the construction of Silbury Hill, or the shaping and erection of the sarsen trilithons at Stonehenge, the conclusion is the same. Throughout the whole period of the Later Neolithic and Early Bronze Ages, there was a succession of major projects of which any community could have been proud. Why should we, confronted by these many examples of clever civil engineering, not be willing to believe their builders capable of elementary arithmetic and geometry, or of making systematic observations of the sun and moon? The latter activities require no more intelligence than the former.

Some archaeologists have been reluctant to accept the idea of a 'home-grown' origin for the geometrical and astronomical knowledge because of the lack of a written language. I shall return to this point shortly. Several writers have rejected the possibility of even the megalithic monuments being constructed by the indigenous people of the area, and have gone to enormous lengths to seek evidence for outside influence. For some years, following the discovery of the dagger carvings on the Stonehenge sarsens, the design of Stonehenge IIIa was attributed to the Myceneans. The sarsen circle was at that time dated to 1600 BC, but it is now known to be older by at least 300 years and the connection has been abandoned. Nevertheless, the idea of a band of cultured visitors instructing the natives in megalithic architecture still flourishes. John Ivimy's book *The Sphinx and the Megaliths* typifies this genre of romantic Stonehenge literature. Ivimy sets out to 'explain' how the neolithic peoples of Britain came by their knowledge of astronomy and geometry, assuming without hesitation that it was imported from Egypt because that was the most advanced civilization of the day.

His fanciful story of the origin of megalithic science begins with the priests of the Egyptian god Ra, who had been responsible for predicting eclipses of the sun and moon 'since the dawn of civilization'. Alas, their predictions gradually became inaccurate, because they were using Chaldean eclipse cycles without understanding them. Learning from his mathematicians that observations of the moon could be made more precisely in higher latitudes than Heliopolis, the High Priest decided to send an expedition to northern lands. The voyagers landed eventually at Milford Haven and there set up an observatory, built of bluestones from the nearby mountain of Preseli. Unfortunately clouds and rain prevented satisfactory observations, so they were forced to change their site; hence the observatory was taken down, transported to the more favourable location of Salisbury Plain, and re-erected. When the leader of the expedition died, he was so greatly honoured that his people buried him under a large mound, Silbury Hill, in imitation of the royal pyramids of Egypt. The astronomers founded and settled in a town near Stonehenge, which they called Abaris (now Avebury), a word mentioned by Diodorus Siculus (page 4) as being the name of one of the later priests of the Hyperboreans.

Stories of this sort, though entertaining, may, when presented in the guise of academic study, seriously mislead their readers. It is not necessary in this book to refute Ivimy's ideas in detail; the confusion of chronology is sufficient to reveal the weaknesses. The book has been cited mainly because of the clear way the author expresses a view held by many writers on the fringe of accepted science. 'The test by which such speculation should be judged is not the same as that by which the validity of scientific theories is properly judged. The question to be asked is not: what solid evidence exists to prove that these ideas are right; but rather does any solid evidence exist to prove them wrong . . . ?'

Unfortunately it is not always possible in archaeology to produce evidence to support speculative interpretations of sites and their interrelationships. There are several examples of this lack in archaeo-astronomy, and the sceptic might very well argue that interpreting stone fans as extrapolation sectors, for example, has no more support than the hypothesis put forward by Ivimy. In the end we have to accept (or reject) both interpretations by the same criteria: do they conflict with more solidly based knowledge of the period, and do reasonable deductions from these ideas lead to conflict or improbabilities? Applying this latter test to Ivimy's suggestion that Stonehenge was built by an Egyptian expeditionary force, leads to the astounding conclusion that, since no Egyptian artefact has ever been discovered in southern Britain in a sealed layer dating from the Neolithic or Early Bronze Ages, we can only suppose they were unfailingly meticulous in keeping all their possessions together and over hundreds of years never lost any, and that finally they took everything with Egyptian connotations back to Egypt. The human race is not normally so careful.

Megalithic monuments have captured the popular interest as have no other branches of archaeology, and a spate of pseudo-scientific books putting forward mystical ideas has appeared in recent years. They often draw inspiration from a book first published in 1925, *The Old Straight Track* by Alfred Watkins. He was a merchant, photographer, naturalist, and amateur archaeologist, who lived in Herefordshire and had an intimate knowledge of the area. One day in 1920, at the age of 65, he was riding over the hills when a revelation came to him—across the countryside was a complex network of lines, connecting together the sites of prehistoric standing stones, burial mounds, hill forts, fords, churches, lengths of road, and certain place-names. He regarded his lines as indications of prehistoric trackways, and he devoted the rest of his life to investigating the 'leys', as he called them, searching for evidence to back his theory and withstanding the verbal onslaughts of professional archaeologists who thought it was all rubbish. Indeed, there is little to be said in favour of Watkins's hypothesis. To begin with, there is no reason to suppose that prehistoric trackways were dead straight; one would have expected them to follow the easy path, as do the well-attested Neolithic and Bronze Age tracks, such as the one along the Dorset Downs. Watkins pays no regard to the period of the markers along his leys, arguing that if a modern church lies on the line, it is proof that the church was built on the site of a prehistoric marking point. Furthermore, he sets no criteria for what is on a line or not, and is quite willing to allow 'near misses', as well as permitting leys to pass along the boundaries of enclosures, or through their centres, whichever looks the better. With rules as flexible as these, it is not difficult to find alignments in any part of the country, using nothing more than a large-scale map and a long ruler.

In the course of his studies of alignments, Watkins paid some attention to midsummer sunrise orientations, and concluded that they were part of the ley system. Understandably, modern devotees of Watkins have seized on Professor Thom's work for the existence of alignments in general, and by implication for ley lines, whether astronomically orientated or not. Some of the alignments cited by Alfred Watkins are of course genuine, and we assume intentional (for example the linear arrays of round barrows and long stretches of Roman roads), and some of his astronomical alignments have been substantiated by later work, but this is no confirmation that his basic theory is correct. There is a world of difference between the precise, numerical, and statistically supported work of Alexander Thom and the diffuse, non-numerical, subjective approach of Alfred Watkins.

However, Watkins himself would doubtless be surprised at the modern ramifications of his theory, for it has been taken over by people whose interest is more mystical than archaeological. In their eyes ley lines are the manifestations of channels of some mysterious force, unknown to contemporary science but thoroughly understood by the ancients, who, being close to nature, had knowledge which is denied to modern man. Nevertheless, the secret forces are strong enough for extra-terrestrial beings, in their flying saucers, to use them for navigation over the chalk uplands of southern England. Associated with these ideas one usually finds a willing acceptance of magic, dowsing, extrasensory perception and the occult, and indeed of almost anything with an air of mystery about it, whether it be the Loch Ness Monster or previous visitations from outer space. Writings on these topics frequently reveal an escapist belief in a Golden Age, now lost owing to the materialism of technological progress. The evidence put forward by such writers is unsubstantiated and never subjected to reasonable critical examination, even though it may be directly contrary to the whole structure of contemporary science. Unfortunately these ideas go largely unchallenged, because scientists are reluctant to divert their attention from productive work to what they see as sterile argument, unlikely to lead to any useful conclusion. Views based on emotional needs are not changed by rational discussion.

Studies of the astronomical and geometrical attainments of the people of the Neolithic and Early Bronze Ages have suffered greatly from the writings of the 'lunatic fringe', whose interest has for a long time discouraged reputable archaeologists from considering archaeo-astronomy seriously. Hence the conclusions of Professor Thom and others have not, until very recently, been taken into account in reviews of our knowledge of prehistoric culture and society. The situation is changing rapidly. Two archaeologists in particular, Professor Colin Renfrew and Dr Euan MacKie, have been the first to attempt to produce a composite picture of neolithic life. Their ideas are stimulating and I shall discuss them shortly, but first it is necessary to recapitulate the conventional view of Neolithic and Early Bronze Age society as it was held only a few years ago.

Visitors to the great museums of the world are left in no doubt about the origins of civilization. Gallery after gallery of the Louvre and the British Museum are filled with archaeological treasures from the eastern Mediterranean, from Egypt and Sumer, Assyria and the Aegean. There are inscriptions, statues, golden ornaments, glassware and jewellery, the happy results of artistic genius and exquisite craftsmanship. The dry climate of the Nile valley permitted even wooden objects to survive, and the stylish lines of Egyptian tables and chairs are elegant compared with much of our modern furniture. The contrast with western European remains is stark: in the collections of finds from the Neolithic Period there are only rows of polished axes, dull brown pottery to hold the evening stew, and flint scrapers for removing the grease from the insides of animal skins. Compared with the Near East, living standards in the British Neolithic Period seem miserably poor. It was natural, almost inevitable, to assume that tribes who were incapable of producing a higher quality of material goods would also be culturally backward, brutish, rough, and barbarian.

Until the mid nineteen-sixties no one had any real doubts about this view, in spite of the large earthworks and stone monuments. Neolithic communities in Britain were seen as tribes of savages, on the remote fringes of the Mediterranean world, and their advancement, so far as it went, was through the slow diffusion of new ideas and technology, westwards from the superior civilizations of the Near East. The diffusionist theory, as it was called, was the basis of the whole framework of Neolithic and Bronze Age archaeology in western Europe. It was explored in detail by many archaeologists and set out by Gordon Childe in a scholarly book which had immense influence, *The Dawn of European Civilisation* (published, as it happened, in the same year as *The Old Straight Track*). According to this theory, not only did bronze come from the Near East (via the Aegean, the Balkans, and central Europe), but every other development as well. Thus passage graves were thought to have been ultimately derived from Cretan round tombs, the style having been brought by migrations of people to Spain, Brittany, and eventually to Ireland and northern Scotland. Likewise, the spiral decorations on megaliths were thought to have their remote origins in Malta, where there are similar carvings at temples such as Tarxien. Since there was a known chronology for the eastern civilizations, and diffused technology must obviously lag behind its origins, this fixed a timescale for the archaeological periods in western Europe. The British Neolithic Period was believed to have begun about 2400 BC, a date which we now realize was nearly 2,000 years too late.

The breakdown of the diffusionist theory came with the development of radiocarbon dating, which allowed for the first time an independent check of the age of wood, charcoal, and bone. The first dates for the British Neolithic Period were received with dismay, because they were much earlier than had ever been expected, but they have been substantiated many times, and later revisions of the radiocarbon technique have pushed the dates even further into the past. Archaeologists eventually had to accept that the neolithic culture of western Europe owed nothing to the traditions of the Near East. Perhaps this ought to have led at once to a revision of the ideas of the capabilities of these 'backward' communities on the Atlantic coast. We could no longer account for the architecture of the corbelled tombs by saying the builders had learnt the techniques at second or third hand from the Aegean, or explain away the design of Stonehenge IIIa as the product of an itinerant architect from Mycenae. For all the poor quality of their material possessions, the local tribes could not have been mere barbarians, as archaeologists had believed.

The impact of the 'radiocarbon revolution' has been reviewed by Colin Renfrew in his book *Beyond Civilisation*. After setting out the case for the new and extended chronology, he explored its consequences, particularly in relation to our interpretation of neolithic society. With the diffusionist theory no longer tenable, the visible remains of the period appear in a new light. The custom of communal burial, at one time regarded as evidence for a cultural unity in north-west Europe, now seems only a factor which several different traditions have in common. By studying the typology and the dates of megalithic tombs and earthen long barrows, Renfrew concludes that they can be separated clearly into four, or possibly five, groups, reflecting quite independent developments in tomb building: Iberia, Brittany, northern Germany, Britain and Ireland. If this is the case, we are bound to ask what forces were operating in western Europe in the Neolithic Period which made it necessary for societies to build these large structures, and what their communal graves represented to the societies who built them.

One answer to both these questions may be that when societies became agricultural and therefore less nomadic they required territorial markers, not only to indicate which was their land but also to act as a ceremonial centre and focus for the social life of the community. The communal grave, whether long barrow or stone tomb, was not, in general, too large to have been constructed by a small group of people, for it is estimated that one could have been built in about 80 man-months, using the tools available at the time. At this period in the early part of the fourth millennium BC, each community was probably composed of a single extended family. Here then is the context of the first signs known to us of an awakening interest in astronomy. The communities who orientated their long barrows and passage graves crudely towards the midsummer or midwinter sunrises were probably families of farmers, who practised a form of sun-worship in the belief that it would foster their crops and their animals. They were not astronomers, nor scientists, and at this stage in the development of society there is no reason to assume they even had wise men or priests.

As society developed, the social units became larger. By about 3500 BC the first causewayed camps were being built in southern England, maybe for cattle-herding or ceremonial activities, or possibly for both purposes. The geographical distribution of these is interesting, and probably very significant. They are widely separated, and each one is surrounded by a group of as many as thirty long barrows. The construction of the causewayed camps is seen by Renfrew as a sign of the emergence of neolithic chiefdoms; the beginning of the organization of society into larger groups, a process which continued throughout the Neolithic Period.

Clues to the pattern of life in prehistoric societies can sometimes be obtained from studies of primitive tribes in modern times, although it is wise to use them only as examples of what could have happened and not to draw rigid conclusions from them. Nevertheless, ritual and ceremony are often important in chiefdoms, and this type of society usually has a specialist priesthood. In neolithic Britain the priests would have been the custodians of the gradually accumulating know-ledge of the movements of the sun and moon. Renfrew quotes an interesting account of the Hopi Indians of the southern USA, who used a horizon calendar in the same way as we assume the neolithic communities of Britain did. The Hopis appointed a religious official, called a Sun Watcher, who kept track of the movements of the sun along the horizon and whose duties included warning the people of important dates. He kept a tally of the passing of days on a notched stick; perhaps the neolithic Britains did too.

During the period from 3500 BC to 2500 BC there seems to have been a steady development, in both centralization of society and sophistication of constructions. New Grange, Silbury Hill, Stonehenge I, the Dorset Cursus, and Avebury all belong to this period, and indicate the ability of chieftains to call on larger numbers of people for communal projects and the existence of specialist knowledge in civil engineering, most likely held by the same priests who organized the religious life. Other works of the period include the first stone circles, usually large and truly circular at this time, in the western half of the British Isles. In the eastern half of Britain they built henges, and at a few sites, like Durrington Walls and the Sanctuary, small circular wooden huts, probably roofed with turf or thatch, and looking, we suppose, like the native huts of parts of Africa.

The really dramatic events in the Neolithic Period took place around, or just before, 2500 BC. Euan MacKie, in *Science and Society in Prehistoric Britain*, has drawn together the results of many recent radiocarbon datings, the information from the excavations by Dr Geoffrey Wainwright of the large Class II henges, and the discoveries of Professor Thom, to produce a cohesive account of the final centuries of the Neolithic Period. He shows how the steady progress of the earlier centuries suddenly gave way to an outburst of building. The small wooden huts like the Sanctuary were replaced by larger and grander roundhouses at Mount Pleasant, Marden, and Durrington Walls. The new buildings at Marden and Durrington were surrounded by huge earthworks, and some time later so was the roundhouse at Mount Pleasant. A century or so behind the others, the complex and subtly designed egg-shaped house of Woodhenge was erected, just outside the main enclosure of Durrington Walls.

This large increase in building activity must have led to an enormous demand for deer antlers for digging the earthworks, and bands of men must have searched the forests for them when they were shed annually by the stags. There would have been great need, too, for stone axes, so that the trees could have been felled and the timbers shaped and jointed. There is no doubt that the axes came from the neolithic flint mines at Grimes Graves in Norfolk. Excavations there have produced datable material—antlers and charcoal—which confirms that the mines were being worked around 2500 BC, but there is an even stronger link than just this: the discovery of the same type of pottery, grooved ware, in the mines and in the ditches of the large henges. The distribution of grooved ware is one of the most significant pieces of evidence in the puzzle of the Late Neolithic Period.

The normal pottery of this time is the round-bottomed 'baggy' type known as Peterborough ware. Grooved ware is flat-bottomed and decorated with patterns of straight lines, or occasionally circles and spirals. It has been found in Ireland, inside a stone ring at Lios, County Limerick; in Orkney at two neolithic village sites, Skara Brae and Rinyo; and at many places in the south and east of England. It is particularly strongly associated with ceremonial sites, for in addition to the large quantities found in the Class II henges, it has been recovered from the ditch bottom at Avebury, from the Sanctuary, Woodhenge, and a few other henges. The origins of this pottery have never been explained. It appears first, apparently without antecedents, in the ditch of Stonehenge I, in association with material dated to about 2800 BC. Unlike other types of neolithic pottery, no piece has yet been discovered with impressions of grain in its surface, suggesting that it was not made in a domestic environment but in its own potteries. The importance of grooved ware is that it firmly links together the larger henges of southern Britain, the neolithic sites in Orkney, and the flint mines of Grimes Graves. They were all connected with the upsurge of activity towards the end of the Neolithic Period.

MacKie relates these diverse facts to the idea of a strong priestly élite in neolithic society. He sees the wooden huts and the later roundhouses of the super-henges as the centres of a cult, permanently occupied by priests and their followers. The grooved ware is special, as befits the ruling classes, and its distribution shows their influence and their control. In the far north, where timber was unobtainable, the priests lived in the stone houses of Skara Brae, in conditions of much greater comfort than the ordinary population of the time. They had stone furniture, surely an indication that their counterparts in the south had wooden tables, chairs, and shelving. This accounts for the flat-bottomed pottery; the normal round-bottomed ware is convenient for setting in the soft ashes beside the camp fire, but not for placing on the kitchen dresser.

The inhabitants of the roundhouses seem to have had different food from the rest of the population. At Durrington Walls they ate mainly pork, as can be seen from the animal bones in the middens, whereas the seasonal visitors to Windmill Hill at the same period ate mainly beef. The middens contained very few animal skulls, implying that meat was brought into the enclosure already cut into joints, and possibly the bread was prepared outside as well, because no querns for grinding grain were found, nor any charred grains of cereal. All this evidence strongly suggests that the inhabitants of the roundhouses were a special group within the community. They were not engaged in the normal practices of agriculture, and presumably would have been occupied with something else. They were, in MacKie's view, astronomer–priests, the wise men who kept alive the arcane knowledge of geometry and astronomy while the rest of the population clothed them, fed them, and worked for them.

There are historic parallels for this idea. One thinks almost immediately of the monasteries in the Middle Ages, where learning and study flourished in the midst of general illiteracy. A closer analogy is to be found in the Mayan civilization of central America, where for several hundred years (AD 200 to AD 900) the peasants were ruled by an upper class who lived in luxurious ceremonial centres, while the rest of the population inhabited wooden huts. This was a stone-age society, for they had not discovered metal-working, but the Mayans became exceptionally skilled in astronomy, geometry, architecture, and sculpture. Their elaborate carvings and inscriptions reveal that they had devised an accurate calendar and discovered astronomical periodicities in the movements of the planets as well as those of the moon, and that they could predict lunar and solar eclipses. The Mayan élite even had its own pottery, which was not used by the common people. Of course, the achievements of the Mayan civilization far exceed anything that is claimed for Neolithic or Early Bronze Age Britain, but the parallel is interesting because it shows that a highly stratified society could exist for a long period. It demonstrates equally that when this type of society collapses, it can do so completely and with great speed.

If the roundhouses of neolithic Britain were the living-quarters of the astronomer–priests, we should expect them to be located near the ceremonial centres, and this seems to be the case. Durrington Walls and Woodhenge are a mere 3 km from Stonehenge; the Sanctuary is but 2½ km from Avebury (and was connected to it by a processional way); Marden is almost exactly mid-way between Woodhenge and the Sanctuary. No important ceremonial or astronomical site has been discovered near Mount Pleasant, but there is a possible candidate only 2 km to the west, a small henge called Maumbury Rings in the town of Dorchester, where grooved ware has been found. Unfortunately this henge has been so greatly changed, having at one time been a Roman amphitheatre and later converted to a gun emplacement in the English Civil War, that very little of its original construction still remains. The neolithic village of Skara Brae is only 10 km from the two important ceremonial and astronomical sites of the Ring of Brodgar and the Stones of Stenness. Both are circles of very large stones within henges; Brodgar is the same diameter (103·6 m, equivalent to 125 MY) as the inner rings of Avebury, and has several sun and moon alignments with distant foresights. The association between the supposed habitations of the astronomer–priests and the ceremonial centres is well-founded, but there are many important astronomical sites where no sign of an élite residence has yet been discovered.

If MacKie is correct about the priestly upper class, one of the objections to the whole of the archaeo-astronomical hypothesis is resolved. His theory explains how knowledge could have been retained and passed on from one generation to another. Critics of the astronomical hypothesis point out that a large amount of complicated geometrical and astronomical data would have had to be recorded. There would have been many rules and detailed procedures, for laying out the complicated geometrical shapes, for setting out and observing with the astronomical alignments, and, most complex of all, for designing and using the extrapolation sectors. We have absolutely no evidence of any writing or system for recording numbers in the Neolithic Period, though there is no doubt about the ability to count as far as the hundreds. The only non-literate way of remembering the data is therefore to ritualize the tasks, so that they can be made 'word perfect', with every repetition exactly the same as the one before. This is not as difficult as it sounds; in the twentieth century only actors and priests need to remember large amounts of prose, but in more primitive societies the village sages can recall details of ancestry going back many generations, or the history of the tribe and its mythology, and constant repetition keeps it fresh in the mind. An élite class of astronomer–priests, living in a separate community, with their schools of novices taught by older men, would provide just the environment for the continuation of a strong and precise oral tradition.

However, learning by heart is insufficient to account for the process of discovery. Even to be sure of the basic 18·6-year cycle of the moon would require observations spread over many years, longer no doubt than the adult lifetime of a neolithic man. The causeway posts at Stonehenge show one way the observations could have been made and the moonrise directions recorded, but surely there must have been some permanent numerical record of the passing of the years to make it all intelligible? Discovering the lunar cycles is much more difficult than passing on accepted knowledge. It may be that they used wooden tally sticks, like the Hopi Indians, and that none of the sticks remains; or that perhaps the cup and ring marks hold the clue and we have not yet learned to decipher them; or even that events may have been recorded by arrangements of stones on the ground, which have not yet been recognized.

The picture presented by this new interpretation is of a priestly hierarchy, emerging with the development of chiefdoms during the time of the causewayed camps, having its own centres before 3000 BC at Marden and Durrington Walls, and becoming by 2700 BC an identifiable and strong élite, able to undertake the building of Stonehenge I and Silbury Hill. At present we have no explanation for the new wave of roundhouse building from 2700 BC onwards. Violent changes in society are the consequences of either internal tensions or external pressures; in Late Neolithic times changes were already occurring on the continent of Europe, with the introduction of bronze implements and weapons. It would be a tidy situation if we could say that the construction boom of the astronomer–priests was due to the cult having been adopted and revitalized by the Beaker Folk immigrants of the Early Bronze Age, but this appears not to be the case. They arrived just too late to be responsible for the building of the new roundhouses at Durrington Walls, Mount Pleasant, and Marden, for the pottery on the bottoms of the ditches is all grooved ware, and Beaker sherds occur only after the ditches had silted for some time.

Euan MacKie's reinterpretation of the Late Neolithic Period has therefore highlighted a new problem. The Beaker immigrations from 2400 BC onwards resulted in new materials, new practices in agriculture, and different burial styles, all of which replaced the neolithic culture. At the same time, the neolithic astronomer–priests were apparently still powerful, and they continued to live in their secluded roundhouses for perhaps another 200 years. It is strange that with such a stable ruling class, Late Neolithic society should have been so open to cultural change.

There are signs that the Beaker Folk rapidly adopted the ideas of the astronomer–priests and became proficient themselves in geometry and astronomy. Their pottery is found in the later occupation levels of the roundhouses, it is often associated with stone circles and they are believed to have built Stonehenge II. Beaker pottery and grooved ware are both found in the lowest levels at Woodhenge, implying a merging of the two cultural traditions before 2250 BC.

Ultimately the wooden posts holding up the roundhouses decayed away. Estimates of the length of time these structures would have lasted range up to 300 years. The Sanctuary was rebuilt several times during its period of occupation, and finally the wooden posts were replaced by a stone circle, dated by Beaker pottery to around 2100 BC. At Mount Pleasant the site of the disused roundhouse was marked with a three-sided square of sarsen stones, open towards the south-west, with two of its sides parallel to the axis of the original building. At Woodhenge a recumbent sarsen stone was placed on the south side just within the outermost ring of rotted posts. The sites of the roundhouses were clearly considered significant even after they had ceased to be habitable.

However, the decay of the roundhouses did not lead to the end of megalithic astronomy. The Scottish sites at Kintraw, Ballochroy, and Temple Wood are dated astronomically to around 1800 BC. The sites in the Western Isles from which Professor Thom deduced the 16-month calendar are well into the Early Bronze Age. The Dartmoor alignments of Cholwichtown and Lower Piles were marked by egg-shaped stone rings, which are also towards the end of stone-circle development. These examples, and, of course, Stonehenge itself, show that astronomical observations were continued for several hundred years into the second millennium

BC. There is a tendency for the observational methods to become more refined; they are reduced to the barest essentials for marking the setting of the sun or moon, and in many cases, as we have seen, this is no more than a single oriented stone from which the observer sights on a notch on the distant horizon.

In the period from 1700 BC onwards, astronomical activity seems to have declined. No solar or lunar observatories have been dated as late as 1600 BC, by either astronomical or archaeological methods. The latest construction which we would attribute to the same tradition of science and geometry is the final phase of Stonehenge, about 1550 BC. It was a period of uncertainty, with changes of plan shown by the abandoning of the Y and Z holes before the spiral rings were completed; and the modifications to the bluestone settings appear not to have any astronomical significance. By this time the deterioration of the climate had set in. The increased cloudiness would have hampered the observations, ultimately making it impossible to continue precision measurements such as the study of the minor perturbation. Concurrently the crops would have begun to fail, the uplands would have become less and less habitable, and the pressures for survival would have left little or no time for inessentials. Indeed, there are signs that many people did not survive, because the familiar Early Bronze Age pottery types, beakers, urns, and food vessels, all disappear from later excavation layers. So do the flint arrowheads and other small stone implements characteristic of the time, and the people no longer kept the same burial customs. By the time the Middle Bronze Age cultures appear in the archaeological record, they are different in almost every respect from those of their predecessors.

If the Early Bronze Age societies perished in the middle of the second millennium BC, was all the astronomical and geometrical knowledge lost for good? According to Euan MacKie, megalithic mathematics lingered on in northern Scotland until the Iron Age. He studied the dimensions of a type of fortification known as brochs. These remains are peculiar to Scotland; they are essentially hollow round towers of drystone walling, which may be up to 13 m high. The walls themselves are hollow and contain rooms and staircases. MacKie surveyed the inner courtyards of 37 brochs, finding 30 to be accurately circular, 4 to be non-circular, and 3 were buried under too much debris to permit the exact shape to be determined (though they were suspected of not being true circles). He applied statistical analysis to the diameters of the circular brochs, and deduced a 'broch yard' of 0·837 m. This is only 1 per cent greater than the megalithic yard. Two of the non-circular brochs were elliptical, and their major and minor axes were simple numbers in megalithic yards, i.e. $14\frac{1}{2}$ MY $\times$ $13\frac{1}{2}$ MY and 14 MY $\times$ 10 MY. The ground plans of the other two brochs were very similar to a flattened circle and a Type I egg, but they were not quite the normal shapes, since the non-circular part of the flattened circle was a half ellipse with axes 13 MY $\times$ 10 MY. The normally semicircular portion of the egg was also a half ellipse with axes 8 MY $\times$ 6 MY. In view of the long time lapse and the changing cultures it is rather surprising that any trace of megalithic geometry should remain, but the similarity of the last two shapes is surely too great to be accidental. We can only presume that a verbal tradition of some shapes being of special significance lingered on for fifteen centuries or more.

Astronomical knowledge was more easily lost once the weather conditions had frustrated observations and the population was forced to move away from many of their sites on the higher ground. Nevertheless, in the extract from Diodorus Siculus, quoted in Chapter 1, there is a reference to a circular enclosure and a temple dedicated to the sun god Apollo in the island of the Hyperboreans. Many authors have interpreted this passage as referring to Avebury and Stonehenge respectively, and take it as evidence for continued use of Stonehenge into the Early Iron Age. Diodorus also says that Apollo visited the island every 19 years, a statement which is thought to refer to the Metonic cycle (page 74), i.e. the repetition after a 19-year interval of the phases of the moon on the same day of the year. This implies that some astronomical knowledge and an accurate calendar were still retained in the 4th century BC, but it does not follow that the inhabitants of Britain had kept alive the more sophisticated astronomical learning of the Late Neolithic and Early Bronze Ages.

The priestly sect of the Iron Age in Britain and northern France was the Druids, made famous by Julius Caesar in his books known collectively as *The Gallic War*. He describes them as one of the two privileged classes—the other was the Knights—and their duties were to officiate at the worship of gods, regulate public and private sacrifices, and give rulings on all religious matters. The tenets of Druidism were not written down but were learned by heart, even though pupils had to spend as much as twenty years memorizing their verses. Caesar also comments on their long philosophical discussions about the physical constitution of the world, the size of the universe, and about the heavenly bodies and their movements. The Druids were the Iron Age successors to, if not the descendants of, the priestly society of learned men of the Late Neolithic Period. It is amusing to speculate, in view of the vehemence of denials by archaeologists that the Druids had anything to do with Stonehenge, that they very possibly made use of its decaying remains for ceremonies, even though its more subtle features would have long since been forgotten.

The work of the new generation of archaeologists on combining our knowledge of the geometry and astronomy of the Neolithic and Early Bronze Ages with conventional archaeological data is only the first step towards compiling a new and more complete picture of the period. It has to proceed at two levels. These are: broad theoretical studies of the nature of neolithic society, integrating the whole gamut of discoveries; and detailed work on particular aspects to provide a surer foundation for archaeological speculation. Archaeologists will be looking for sites in the north and west of Britain which could have been the equivalents of roundhouses in the south, because if a priestly élite existed at all, we should expect it to have been just as active in the mountain zone where megalithic remains are so very numerous. The origins of grooved ware will no doubt be sought, using modern techniques of chemical and petrological analysis; the pattern will become much clearer when we know where it was made and we can see how it related to the Beaker pottery which covered almost the same span of time.

We believe that in the past, as in modern times, ideas and techniques had their origins, were developed to a peak, and then slowly declined as they lost relevance for the society which created them. With this in mind it should be possible to trace the evolution of geometrical and astronomical ideas and to relate them specifically to other aspects of life. There must for example have been some evolutionary process which led to the different shapes of stone rings; and ultimately, it is to be hoped, when the chronology of stone circles is better known, each type of ring will be related to its own time span and geography, and connected with other cultural features. Eventually the shape of stone rings, which have now no clear pattern in time and space, could become one of the clues by which we recognize the progression of cultural characteristics from one community to another. Similarly it ought to be possible to reconstruct the development of astronomical techniques in detail, from the ceremonial and inaccurate orientations of the early megalithic tombs to the precise and austere alignments marked by the single standing stones. The result of research into the science of the Neolithic and Early Bronze Ages in north-west Europe has been a repainting of the traditional picture, but the new version is far more interesting and exciting. We now have a prospect which is unique in archaeology and particularly attuned to our own time. We are discovering the first traces of the development of science in one of the most remarkable periods in the whole of man's history.

Appendix A
Mathematical Proofs

Derivation of the extrapolation distance

This is the derivation of the quantity η used in Chapter 7 (see page 122). Figure A.1 is essentially the same as Figure 7.3, with the position of the stakes plotted as a function of the time before and after the time of maximum declination. Two stake positions are indicated by A and B, at times t_1 before and t_2 after the time of maximum declination, and they are at distances y_A and y_B from the stake position corresponding to maximum declination. Note that y_A and y_B are not known, only the distance between them, $2p$.

We introduce the unknown constant k to describe the parabola by the equation $y = kt^2$. We also make $t_1 = a-b$ and $t_2 = a+b$.

Then
$$y_B = kt_2{}^2 = k(a+b)^2 = ka^2+kb^2+2kab, \tag{1}$$
and
$$y_A = kt_1{}^2 = k(a-b)^2 = ka^2+kb^2-2kab. \tag{2}$$

Then, by subtraction, $y_B-y_A = 4kab$, but this is also equal to $2p$,

hence
$$k = p/2ab. \tag{3}$$
Similarly,
$$\eta = ED = kb^2. \tag{4}$$

The total distance to be extrapolated from the mid-position of the two stakes, $G+\eta, = \frac{1}{2}(y_A+y_B)$, which by addition of (1) and (2) becomes $k(a^2+b^2)$. Using (4), we get $G = ka^2$.

Now since a is half a day in time, G must be the distance the stake would be from the maximum declination position if the stakes were put in exactly half a day before or after the time of maximum declination. By eliminating k, using (3), we find that

$$G = ka^2 = ap/2b = \tfrac{1}{2}p(a/b),$$
and
$$\eta = kb^2 = bp/2a = \tfrac{1}{2}p(b/a),$$
whence
$$\eta = p^2/4G.$$

The total distance to be extrapolated from the mid-point of the two stakes is therefore $G+p^2/4G$ and it also follows that the distance to be extrapolated from the further stake is $G+p^2/4G-p$.

Extrapolation from three successive nights' observations

Extrapolation from observations of the moon on three successive nights is the method possibly used in Brittany (Chapter 8). The three stake positions are represented by C, A, and B on Figure A.1, at times $2a+t_1$ and t_1 before the maximum, and $2a-t_1$ after the maximum. The distances y_C, y_A, and y_B are the distances from the stakes to the position corresponding to maximum declination. Note that y_C, y_A, and y_B are not known, only the spacings between them, $2p$ and $2q$.

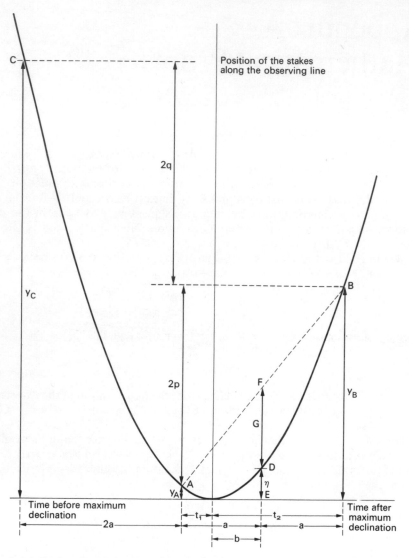

FIG. A.1   Stake positions in relation to the time before and after maximum declination

Using the same constant k to describe the parabola as was used when discussing two nights' observations, we have

$$y_A = kt_1^2,$$
$$y_B = k(2a - t_1)^2 = k(4a^2 + t_1^2 - 4at_1),$$
$$y_C = k(2a + t_1)^2 = k(4a^2 + t_1^2 + 4at_1).$$

By subtraction,

$$2q = y_C - y_B = 8kat_1, \quad \text{hence} \quad q = 4kat_1 \quad \text{and} \quad k = q/4at_1.$$

We know, from the first proof in the Appendix, that $G = ka^2$.

Therefore
$$G = \frac{qa^2}{4at_1}, \text{ and } t_1/a = q/4G.$$

But
$$y_A = kt_1^2, = \frac{qt_1^2}{4at_1} = \frac{q}{4}(t_1/a).$$

This leads to
$$y_A = q^2/16G.$$

In Chapter 8, the symbol η' is used instead of y_A for the distance to be extrapolated from the furthermost stake. Note that these symbols differ from those used by Professor Thom in his original papers, in order to avoid having in this book the same symbol for different quantities.

To find the 'best fit' circle for the Merrivale method of extrapolation

The required circle should be tangential to the line OM of Figure 7.14 and should pass through the point L.

Since
$$OL = G \text{ and } OM = 2G, LM = \sqrt{5}G.$$

Now   NM/PM = LM/LO by similar triangles,

therefore $NM = PM \times LM \div LO, = \frac{1}{2}\sqrt{5}\,G \times \sqrt{5}\,G \div G = 2\frac{1}{2}\,G.$

More generally, if OM represents a fraction r of the spacing between the two stakes, the radius of the best fit circle becomes

$$NM = \frac{1}{2}(1+16r^2)G.$$

$NM = 2\frac{1}{2}G$ is a special case of this solution for $r = \frac{1}{2}$. When $r = 1$, $NM = 8\frac{1}{2}G$, and when $r = \frac{3}{4}$, $NM = 5G$.

Appendix B
A Note on Dating

Dates in this book are given in calendar years BC. Some of the dates were found by Lockyer's astronomical method, but the majority are based on radiocarbon measurements published in various books and journals. Neither of these methods of dating leads to an absolutely accurate date, because there are always unavoidable inaccuracies in making the measurements. There is, however, an important difference between astronomical and radiocarbon dates—when the inaccuracies are reduced to the smallest possible, the astronomical method gives the true date BC but the radiocarbon date does not. These dates are normally published as 'radiocarbon years' which are not the same as true years. To distinguish them from calendar dates, radiocarbon dates are expressed with small letters bc after

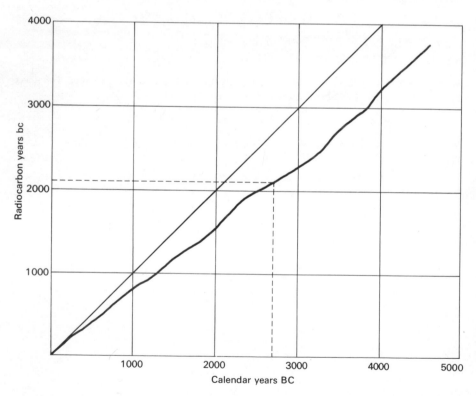

FIG. B.1   An approximate radiocarbon calibration curve

the date, for example 2450 bc. For the purpose of this book, dates bc have been converted to dates BC by using Figure B.1.

Radiocarbon dating is a method of estimating the age of an archaeological sample by measuring its radioactive properties. It gives a date which is quite independent of any archaeological associations and it is therefore particularly valuable when traditional dating methods, such as cross-linking with dated civilizations, cannot be applied. The method was devised by Professor Willard Libby in the nineteen-fifties when he was working at the Institute of Nuclear Studies in Chicago, and in 1960 he was awarded a Nobel Prize for his discovery.

Radiocarbon is a variety of ordinary carbon, the difference between it and normal carbon being only in the number of particles in the nucleus of the atom. Ordinary carbon has six protons and six neutrons in its nucleus; it is therefore known as carbon 12. Radiocarbon has six protons and eight neutrons and is often called carbon 14. The chemical properties of atoms are determined by the number of protons, not the number of neutrons, and the two types of carbon therefore have identical chemical behaviour. They are quite indistinguishable in the way in which they interact with other atoms to form organic compounds in living material. They differ, however, in their physical properties, because, apart from radiocarbon atoms weighing 17 per cent more than the others, the radiocarbon nucleus is unstable and decays away to nitrogen 14 (seven protons and seven neutrons) by emitting an electron.

These electrons are shot out like small bullets and they can be detected by sensitive equipment. It is possible to measure the amount of radiocarbon in a sample of wood, charcoal, or bone by counting the rate of emission of electrons.

All living material contains a small amount of radiocarbon, in the proportion of one radiocarbon atom to every million million atoms of carbon 12. The origin of radiocarbon is in the upper atmosphere, where the atoms of the air are perpetually under bombardment from high-speed particles coming in from space (the cosmic rays). Sometimes these particles collide with atoms of the atmosphere and eject neutrons. These neutrons, in their turn, may collide with nitrogen 14 nuclei to produce yet another nuclear reaction which results in radiocarbon and the emission of a proton. The radiocarbon mixes thoroughly with ordinary carbon and eventually it finds its way into every living thing which contains carbon, always in the same small proportion of one radiocarbon atom to every million million of carbon 12. As long as an object is alive, the chemical reactions of breathing, taking in food, etc., ensure that its radiocarbon fraction remains constant.

When an object dies, it no longer interacts with its environment in the same way. It ceases to take in carbon, and the radiocarbon within it steadily decays away. The rate of decay is quite slow, for half the radiocarbon atoms revert to nitrogen in about 5,600 years, three-quarters have reverted after 11,200 years, seven-eighths after 16,800 years, and so on. Measuring the radiocarbon content gives an estimate of the time since the death of the sample under test.

There is always some statistical uncertainty in radiocarbon dates. The electrons are emitted randomly, and the number of emissions has to be counted over many hours before the true emission rate is known. The longer the counting time, the more accurate the dating, but this puts up the cost of the tests because the expensive equipment is in use for a longer period. Radiocarbon dates are always accompanied by an indication of their statistical accuracy, for example 1560 ±30 bc. This simply means that the radiocarbon date has a 50 per cent chance of being between 1590 bc and 1530 bc.

When the first radiocarbon dates were obtained from British prehistoric periods they were, as explained in Chapter 10, very surprising. The Neolithic and Early Bronze Ages were much earlier than had been expected on archaeological grounds. But it soon became apparent, as more dates were collected, that the new chronology was not right either. Radiocarbon dates for Egyptian samples did not agree with the historic dates, because the radiocarbon dates were apparently too recent. The older the sample the bigger the discrepancy became.

The disagreement has now been resolved by the independent calibration of radiocarbon dates. Fortunately for archaeology there is a very long-lived tree, the Bristlecone Pine, which grows in the White Mountains of California. The Laboratory of Tree-Ring Research at the University of Arizona has laboriously built up a continuous tree-ring sequence from the timber of many trees, extending back more than 8,000 years. As far as chemical changes are concerned, the wood of each ring is effectively dead, and receives no new radiocarbon after the year in which it grew. The age of a ring is found by counting its position in the sequence, and the radiocarbon content of the ring provides the data for a direct calibration of the method.

Calibration results have been published by Professor Hans Suess. From 1500 BC to the present time there are only small differences between calendar years and radiocarbon years, and the method gives a nearly true date. Before 1500 BC there are significant divergences, and they are larger for the earlier dates. At 2000 BC the error is about 500 years, and at 3000 BC it is 700 years. The reason for the errors is that in the third millennium BC the amount of radiocarbon in the atmosphere was greater than it is now. This was not known when the radiocarbon dating method was first developed, and everyone had made the assumption that the proportion of radiocarbon was the same in the past as it is now.

To find calendar dates from radiocarbon dates we must make a correction. An easy method is to use a calibration curve, such as Figure B.1. The dotted lines show that 2100 bc is equivalent to 2700 BC. This curve is based on one by Suess, but it has been greatly simplified to make it easier to use, by ironing out the short period undulations. The loss of accuracy is not important in a book of this sort, especially in view of the statistical counting errors inherent in radiocarbon dates; however, readers should bear in mind that Figure B.1 is only an approximate calibration curve.

Appendix C
Trigonometrical Ratios

In Chapter 4 the trigonometrical ratios sin and cos (short for sine and cosine) were used in equations (1) and (2). The sine and cosine are ways of indicating numerically the size of an angle. In many mathematical problems they are more convenient than degrees.

The definitions of sine and cosine are based on the ratios of the lengths of sides of right-angled triangles. If we wish to find the sine of an angle, we can draw a right-angled triangle of any size incorporating that angle; the sine of the angle is the length of the opposite side divided by the length of the hypotenuse. Thus in Figure 3.1,

$$\sin B = b/a \text{ and } \sin C = c/a.$$

The cosine of an angle is the length of the adjacent side divided by the length of the hypotenuse. Thus in Figure 3.1,

$$\cos B = c/a \text{ and } \cos C = b/a.$$

Sines and cosines are conveniently found from standard tables of trigonometrical functions. Commonly occurring values are

$$\sin 0° = 0{\cdot}000 \qquad \cos 0° = 1{\cdot}000$$
$$\sin 30° = 0{\cdot}500 \qquad \cos 30° = 0{\cdot}866$$
$$\sin 45° = 0{\cdot}707 \qquad \cos 45° = 0{\cdot}707$$
$$\sin 60° = 0{\cdot}866 \qquad \cos 60° = 0{\cdot}500$$
$$\sin 90° = 1{\cdot}000 \qquad \cos 90° = 0{\cdot}000$$

Bibliography

Chapter 1

ATKINSON, R. J. C., *Stonehenge*. Pelican, London (1960).
— 'Moonshine on Stonehenge', *Antiquity*, **40**, 212–16 (1966).
— 'Hoyle on Stonehenge: some comments', *Antiquity*, **41**, 92–5 (1967).
— 'Megalithic astronomy: a prehistorian's comments', *Journal for the History of Astronomy*, **6**, 42–52 (1975).
HADINGHAM, E., *Circles and Standing Stones*. Heinemann, London (1975).
HAWKINS, G. S., 'Stonehenge decoded', *Nature*, **200**, 306–8 (1963).
— 'Stonehenge: a Neolithic computer', *Nature*, **202**, 1258–61 (1964).
— *Stonehenge Decoded*. Souvenir Press Ltd., London (1966); Fontana Books, London (1970).
HOARE, R. COLT, *The Ancient History of Wiltshire* (1812).
HOYLE, F., 'Stonehenge: an eclipse predictor', *Nature*, **211**, 454–6 (1966).
— 'Speculations on Stonehenge', *Antiquity*, **40**, 272–6 (1966).
KENDALL, D. G., PIGGOTT, S., KING-HELE, D. G., and EDWARDS, I. E. S. (organizers), and HODSON, F. R. (editor), *The Place of Astronomy in the Ancient World*. A Joint Symposium of The Royal Society and The British Academy. Oxford University Press (1974); also published, in a paper-bound edition, by the Royal Society in its series *Philosophical Transactions A*, **276**, no. 1257.
LOCKYER, N. J., *Stonehenge and other British Stone Monuments Astronomically Considered*. Macmillan, London (1906).
MACKIE, E. W., 'Archaeological tests on supposed prehistoric astronomical sites in Scotland', in KENDALL *et al.*, *The Place of Astronomy in the Ancient World*, 169–91.
NEWALL, R. S., *Stonehenge*. HMSO, London (1959).
NEWHAM, C. A., in the *Yorkshire Post*, 16 March 1963.
— *The Enigma of Stonehenge*. John Blackburn Ltd., Leeds (1964).
— *The Astronomical Significance of Stonehenge*. John Blackburn Ltd., Leeds (1972).
RUGGLES, C., 'Megalithic observatories: a critique', *New Scientist*, 577–9, 16 September 1976.
THOM, A., 'Megaliths and mathematics', *Antiquity*, **40**, 121–8 (1966).
— *Megalithic Sites in Britain*. Clarendon Press, Oxford (1967).
— *Megalithic Lunar Observatories*. Clarendon Press, Oxford (1971).

Chapter 2

ATKINSON, R. J. C., 'The Dorset Cursus', *Antiquity*, **29**, 4–9 (1955).
— 'Silbury Hill 1969–1970', *Antiquity*, **44**, 313–14 (1970).
BRADLEY, R., 'Where have all the houses gone? Some approaches to Beaker settlement', *Current Archaeology*, **2**, 264–6 (1970).

BURL, A., *The Stone Circles of the British Isles*. Yale University Press, New Haven and London (1976).

DYER, J., *Southern England: an archaeological guide*. Faber and Faber Ltd., London (1973).

MACKIE, E. W., *Scotland: an archaeological guide*. Faber and Faber Ltd., London (1975).

RENFREW, C., *Before Civilisation*. Jonathan Cape Ltd., London (1973).

— *British Prehistory: a new outline* (editor). Gerald Duckworth and Co. Ltd., London (1974).

SELKIRK, A. and W., 'New Grange', *Current Archaeology*, **2**, 297–300 (1970).

STONE, J. F. S., *Wessex Before the Celts*. Thames and Hudson Ltd., London (1958).

Chapter 3

BROADBENT, S. R., 'Quantum hypotheses', *Biometrika*, **42**, 45–57 (1955).

— 'Examination of a quantum hypothesis based on a single set of data', *Biometrika*, **43**, 32–44 (1956).

CUNNINGTON, M. E., *Woodhenge*. George Simpson, Devizes (1929).

FREEMAN, P. R., 'A Bayesian analysis of the megalithic yard', *Journal of the Royal Statistical Society A*, **139**, 20–55 (1976).

— 'Thom's survey of the Avebury ring', *Journal for the History of Astronomy*, **8**, 134–6 (1977).

KENDALL, D. G., 'Hunting quanta', in KENDALL *et al.*, *The Place of Astronomy in the Ancient World*, 231–66.

PORTEOUS, H. L., 'Megalithic yard or megalithic myth?', *Journal for the History of Astronomy*, **4**, 22–4 (1974).

ROY, A. E., MCGRAIL, N., and CARMICHAEL, R., 'A new survey of the Tormore Circles', *Transactions of the Glasgow Archaeological Society*, **15**, 59–67 (1963).

THOM, A., 'A statistical examination of the megalithic sites in Britain', *Journal of the Royal Statistical Society A*, **118**, 275–95 (1955).

— 'The egg-shaped standing stone rings of Britain', *Archives Internationales d'Histoire des Sciences*, **14**, 291–303 (1961).

— 'The geometry of megalithic man', *Mathematical Gazette*, **45**, 83–93 (1961).

— 'The megalithic unit of length', *Journal of the Royal Statistical Society A*, **125**, 243–51 (1962).

— 'The larger units of length of megalithic man', *Journal of the Royal Statistical Society A*, **127**, 527–33 (1964).

— 'Megaliths and mathematics'.

— 'The metrology and geometry of cup and ring marks', *Systematics*, **6**, 173–89 (1968).

THOM, A., and THOM, A. S., 'A megalithic lunar observatory in Orkney', *Journal for the History of Astronomy*, **4**, 111–23 (1973).

— 'Avebury (2): the West Kennet Avenue', *Journal for the History of Astronomy*, **7**, 193–7 (1976).

THOM, A., THOM, A.S., and FOORD, T. R., 'Avebury (1): A new assessment of the geometry and metrology of the ring', *Journal for the History of Astronomy*, **7**, 183–92 (1976).

Chapter 4

COLTON, R., and MARTIN, R. L., 'Eclipse cycles and eclipses at Stonehenge', *Nature*, **213**, 476–8 (1967).

HAWKINS, G. S., 'Stonehenge: a Neolithic computer'.

HOYLE, F., 'Stonehenge: an eclipse predictor'.

NEWTON, R. R., 'Introduction to some basic astronomical concepts', in KENDALL *et al.*, *The Place of Astronomy in the Ancient World*, 5–20.

SADLER, D. H., 'Prediction of eclipses', *Nature*, **211**, 1119–21 (1966).

THOM, A., *Megalithic Lunar Observatories*.

Explanatory Supplement to the 'Astronomical Ephemeris' and the 'American Ephemeris' and the 'Nautical Almanac'. HMSO, London (1961).

Chapter 5

BAILEY, M. E., COOKE, J. A., FEW, R. W., MORGAN, J. G., and RUGGLES, C. L. N., 'Survey of three megalithic sites in Argyllshire', *Nature*, **253**, 431–3 (1975).

BIBBY, J. S., 'Petrofabric analysis', Appendix to paper by MACKIE, E. W., in KENDALL *et al.*, *The Place of Astronomy in the Ancient World*, 191–4.

COOKE, J. A., FEW, R. W., MORGAN, J. G., and RUGGLES, C. L. N., 'Indicated declinations at the Callanish megalithic sites', *Journal for the History of Astronomy*, **8**, 113–33 (1977).

HAWKINS, G. S., 'Callanish: a Scottish Stonehenge', *Science*, **147**, 127–30 (1965).

MACKIE, E. W., 'Duntreath', *Current Archaeology*, **4**, 6–7 (1973).

— 'Archaeological tests on supposed prehistoric astronomical sites in Scotland'.

PATRICK, J., 'Midwinter sunrise at New Grange', *Nature*, **249**, 517–19 (1974).

PENNY, A., and WOOD, J. E., 'The Dorset Cursus complex: a Neolithic astronomical observatory?' *Archaeological Journal*, **130**, 44–76 (1973).

SOMERVILLE, B., 'Astronomical indications in the megalithic monument at Callanish', *Journal of the British Astronomical Association*, **23**, 83–96 (1912).

THOM, A., *Megalithic Lunar Observatories*.

Chapter 6

DAVIDSON, C. J., and SEABROOK, R. A. G., 'Stone rings on south-east Dartmoor', *Proceedings of the Devon Archaeological Society*, **31**, 22–44 (1973).

NEWHAM, C. A., 'Stonehenge: a Neolithic "observatory"', *Nature*, **211**, 456–8 (1966).

— *The Astronomical Significance of Stonehenge*.

PENNY, A., and WOOD, J. E., 'The Dorset Cursus complex: a Neolithic astronomical observatory?'

THOM, A., *Megalithic Lunar Observatories*.

Chapter 7

HEGGIE, D. C., 'Megalithic lunar observatories: an astronomer's view', *Antiquity*, **46**, 43–8 (1972).

THOM, A., *Megalithic Lunar Observatories*.

WOOD, J. E., and PENNY, A., 'A megalithic observatory on Dartmoor', *Nature*, **257**, 205–7 (1975).

Chapter 8

ATKINSON, R. J. C., 'Megalithic astronomy—a prehistorian's comments', *Journal for the History of Astronomy*, **6**, 42–52 (1975).

FREEMAN, P. R., 'Carnac probabilities corrected', *Journal for the History of Astronomy*, **6**, 219 (1975).

HADINGHAM, E., *Circles and Standing Stones*.

PATRICK, J., and BUTLER, C. J., 'On the interpretation of the Carnac menhirs and alignments by A. and A. S. Thom', *Ulster Journal of Archaeology*, **35**, 29–44 (1976). (With reply by A. and A. S. Thom.)

THOM, A., and THOM, A. S., 'The astronomical significance of the large Carnac menhirs', *Journal for the History of Astronomy*, **2**, 147–60 (1971).

— 'The Carnac alignments', *Journal for the History of Astronomy*, **3**, 11–26 (1972).

— 'The uses of the alignments at Le Menec, Carnac', *Journal for the History of Astronomy*, **3**, 151–64 (1972).

— 'The Kerlescan cromlechs', *Journal for the History of Astronomy*, **4**, 168–73 (1973).

— 'The Kermario alignments', *Journal for the History of Astronomy*, **5**, 30–47 (1974).

THOM, A., THOM, A. S., and GORRIE, J. M., 'The two megalithic lunar observatories at Carnac', *Journal for the History of Astronomy*, **7**, 11–26 (1976).

Chapter 9

ATKINSON, R. J. C., *Stonehenge*.

— 'The Stonehenge stations', *Journal for the History of Astronomy*, **7**, 142–4 (1976).

BRINCKERHOFF, R. F., 'Astronomically orientated markings on Stonehenge', *Nature*, **263**, 465–9 (1976).

DIBBLE, W. E., 'A possible pythagorean triangle at Stonehenge', *Journal for the History of Astronomy*, **7**, 141–2 (1976).

HAWKINS, G. S., *Stonehenge Decoded*.

NEWHAM, C. A., *The Astronomical Significance of Stonehenge*.

THATCHER, A. R., 'The Station Stones of Stonehenge', *Antiquity*, **49**, 144–6 (1975).

THOM, A., THOM, A. S., and THOM, A. S., 'Stonehenge', *Journal for the History of Astronomy*, **5**, 71–90 (1974).

— 'Stonehenge as a possible lunar observatory', *Journal for the History of Astronomy*, **6**, 19–30 (1975).

Chapter 10

BEACH, A. D., 'Stonehenge I and lunar dynamics', *Nature*, **265**, 17–21 (1977).

CAESAR, JULIUS, *The Conquest of Gaul* (translated by S. A. Handford). Penguin Books Ltd., Harmondsworth (1971).

CHILDE, V. G., *The Dawn of European Civilisation*. Routledge and Kegan Paul Ltd., London (1925); Paladin, St Albans (1973).

EVANS, J. G., *The Environment of Early Man in the British Isles*. Paul Elek, London (1975).

IVIMY, J., *The Sphinx and the Megaliths*. Turnstone Books Ltd., London (1975); Abacus, London (1976).

LAMB, H. H., 'Climate, vegetation and forest limits in early civilised times', in KENDALL et al., *The Place of Astronomy in the Ancient World*, 195–230.

MACKIE, E. W., *Science and Society in Prehistoric Britain*. Paul Elek, London (1977).

PARKER, R. A., 'Ancient Egyptian astronomy', in KENDALL et al., *The Place of Astronomy in the Ancient World*, 51–65.

RENFREW, C., *Before Civilisation*.

SACHS, A., 'Babylonian observational astronomy', in KENDALL et al., *The Place of Astronomy in the Ancient World*, 43–50.

WAINWRIGHT, G. J., 'Excavations at Marden, Wiltshire, 1969', *Antiquity*, **44**, 56–7 (1970).

— 'Mount Pleasant', *Current Archaeology*, **2**, 320–4 (1970).

— 'Durrington Walls: excavations 1966–68', *Reports of the Research Committee of the Society of Antiquaries, No. 29*, London (1971).

— 'The excavation of a Late Neolithic enclosure at Marden, Wiltshire', *Antiquaries Journal*, **51**, 177–239 (1971).

WATKINS, A., *The Old Straight Track*. Methuen and Co. Ltd., London (1925); Abacus, London (1974).

Appendix B

RENFREW, C., *Before Civilisation*.

SUESS, H. E., 'Bristlecone Pine calibration of the radiocarbon time-scale 5200 BC to the present, in radiocarbon variations and absolute chronology', in *Proceedings of the 12th Nobel Symposium* (edited by I. U. Olsson), 303–12. Wiley, London and New York (1970).

Index

The numbers in parentheses after some entries are the National Grid Coordinates. They may be useful in locating places in Great Britain on Figs. 2.1 and 2.2, but are included primarily so that the sites can be found precisely on large-scale maps.